W9-AYC-991

BARBECUE
SAUCES
RUBS AND MARINADES
BASTES, BUTTERS, *and* GLAZES, TOO

STEVEN RAICHLEN

WORKMAN PUBLISHING
NEW YORK

Portions of this book were originally published in 2000 as *Barbecue! Bible® Sauces, Rubs, and Marinades, Bastes, Butters & Glazes.*

BARBECUE! BIBLE is a registered trademark of Steven Raichlen and Workman Publishing Co., Inc.

WORKMAN is a registered trademark of Workman Publishing Co., Inc.

Library of Congress Cataloging-in-Publication Data is available

ISBN 978-1-5235-0081-9

Cover and book design by Becky Terhune
Original photography by Matthew Benson
Food styling: Nora Singley
Prop styling: Sara Abalan
Additional photos: © fotolia: pages iv, 15, 17, 19, 20, 27, 28, 39, 40, 43, 47, 52, 60, 67, 70, 71, 79, 82, 86, 89, 93, 99, 100, 104, 113, 118, 127, 131, 137, 139, 141, 151, 154, 164, 169, 172, 177, 178, 183, 185, 188, 194, 197, 199, 206, 211, 218, 229, 236, 242, 252–254, 258, 267, 274, 282, 289, 295, 296, 305, 309, 312, 315, 319, 324, 329, 332.
© Sann von Mai/Shutterstock: page 194

Author photo on cover: Roger Proulx

Steven Raichlen is available for select speaking engagements. Please contact speakersbureau@workman.com.

Workman books are available at special discounts when purchased in bulk for premiums and sales promotions as well as for fund-raising or educational use. Special editions or book excerpts can be created to specification. For details contact the Special Sales Director at the address below.

Workman Publishing Company, Inc.
225 Varick Street
New York, NY 10014-4381

Printed in the United States of America
First printing April 2017

10 9 8 7 6 5 4

To Suzanne Rafer, dotter of i's, crosser of t's, and my longtime editor and friend at Workman Publishing, whose editorial finesse is surpassed only by her impeccable taste in books!

ACKNOWLEDGMENTS

No man is an island and no book is written alone. The best part of writing a book is thanking the people who helped make it possible:

Editorial: Suzanne Rafer, Susan Bolotin, Dan Reynolds, Kate Karol, Beth Levy, Molly Kay Upton, and Joanna Eng

Art: Becky Terhune (design), Anne Kerman (photo editor), Matthew Benson (photographer), Nora Singley (food stylist), Sara Abalan (prop stylist), Doug Wolff (production), Barbara Peragine (type)

Culinary: Robb Bass (fire wrangler and recipe tester) and Chris Lynch (chef)

Publicity: Rebecca Carlisle and Selina Meere

Keeping the home fires burning: Jake Klein; Betsy, Ella, Mia, and Julian Berthin

A huge thanks to my indefatigable assistant, recipe tester, and editor extraordinaire, Nancy Loseke

And last, but certainly not least: my amazing wife, Barbara, from whom emanate all the good things that happen to me.

Steven Raichlen
Miami, Florida

CONTENTS

INTRODUCTION:
BUILDING BETTER BARBECUE: THE FLAVOR FACTOR 1

SEASONINGS AND RUBS 11

MARINADES, WET RUBS, SPICE PASTES,
CURES, AND BRINES 51

BASTES, MOPS, BUTTERS, AND SO MUCH MORE 109

AMERICAN BARBECUE SAUCES 157

WORLD BARBECUE SAUCES 191

SLATHER SAUCES FROM KETCHUP AND MUSTARDS
TO AFTER-MARINADES AND BOARD SAUCES 239

SALSAS, RELISHES, SAMBALS, AND CHUTNEYS 291

CONVERSION TABLES 333

INDEX 334

BUILDING BETTER BARBECUE
THE FLAVOR FACTOR

They're the foundation of world-class barbecue, the cornerstones on which unforgettable live-fire flavors are built. I'm talking about the barbecue sauces, rubs, spice pastes, marinades, and mops that transform ordinary grilled meats and seafood into barbecue of the highest distinction. They're the essential seasonings that give grilled fare its character, personality, and soul.

And they're about to make you, the grill master, look like a million bucks.

One thing's for sure: Never has interest been keener in these not-so-subtle boosters of flavor. Spice and chile sales continue to skyrocket as we hunger for big-flavor foods that pack a wallop to the taste buds. In the realm of barbecue sauces, there are now literally thousands of different commercially bottled varieties to choose from.

Despite the proliferation of barbecue sauces, rubs, marinades, and bastes, a great deal of confusion surrounds them. What's the difference between a dry rub and a wet rub? When do you use a spice mix or a marinade? How long should you marinate your favorite meat or seafood? What's the best way to baste or glaze? When should you apply the barbecue sauce? What do fire masters in other countries serve with grilled fare? How do the pros use rubs, marinades, and sauces to make championship barbecue every time?

This book explores the answers to these and other questions. For rubs, marinades, and sauces can make all the difference between serviceable grilled fare and world-class barbecue. There's no shortage of commercial versions of all of these, and many will produce tasty results. But if you want to express your culinary creativity to its fullest, you'll want to concoct your own.

First, a word about nomenclature. Oceans of ink have been spilled about the true meaning of barbecue. To some, it's a catchall term for anything cooked on a grill or in a pit. For others, barbecue refers to a specific type of meat (usually pork or beef) cooked by means of an equally distinctive cooking technique—long, slow smoking with indirect fire. Yet others use the word *barbecue* to describe a cooking device (the so-called barbecue grill), a dish (pulled pork in North Carolina, for example, or brisket in Texas), or even a cookout.

In Miami, where I live, and on the American East and West Coasts in general, barbecue refers to any sort of food cooked with live fire. The method can be direct or indirect. This is the way I use the term in this book. I acknowledge that this isn't the way certain Texans, Kansans, and North Carolinians see matters, but for the sake of expediency, please work with me.

A STRONG FOUNDATION

Anyone can grill a steak or smoke a brisket. But cooking great barbecue involves an intimate knowledge of fuels and fire control as well as considerable expertise in using rubs, marinades, bastes, glazes, and sauces. In a way, the process is similar to building a house. The contractor has to know how to select a site, dig a foundation, build a frame, do the finishing work, paint, decorate, and landscape, using the proper tools and construction methods.

Building great barbecue also requires the right tools (smokers and grills), the proper methods (smoke and heat control), a solid foundation (the rubs and marinades), good finish work (the bastes and glazes), attractive paint (the barbecue sauce), and pleasing landscaping (the salsas, relishes, chutneys, mustards, ketchups, and other condiments served as accompaniments). Get these elements right and your barbecue will be very much at home on the plate, on your tongue, and in your belly.

Not every dish requires all of these elements. That would be overkill. But a lot of traditional American barbecue (Kansas City-style ribs, for example) features a soak in a marinade, a dusting with a rub, a generous basting during cooking, a glaze during the final grilling, and a barbecue sauce for serving.

Some years ago, I had the opportunity to watch one of the most decorated teams on the American barbecue competition circuit—Apple City from Murphysboro, Illinois—prepare the ribs that won the grand championship at the Memphis in May World Championship Barbecue Cooking Contest. The process was illuminating! Each rack of ribs was painstakingly trimmed with a scalpel, then marinated overnight in a tenderizing bath of lemon juice and apple cider. No baby was ever toweled dry more gently than those ribs or more lovingly dusted with baby powder than the way the guys from Apple City sprinkled the bones with an eighteen-ingredient spice mix affectionately dubbed Magic Dust. (The formula is such a closely held secret, quipped the team captain, Pat Burke, that "no team member knows more than three of the ingredients.")

Once in the smoker, the ribs were sprayed repeatedly with apple cider to keep them moist, re-seasoned with rub for extra flavor, and varnished with a barbecue sauce—flavored with apple cider (what else?!)—to give them a handsome sheen. Come time for the judging, the sauce was served on the side to allow the judges to experience the extraordinary flavor of the ribs without distraction.

Americans aren't the only barbecue masters to make such elaborate use of marinades, bastes, and sauces. On one trip to New Delhi, I watched tandoori masters marinate lamb first in a tenderizing marinade of palm vinegar and lemon juice, then a flavorizing paste of yogurt, aromatics, and spices. The meat was basted with butter during grilling and served with mint and onion chutneys by way of barbecue sauce and a cooling yogurt dip called raita.

All this may sound complicated. It *is* complicated —it's supposed to be—but you needn't feel intimidated. As you read the chapters in this book, you'll learn everything you need to know about rubs and seasonings, marinades and bastes, glazes and finishing sauces, barbecue sauces, relishes, and chutneys. You'll meet some of the greatest living practitioners of the art of live-fire cooking and you'll learn how they use rubs, marinades, and sauces to create winning barbecue every time.

You'll find lots of great recipes—many of them award winners—but even more important, you'll learn how to create your own rubs, marinades, and barbecue sauces. That is the goal of this book: to help you become a more confident, creative grill master yourself.

SOME BASIC DEFINITIONS

This book has seven main chapters, one for each of the flavor-enhancing components of great barbecue. Throughout the book you'll find recipes and boxes that tell you how to put them together. Here's a brief overview in order of when the components are used in the cooking process, along with some basic definitions. Note that there can be considerable overlap between categories:

All wet rubs are marinades, for example, but not all marinades are wet rubs.

SEASONINGS: These are mixtures of salt and spices used to season foods before, during, and after grilling. Seasonings differ from rubs in that salt is always the primary flavoring and that they are applied just prior to and/or during the cooking.

RUBS: These are mixes of salt, spices, herbs, and often sugar or other sweeteners used to give a base flavor to the meat, rather than just season it. Rubs are usually applied to the meat several hours before cooking, so that a marinating effect takes place. Rubs help foster the formation of a savory crust.

DRY RUBS: These contain only dry ingredients. They are sprinkled over the food in powder form.

WET RUBS: Also known as **spice pastes**, these start as dry rubs, but a liquid—often water, oil, or yogurt—is added to create a thick paste. This paste is smeared on the meat, where it works in a way similar to a marinade.

MARINADES: These are liquid seasonings—mixtures

of herbs, spices, aromatic vegetables (such as garlic, onions, and peppers), and flavorful liquids (such as olive oil, lemon juice, soy sauce, vinegar, or yogurt). The essence of a marinade is its wetness: The meat acquires its flavor by means of soaking. Marinades benefit meats in ways other than adding flavor. The acids in the marinade (wine, lime juice, vinegar) tenderize the meat by breaking down muscle fibers. The oil and other liquids keep the meat moist during cooking. Thus, marinades are particularly well suited to lean, dry meats, such as chicken breasts and game.

BRINES: Brines are saline (salt water) solutions used for marinating and curing. (Sometimes sugar is added, too.) The typical salinity is 6 to 7 percent. Brines are used to make bacon, ham, jerky, and kippered salmon, and they're also useful for keeping intrinsically dry meats, like turkey or pork chops, from drying out on the grill.

CURES: Like brines, cures have a high salt content. (The salt "cures" the meat by drawing out moisture. It also imparts a pleasing flavor all its own.) Cures often contain sugar and spices. Unlike brines, they're dry instead of wet.

BASTES: Liquids applied to foods as they cook are called bastes. Basting serves three purposes: It keeps meats moist, adds an extra layer of flavor, and fosters the formation of a savory crust during grilling. A baste can be as simple as apple cider sprayed on ribs with a mister or as elaborate as the lemon-saffron-butter mixture brushed on shish kebab by Iranian grill jockeys. Bastes usually contain some sort of fat—olive oil or melted butter, for example—to keep the meat moist.

FLAVORED OILS: Often used for basting, flavored oils can also serve as marinades, sauces, and decorative drizzles.

GLAZES: Similar to bastes in that they are brushed on the food as it cooks, glazes are applied toward the end of cooking to create a shiny coating. Most contain a sweetener, like sugar or honey, which caramelizes during the cooking process, creating a sweet, flavorful exterior.

FINISHING SAUCE: A uniquely American invention, a finishing sauce is brushed on meat at the end of or after cooking to keep it moist and flavorful until serving. Finishing sauces are usually found on the barbecue competition circuit, where the meat must travel from the pit to the judging station.

BARBECUE SAUCE: To many people, barbecue just isn't barbecue without it. In the United States alone, there are thousands of commercially bottled barbecue sauces and dozens of regional styles. Barbecue sauces range from the sweet smoky red condiment of Kansas City to the mouth-puckering vinegar sauces of the Carolinas and the unusual white mayonnaise-based barbecue sauce in northern Alabama. Like Italy's pasta sauces, barbecue sauces evolved to accompany a specific kind of meat. South Carolina's sharp mustard sauce, for example, counterbalances the fat in a barbecued pork butt. The watery thinness of North Carolina vinegar sauce allows it to be readily absorbed by the pulled (shredded) pork so popular in this region. This book includes a full chapter of

American barbecue sauces and another full chapter of the barbecue sauces popular elsewhere in the world.

SLATHER SAUCE: This catchall category includes condiments that are slathered or spread on grilled fare and barbecue before serving. Ketchup and mustard are slather sauces; so are mayonnaise, aïoli (a creamy garlic sauce from Provence), and romesco (Spanish roasted vegetable and nut sauce). Slather sauces are generally thicker than conventional barbecue sauce. (The exception here is ketchup.) Many contain eggs, oil, or cream: Think tartar sauce, horseradish sauce, or béarnaise sauce.

DIPPING SAUCE: A condiment you dip cooked barbecue into. Thai peanut sauce is one of the quintessential dipping sauces; so are Vietnamese *nuoc mam* and Kentucky black dip. While you find dipping sauces in many parts of the world, Southeast Asia is their epicenter. This makes sense, because for Southeast Asians, barbecue means tiny kebabs and paper-thin slices of meat, which are just perfect for dipping in tiny bowls of flavorful sauce.

CONDIMENTS: Salsas, relishes, pickles, chutneys, and other intensely flavorful accompaniments companion barbecue the world over. As a rule, condiments are too thick to qualify as sauces. They're served a spoonful at a time with simply grilled meats and seafood. Their explosive flavors round out the barbecue experience, particularly in Mexico, India, and Asia.

SALSA: This vibrant Mexican table sauce accompanies barbecue south of the border. Mexican salsas come in a dazzling variety—from the simple *salsas frescas* of northern Mexico to the robust roasted chili and vegetable salsas of Oaxaca and the Yucatán. Mexican salsa inspired many of the fruit salsas served with simple grilled poultry and seafood at contemporary restaurants in North America.

RELISH: Mixtures of chopped vegetables or fruits, relishes are often pickled or seasoned with vinegar and sugar. The sharpness of vinegar or citrus juice in a relish counterpoints the smoke flavor of grilled fare.

CHUTNEY: "A strong, hot condiment compounded of ripe fruit, acids, or sour herbs, and flavored with chiles and spices" is how the *Oxford English Dictionary* defines chutney. That pretty much sums it up, except to say that chutneys were born in India, where they are still traditionally served with curries, stews, and rice dishes. Spoon chutney over a simple grilled salmon steak or chicken breast and you'll see dinner from an entirely new perspective.

ABOUT THE RECIPES IN THIS BOOK

The recipes in this book come from a wide range of sources. Many are traditional, having been perfected over decades, sometimes centuries. It would be impossible to identify their creators. Others I collected during my many travels on the world's barbecue trail. Over the years I've attended a lot of barbecue festivals, including Memphis in May, the Kansas City Royal, and the Jack Daniel's Invitational. In the process, I've made a lot of friends on the barbecue competition circuit. Many have graciously shared the recipes for their prizewinning rubs and sauces.

In the following pages you'll find more than 200 recipes for rubs, spice pastes, marinades, barbecue sauces, ketchups, mustards, salsas, chutneys, relishes— in short, every seasoning and condiment you could possibly need for preparing and enjoying great barbecue. Use them singly or in combinations, with the foods I suggest or following your own inspiration.

I've tried to include something for everyone: basic sauces and seasonings for the neophyte; professional preparations for the expert; classic rubs and barbecue sauces for the traditionalist; cutting-edge flavor combinations for the adventurer; down-home, commonsense seasonings for the basic barbecue guy; and downright exotic ethnic preparations for the culinary globe-trotter. I've also included recipes for dozens of complete dishes, using the sauces, seasonings, and condiments in this book.

There are two ways to use this book: Follow some recipes to the letter and use others as springboards for your imagination. If you don't have a particular ingredient on hand, experiment with another. (Remember: There's no such thing as a mistake in the kitchen, just a new recipe waiting to be discovered.) Add these recipes to your repertory as they are or customize and make them your own. Sometimes, the best dishes are those you make when you cook by the seat of your pants.

And please keep me apprised of your efforts. Ask me questions; share your ideas and results by visiting Barbecuebible.com, my Steven Raichlen Facebook page, or on Instagram and Twitter at @sraichlen.

Remember, barbecue isn't brain surgery. Have fun!

TOOLS OF THE TRADE

You don't need to invest in a lot of specialized gear to make great barbecue. But having the right equipment can go a long way in making barbecue easier and more fun. Here's what you need to become a master baster and sauce maker.

BLENDER: In our rush to modernize our kitchens, many of us have shelved the blender in favor of the more high-tech food processor. The latter is terrific, but there are some tasks that are just better performed in the blender, among them combining herbs and oil to make vinaigrettes and flavored oils for basting. Buy a sturdy blender with a tight-fitting lid and use it for blending liquid concoctions or making smooth purées. Another option is an immersion blender, which you plunge into a liquid-filled bowl or saucepan. When using a blender, add the wet ingredients such as the water or oil first, then the solids.

CAST-IRON SKILLET: Useful for toasting spices and roasting vegetables. The thick metal spreads the heat evenly. And you don't have to worry about scorching a nonstick surface. Cast-iron skillets serve another valuable purpose: They're great for cracking peppercorns and coriander seeds. Loosely wrap the seeds in cloth and crush them under the bottom of the pan.

CHEESECLOTH: Tie loose spices in a square of cheesecloth to add to marinades and sauces. For a high-tech version, wrap the spices in a piece of aluminum foil and perforate the package with a fork.

CONTAINERS FOR MARINATING: These include bowls, baking dishes, roasting pans, disposable aluminum foil pans, and even heavy-duty resealable plastic bags. Be sure to use nonreactive bowls and pans—that is, vessels made of glass, ceramic, plastic, or stainless steel. Do not use aluminum or cast-iron pans; these metals sometimes react with acidic ingredients like vinegar or lemon juice. Note: Anodized aluminum (like Calphalon) or stainless steel-lined aluminum is okay. When using resealable plastic bags, place them in a bowl or baking dish to catch any leaks.

CUTTING BOARDS: Wood or plastic? Good question. Just when I was all set to recommend plastic, which you can run through the dishwasher, the *New York Times* ran an article asserting that you get less bacterial cross contamination with wood. (The exact chemistry of this phenomenon is unclear, but it has been scientifically proven.) It's a good idea to own several cutting boards; that way, you can dice onion or garlic on one and cut up chicken on another. Choose a cutting board large enough to do a clean job, at least 12 by 15 inches. Whichever kind of cutting board you use, place it on a damp dishcloth or paper towel to keep it from sliding on the counter.

FOOD PROCESSOR: When it comes to reducing herbs and vegetables to flavorful seasoning pastes, nothing can beat a food processor. Buy a model with a wide bowl and strong motor. When using a food processor, add the solid ingredients like the onions, tomatoes, and celery first, then the liquids.

INJECTORS: Marinades are great for applying flavor to the surface of a food. But what if you want to put the flavor deep into the heart of the meat? There's a simple tool that looks like an over-size hypodermic needle—the injector—and pit masters use it to make some of the most succulent barbecue in the world. To use a meat injector, draw the marinade or basting liquid into the cylinder and plunge the needle into the center of a turkey breast, pork shoulder, or beef roast. A push of the plunger injects the flavoring deep into the meat. There are many good

brands, including my own Best of Barbecue.

JARS: If you're making a large batch of sauce, my choice for storage is the Ball jar, recognizable by its flat lid and ring-like collar. The sturdy glass jar comes with calibrations on the side so you know exactly how much sauce you have. The flexible lid pops up if the jar is improperly sealed— great if you're preserving the sauce for later use. Ball jars are available at most supermarkets and hardware stores.

KNIVES: Buy good knives and take care of them. Taking care of them means washing and drying by hand (never leave a knife in the sink or put through the dishwasher). Keep the blade honed with a sharpening steel.

MEASURING CUPS AND SPOONS: Accurate measuring may seem like the antithesis of the creative spirit. A pinch of this, a splash of that—aren't these the measurements used by pit masters to create some of their most inspired sauces? True, many great condiments have been whipped up on the spur of the moment, but if you want to be able

to reproduce your results and make a second batch of that exquisite sauce, you need to measure accurately and record your efforts for future use. Get yourself a set of measuring spoons and measuring cups (including some glass cups with spouts for liquids) and use them.

MIXING BOWLS: A set of nested metal mixing bowls is essential for any aspiring sauce master. Choose a bowl that's large enough to allow for vigorous mixing without spilling ingredients all over the work surface. This ought to seem self-evident, but you wouldn't believe how often I've watched a big guy grab a tiny bowl and proceed to scatter the ingredients all over the kitchen.

MORTAR AND PESTLE: Visit an Indonesian or Italian kitchen and you'll find a utensil that's almost as old as cooking itself: a mortar and pestle. Nothing beats this ancient low-tech device for pounding garlic and spices into aromatic pastes used for seasoning barbecue.

Why do a mortar and pestle work better than, say, a blender or food processor? Well, consider for a moment the chemistry of an onion or garlic. The flavor of these ingredients is intensified when the sulfur compounds in them are brought into contact with air. What results is a mild form of sulfuric acid, the compound that makes you cry when you chop onion. The smaller the pieces, the greater the exposure to air and the more forceful the flavor. When you buy a mortar and pestle, look for a deep bowl (at least 6 inches deep) with at least a 4-cup capacity. Small mortars and pestles may look nice, but the ingredients will soon scatter all over the work surface. The best place to buy a serious mortar and pestle is at an ethnic market. Buy them from the people who use them.

SAUCEPANS: You can't make barbecue sauce without them. When choosing the right pan, look at three things: size, material, and construction. The pan should be large enough to allow you to simmer and stir your sauce without it spilling over. This means at least a 3-inch clearance between the surface of the sauce and the rim of the saucepan. But choose a pan that's too big and the sauce will settle in such a thin layer on the bottom, it will either burn or evaporate too quickly.

The pan should be made of a nonreactive material, especially when working with acidic ingredients. Stainless steel, enamel, and anodized aluminum are good candidates. Avoid plain aluminum and cast iron, which tend to react adversely with lemon juice, vinegar, tomatoes, and other acidic flavorings. The construction of the pan is important, too. You want a pan with a thick base and walls, so that the heat spreads evenly. Thin pans tend to have hot spots, which will scorch or even burn your sauce. Finally, the pan should have a firmly attached (riveted) handle, preferably of a nonconductive material, so you don't burn your fingers.

SCALE: Invaluable for accurate measuring—especially for odd-shaped ingredients, like dried chiles. Buy a kitchen scale at a cookware shop.

SPICE MILL: As any Indian knows, the secret to great flavor is to start with whole spices. Toast them in a skillet, then grind them in a spice mill. Most of the major appliance companies sell spice mill/coffee grinders. Once you've designated a coffee grinder for spices, don't use it for coffee (or vice versa).

VEGETABLE PEELER: A must for removing thin strips of lemon and orange zest, as well as for peeling cucumbers, carrots, celery, and so on.

WOODEN SPOONS AND WHISKS: The basic tools for mixing. Buy wooden spoons with long handles to keep your hand away from the heat. You'll also want several sizes of whisks, preferably with thick handles (which are easier to hold than thin ones). Use whisks for mixing both rubs and sauces. And don't forget the ultimate tool for mixing rubs: your fingers. When you mix a rub by hand, you can break up lumps of brown sugar or salt or crumble spices between your fingers.

A WORD ON FOOD SAFETY

My research on barbecue has taken me all over the world. I've eaten satés at street markets in Thailand, chicken *tikka* at tandoori joints in India, and *anticuchos* from itinerant food sellers in Peru. Much of this fare came from street vendors, who work in what would seem to most North Americans like dubious sanitary conditions. But during these years on the world's barbecue trail, I rarely get sick—a tribute to the sterilizing powers of fire as well as to an intuitive understanding of basic notions of food safety on the part of the world's grill jockeys.

The most important risk to avoid is cross contamination. Here are a few basic rules to keep your barbecue safe.

RUBS: Wear disposable rubber or plastic gloves when rubbing meats—especially chicken—with spice mixes. This keeps any surface bacteria off your fingers. Throw the gloves away after each use. Barbecue great John Willingham has a nifty trick: When he plans to handle several different types of meat, he puts on an equal number of gloves, one on top of the other. He peels one glove off after each use, thereby avoiding cross contamination.

MARINADES: Marinades are great flavor enhancers, but they can also carry contaminants. Follow these simple commonsense tips and your food will be safe every time:

- Marinate your food in the refrigerator. Tightly cover the bowl or dish with plastic wrap to keep garlic, onion, or other marinade smells from spreading.
- Most marinades are meant to be used a single time, then discarded. If you want to reuse a marinade, boil it for several minutes first, then let it cool to room temperature. Put it and the food into a clean container. Store, covered, in the refrigerator.
- Some marinades are flavorful enough to be used for basting. There are two ways to do this safely:
  - Set aside a quarter of the marinade before you add the meat or seafood. Use this portion for basting.
  - Boil the used marinade for several minutes before using it for basting.

BASTING AND GLAZING: Basting should be done toward the end of cooking—or at least, after the surface of the food has been seared. If you brush a baste or glaze on uncooked or undercooked food, you run the risk of contaminating the basting brush and any remaining baste.

BARBECUE SAUCES: When serving barbecue sauces, squirt them from squeeze bottles or spoon them over the meat. When serving dipping sauces, place a single serving of sauce in a small bowl or saucer, providing one for each eater. Don't dip cooked meat into a communal bowl of sauce.

CUTTING BOARDS: Never cut cooked meat on the same board on which you cut raw food. Always use different cutting boards for raw meats and any other ingredients you may be using, like vegetables or tofu. Scrub dirty cutting boards with soap and hot water.

PLATTERS AND PLATES: It's so tempting. You bring your steaks to the grill on a platter. You've forgotten to fetch another for serving. So when no one's looking, you grab a paper towel and wipe the offending platter. Don't. Always bring two platters to the grill: one for raw meat and one for the cooked. Never the twain shall meet.

SEASONINGS AND RUBS

I've always been fascinated by the simple alchemy by which assertive seasonings are melded into a harmonious whole. Clearly, I'm not alone. Wherever you find people grilling, you'll find spices, and wherever you find spices, you find signature rubs and spice mixes that give barbecue its personality.

This chapter focuses on the rubs, spice mixes, and seasonings used by grill masters the world over. There's something for everyone: a quick, easy, all-purpose Basic Barbecue Rub (page 19); a Kansas City Sweet and Smoky Rub (page 24); and a fiery Lone Star Steak Rub (page 27).

From beyond America's borders, experience an electrifying kebab spice from Spain (page 41); a fragrant rosemary rub from Tuscany (page 40); and even a pungent seasoning from Bali (page 15).

Whether you're trying to increase the flavor of your barbecue or simply reduce the overall fat, chances are there's a rub or spice mixture in this chapter that can help you. You'll never have to use a commercial blend again.

SEASONED SALTS AND PEPPERS

ALL-PURPOSE SEASONED SALT

YIELD: Makes 1⅓ cups

TRY THIS!

Sprinkle this mixture on steaks, chops, chicken, fish—on just about anything you cook on the grill.

Virtually every recipe cooked on the grill calls for salt and pepper. In a perfect world, you'd dose the salt and grind the pepper fresh every time. This isn't always a perfect world, and having a batch of premixed seasoned salt on hand can save a lot of time and trouble. There's no shortage of commercial seasoned salts, but most of them are loaded with MSG and sugar. The following formula may seem simple, but it reacts in complex ways on your taste buds. The coarse crystals of salt and cracked black peppercorns give you sharp bursts of flavor. The black, white, and cayenne peppers provide three different kinds of heat. Black pepper is the most aromatic; white pepper has a stinging, front-of-the-mouth heat; while cayenne is pure fire that's chiefly experienced deep in your gullet. Put them together and you get a seasoning mix that makes just about everything on the grill taste better. Note that some people like a touch of sweetness in their seasoned salt, others don't, so I've made the sugar optional.

INGREDIENTS

1 cup coarse salt (sea or kosher)

⅓ cup cracked black peppercorns

2 tablespoons freshly ground white pepper

1 tablespoon ground cayenne pepper

1 tablespoon sugar (optional)

Combine all the ingredients in a bowl and stir or whisk to mix. Transfer to a jar, cover, and store away from heat and light. The salt will keep for several weeks.

SMOKED SALT

YIELD: Makes 2 cups

One of the best ways to give foods a smoky barbecue flavor is to season them with smoked salt. You can buy smoked salt, but it's not hard to make your own from scratch. Moreover, you can customize the smoke flavor, from the elegance of oak to the robustness of mesquite. Here are three methods for smoking salt, both indoors and outdoors. Smoked salt keeps well in a sealed jar. If it starts to cake after a few weeks, flake it with a fork.

INGREDIENTS

2 cups coarse salt (sea or kosher)

CHARCOAL GRILL METHOD: Set up the grill for indirect grilling. Add 1½ cups wood chips to the coals. Spread the salt in a thin layer in an aluminum foil drip pan and place it on the grate away from the fire. Cover the grill and adjust the vent holes for medium heat (350°F). Smoke the salt for 30 to 40 minutes. Add the remaining chips to the coals and continue smoking until the salt is bronzed with smoke and intensely smoke-flavored. Repeat as necessary. Cool the salt to room temperature, then transfer it to a jar, cover, and store away from heat and light.

SMOKER METHOD: Light your smoker and preheat to 250°F. Add the wood as specified by the manufacturer. Spread the salt in a thin layer in an aluminum foil drip pan and place it in the smoker. Smoke salt until bronzed with smoke and intensely smoke-flavored, 4 to 6 hours. Cool the salt to room temperature, then transfer it to a jar, cover, and store away from heat and light.

STOVETOP SMOKER METHOD: Place the sawdust in the bottom of a stovetop smoker, like one from Camerons or Nordicware, following the manufacturer's instructions. Place the drip pan in the smoker and the grate lined with aluminum foil on top. Spread the salt out in a thin layer and close the smoker,

TRY THIS!

Sprinkle this smoky salt on anything. I mean anything. Even put it on popcorn, so you can be reminded of barbecue when you're at the movies.

YOU ALSO NEED

If smoking outdoors:
3 cups hardwood chips (or as needed), soaked in cold water for 30 minutes, then drained

If smoking indoors:
Hardwood sawdust

leaving a 1-inch gap. Place the smoker over high heat. When you start to see wisps of smoke, reduce the heat to medium and tightly close the lid. Smoke the salt for 20 minutes. Repeat as needed until the salt is bronzed with smoke and intensely smoke-flavored. Cool the salt to room temperature, then transfer it to a jar, cover, and store away from heat and light. It will keep for several weeks.

SEDUCED BY SALT

It's an edible stone—and a biological necessity—and barbecue would be unimaginably dull without it. I'm talking about the one food we eat daily that's neither plant nor animal, the world's most popular seasoning: salt.

Salt comes in a bewildering array of colors, textures, and tastes.

Indians love black salt (*kala namak*), a blackish-brown or blackish-pink salt with a smoky, almost sulfurous flavor. Talk about reinforcing the smoke flavor of barbecue! When I was in Hawaii, I chanced upon a red salt that was colored with edible clay—the traditional seasoning for the pit-roasted pig at a luau.

Salt comes from two primary sources: mineral deposits in the earth and evaporated seawater. Mineral deposits furnish rock salt; the ocean, sea salt. Freshly mined rock salt is the coarse, gray-white stuff we sprinkle on driveways to prevent them from freezing. To make common table salt, the mineral is dissolved in water, purified, evaporated, and dried.

Sea salt is made by evaporating seawater. Traditionally, the water was channeled into shallow seaside basins, where it evaporated in the sun. Sea salt is loaded with flavorful minerals, including iodine and calcium and magnesium chloride.

The ultimate salt goes by the French name of *fleur de sel* (salt flower). Made by the traditional solar evaporation method, this premium sea salt comes in large flaky crystals with a pleasing crunch and elegant briny flavor. One great example is Maldon salt from Essex, England.

Kosher salt comes in large, flaky pyramid-shaped crystals that are slow to dissolve on food. Because kosher salt doesn't melt right away, it gives you pointillistic bursts of flavor when you bite into a grilled steak or fish fillet. Its coarse texture feels great between your fingers when you take a pinch.

BALINESE SEASONED SALT

YIELD: Makes ⅔ cup

first tasted this seasoned salt at the Amankila resort in Bali. The bold flavors—coriander and cloves for pungency and anise and nutmeg for sweetness—ricochet on your taste buds. Ground red rice gives the rub a striking pink color. It also fosters the formation of a savory crust. Red rice is available at Asian markets and natural foods stores. If it's unavailable, use white rice.

TRY THIS!

Sprinkle this salt on grilled chicken, pork, and seafood. It's also great on grilled vegetables.

INGREDIENTS

2 tablespoons red rice

2 tablespoons coriander seeds

2 teaspoons fennel seeds

½ teaspoon whole cloves

½ teaspoon freshly grated nutmeg

½ cup coarse salt (sea or kosher)

Heat a small dry skillet over medium heat. Add the rice, coriander, fennel, cloves, and nutmeg and toast until fragrant, 2 minutes. Do not brown. Cool the spices, then transfer to a spice mill and grind to a fine powder. Add the salt and pulse the grinder to mix. Transfer to a jar, cover, and store away from heat and light. The salt will keep for several weeks.

CENTRAL ASIAN SEASONED SALT

YIELD: Makes ¾ cup

TRY THIS!

Generously sprinkle on lamb, beef, chicken, or seafood prior to grilling.

The spices in this salt are traditional Central Asian seasonings for grilling.

INGREDIENTS

½ cup coarse salt (sea or kosher)

1 tablespoon cracked black peppercorns

1 tablespoon dried chives

1 tablespoon dried parsley

1 tablespoon dried mint

2 teaspoons ground coriander

2 teaspoons hot paprika

2 teaspoons dried garlic flakes

½ teaspoon ground cinnamon

Combine all the ingredients in a bowl and stir to mix. Transfer to a jar, cover, and store away from heat and light. The salt will keep for several weeks.

SESAME SALT

YIELD: Makes 1¾ cups

TRY THIS!

This Asian-inflected salt makes a colorful seasoning for grilled seafood, chicken, and vegetables. Use it on grilled tofu, seitan, and vegetables.

I love the nutty roasted flavor of this sesame-seasoned salt. Ditto for its appearance: snow-white salt crystals, tan roasted sesame seeds, and jet-black *kuro goma* (Japanese black sesame seeds). The latter are available at Japanese markets and at natural foods stores and gourmet shops.

INGREDIENTS

½ cup white sesame seeds

½ cup black sesame seeds, or additional white sesame seeds

¾ cup coarse salt (sea or kosher)

3 tablespoons cracked black peppercorns

Heat a dry skillet over medium heat. Add the white sesame seeds and toast, stirring occasionally, until fragrant and golden brown, 2 to 4 minutes. Transfer the sesame seeds to a bowl and let cool. Stir in the black sesame seeds, salt, and pepper. Transfer to a jar, cover, and store away from heat and light. The salt will keep for several weeks.

LEMON PEPPER

YIELD: Makes ¾ cup

Many of the rub and sauce recipes in this book call for lemon pepper. You can buy it ready-made, of course, but commercial brands vary widely in quality and are often artificially flavored. It's easy to make your own.

For even more flavor, use fragrant Meyer lemons, which originated in China as a cross between a lemon and a mandarin orange.

TRY THIS!

Sprinkle on as you would normal pepper, but when you want a bright blast of lemon as well. It also works as an ingredient in rubs, marinades, or sauces.

INGREDIENTS

2 lemons

¾ cup black peppercorns

1. Grate the zest (oil-rich outer rind) off the lemons, using a Microplane or box grater. You need about 2 tablespoons.

2. Place the lemon zest and peppercorns in a spice mill. (Don't overcrowd the spice mill—work in several batches if necessary.) Grind the zest and peppercorns to a coarse powder. Transfer to a jar, cover, and store in the refrigerator. The lemon pepper will keep for several weeks.

SIX PEPPER BLEND

YIELD: Makes ¾ cup

TRY THIS!

Use as you would regular pepper—not just on grilled foods. It's better.

When I was growing up, pepper was, well, pepper. Today you can find white, black, green, and pink peppercorns, not to mention pungent Sichuan pepper. Each has a distinct flavor: the earthy heat of black peppercorns; the clean heat of white pepper; the herbal, almost fruity tang of green peppercorns.

Botanically speaking, pink peppercorns and Sichuan peppercorns aren't pepper at all, but the berries of exotic shrubs. The former have a floral fragrance, while the latter possess a piney pungency that has the curious effect of making your tongue feel numb. As for hot pepper flakes, they belong to the capsicum family and add a different sort of heat.

INGREDIENTS

2 tablespoons Sichuan peppercorns

½ cup black peppercorns

2 tablespoons white peppercorns

2 tablespoons green peppercorns

1 tablespoon pink peppercorns (optional)

1 tablespoon red pepper flakes

1. Heat a small dry heavy skillet over medium heat. Add the Sichuan peppercorns and roast until fragrant and just beginning to darken, 2 to 4 minutes, stirring often. Transfer the peppercorns to a bowl to cool. Add the remaining ingredients to the bowl and stir to mix.

2. Grind the pepper mixture in a pepper or spice mill. If using a spice mill, work in small batches to ensure an even grind. Transfer to a jar, cover, and store away from heat and light. The pepper blend will keep for several weeks.

AMERICAN RUBS

BASIC BARBECUE RUB

YIELD: Makes 1 cup

H ere's the granddaddy of all barbecue rubs, but don't let the simple formula fool you. There's a heap of flavor in this simple rub—the molasses sweetness of the brown sugar, the heat of the pepper, the vegetal sweetness of the paprika, and the slow burn of the cayenne. Use this basic formula as a springboard for your own creativity (see page 20). Note: There are two ways to use this or any rub—sprinkle it on right before grilling or smoking as you would a seasoned salt. Or apply it several hours or even the day before to cure the meat as well as season it.

TRY THIS!

Sprinkle this rub on pork, beef, chicken, and robust fish, like salmon. You can cook the meat at once or, for an even richer flavor, let it marinate for 2 to 4 hours first.

INGREDIENTS

¼ cup coarse salt
   (sea or kosher)

¼ cup packed brown sugar
   (light or dark—your choice)

¼ cup sweet paprika

2 to 4 tablespoons freshly
   ground black pepper

OPTIONAL FLAVORINGS:

1 tablespoon garlic powder

1 tablespoon onion powder

½ teaspoon ground cayenne
   pepper

½ teaspoon celery seeds

Combine all the ingredients in a bowl and stir or whisk to mix. Transfer to a jar, cover, and store away from heat and light. The rub will keep for several weeks.

HOW TO CUSTOMIZE A BARBECUE RUB

THE BASIC BARBECUE RUB: ADDS AND SUBS

- For a Tex-Mex-style rub, add 2 tablespoons chile powder and 1 tablespoon each ground cumin, oregano, and unsweetened cocoa.

- For a West Indian rub, add 1 tablespoon each onion and garlic powder; 1 teaspoon ground allspice; and ½ teaspoon each ground cinnamon, nutmeg, and Scotch bonnet chile powder or ground cayenne pepper.

- For a Spanish-style rub, substitute smoked paprika (pimentón) for the sweet paprika in the Basic Barbecue Rub. Add 1 tablespoon each ground cumin and ground coriander and 1 teaspoon grated orange zest.

- For a seafood rub, use only half the salt in the Basic Barbecue Rub, replacing the other half with Old Bay Seasoning (or add to taste).

THE FLAVOR COMPONENTS: WHEN STARTING FROM SCRATCH

Barbecue rubs are all about balance, blending sweet, salty, sour, and hot into a harmonious whole. Here are options for each of these flavor components:

Sweet: Sugar, brown sugar, maple sugar, palm sugar, or freeze-dried sugarcane juice (like Sucanat)

Salty: Sea salt, kosher salt, smoked salt, or specialty salts, like Indian black salt or Alaskan spruce salt

Sour: Lemon pepper, fresh or dried lemon, lime or orange zest, sumac, and so on

Heat: Black pepper, green peppercorns, pink peppercorns, Sichuan pepper, white pepper, dried chile flakes or powder, ginger, wasabi, hot paprika

DALMATIAN RUB / NEWSPAPER RUB

YIELD: Makes 1 cup

S ometimes less is more. Consider the "Dalmatian" Rub used by new wave pit masters to turn out world-class briskets and beef ribs. Combine equal parts coarse salt (sea or kosher) and cracked black peppercorns and you get a white and black rub that's speckled like a Dalmatian. Add hot red pepper flakes and you get a "Newspaper" rub—black and white and red (read) all over. Use either to make superlative grilled and smoked beef.

INGREDIENTS

½ cup coarse salt
  (sea or kosher)

½ cup cracked black
  peppercorns

¼ cup red pepper flakes
  (optional)

Combine the salt, pepper, and red pepper flakes (if using) in a bowl and mix with your fingers or a small whisk. Store any unused rub in a jar with a tight-fitting lid away from heat or light. It will keep for several weeks.

TRY THIS!

Apply this simple seasoning the next time you grill a steak or smoke a brisket or beef ribs. Pretty terrific on pork, lamb, and veal chops, too.

🔥 HOW TO CRACK BLACK PEPPERCORNS

G round black pepper works well in rubs. For seasoning steaks and other meats, I prefer partially pulverized black peppercorns, better known as cracked pepper. To crack peppercorns in a pepper mill, set the mill on the largest grind. To crack peppercorns by hand, wrap a couple of tablespoons of peppercorns in a dish towel and crush them with a heavy object, like a rolling pin or the bottom of a cast-iron skillet. A heavy-duty mortar and pestle work well, too. the French call cracked black peppercorns *mignonettes* and use them to make steak *au poivre*.

DALMATIAN RIBS
SALT AND PEPPER BEEF RIBS

YIELD: Serves 4

YOU ALSO NEED

Hickory, oak, or your favorite hardwood

These may be the simplest ribs you'll ever make, but simple doesn't mean simplistic. The salt-pepper seasoning forms a savory crust while keeping the focus on the beef. I call for beef short ribs here, but you can also use beef long ribs or full beef plate ribs. (Increase the cooking time to 6 to 8 hours for the latter.)

INGREDIENTS

4 pounds beef short ribs (choose large ribs with lots of meat on them)

½ cup Dalmatian Rub/ Newspaper Rub, or as needed

Lean-and-Mean Texas Barbecue Sauce (optional; page 167)

1. Set up your smoker following the manufacturer's instructions and preheat to 250°F. If working on a charcoal grill, use only half a chimney of charcoal.

2. Generously season the short ribs on all sides with Dalmatian Rub/Newspaper Rub. Place the ribs meat side up on the smoker rack.

3. Smoke the ribs until darkly browned and cooked through and tender, 3 to 4 hours. When cooked, the meat will have shrunk back from the ends of the bones by ½ to 1 inch and the internal temperature will be about 200°F.

4. Transfer the short ribs to a platter. Loosely tent them with aluminum foil and let rest for 15 minutes. Pass the Lean-and-Mean Texas Barbecue Sauce.

NOTE: For even more flavor, set up your grill for direct grilling and preheat to high. Brush and oil the grill grate. Just before serving, brush the cooked short ribs on all sides with the barbecue sauce and grill over a hot fire to sizzle the sauce into the meat (2 to 4 minutes per side). Serve the remaining sauce on the side.

KANSAS CITY SWEET AND SMOKY RUB

YIELD: Makes about 2½ cups

TRY THIS!

Sprinkle on ribs, pork shoulders, briskets, and chicken 30 minutes to 2 hours before smoking. If desired, sprinkle on more rub during cooking and give a final hit just before serving.

This Kansas City rub is the most ecumenical of barbecue seasonings. Sweet rather than salty, flavorful rather than fiery, it contains mustard in the style of a Memphis rub and chili powder in the style of Texas. This open-mindedness reflects KC's central geographic location. Beef and pork are equally popular here and sauces and seasonings tend to be mild and sweet, rather than strongly flavored or spicy. A well-mannered rub, this recipe—from my friends at the Kansas City Barbecue Society (KCBS), the source of so much good information about barbecue—will produce the sort of sweet, smoky ribs most of us would identify as perfect barbecue. Note the use of smoked salt to add a smoky dimension to the rub. You can make your own (page 13) or use a good commercial brand.

INGREDIENTS

⅔ cup packed light brown sugar

⅔ cup granulated sugar

½ cup sweet or smoked paprika

¼ cup seasoned salt, preferably All-Purpose Seasoned Salt (page 12), or a good commercial brand, such as Lawry's

¼ cup Smoked Salt (page 13), or a good commercial brand

¼ cup onion salt

¼ cup celery salt

2 tablespoons freshly ground black pepper

2 tablespoons pure chile powder (not a blend)

2 teaspoons mustard powder

1 teaspoon poultry seasoning

1 teaspoon ground ginger

½ teaspoon ground allspice

½ teaspoon ground cayenne pepper

Combine all the ingredients in a bowl and stir or whisk to mix. Transfer to a large jar, cover, and store away from heat and light. The rub will keep for several weeks.

HOW TO MAXIMIZE YOUR RUB'S PERFORMANCE

Buy the freshest possible spices and dried herbs. After 3 months, most dried herbs, especially delicate herbs like chervil or tarragon, will have lost their punch. Buy replacements at a store that has a high turnover. When possible, grind whole spices yourself right before you use them. Use a small electric coffee grinder reserved for this purpose. Use another grinder for coffee.

- Date the rub and indicate the shelf life: If kept away from light and heat, most rubs will be at their peak for 1 to 2 months.

- Use a cautious hand when adjusting flavors. Remember—the male brain is wired to think, "If some is good, more must be better." Too much of any spice can ruin a great batch of rub.

- Take your rub for a test drive. Remember, a rub will taste different on your finger than it will on meat sizzling away on a grill. Try the rub on a neutral-tasting piece of meat, like a steak or chicken breast, so you know how it behaves on the grill.

- Strive for balance. A good rub will play like a musical chord on guitar or piano.

- If not following a recipe, be sure to record the ingredients you use along with accurate measurements. You want to be able to replicate your successes. And share them with us on the Barbecue Board (barbecuebible.com).

- When giving rubs as gifts, package in airtight containers or shaker jars. These can be purchased in some cookware shops or restaurant supply stores. Design a label—easy using a computer. Include instructions for use.

- As a general rule, figure on 2 to 4 teaspoons of rub per pound of meat, poultry, or fish.

So, how do you use your rub? There are two ways.

As a seasoning, like you would salt and pepper, and apply it just before grilling. Sprinkle it on, or rub it in with your fingertips. (That's why it's called a rub.) You can sprinkle on some more just before serving to reinforce the flavor.

As a cure: You'll achieve a more complex flavor if you use the rub as a cure or marinade: Apply the rub to food several hours ahead of time (up to 1 to 2 days ahead for large cuts of meat), and refrigerate, covered, until ready to grill.

5-4-3-2-1 RUBS EAST AND WEST

The 5-4-3-2-1 Rub has been a mainstay on the American barbecue competition circuit—not to mention an easy way to remember the formula for a complex flavored rub equally well suited to pork, beef, lamb, and poultry. That set me thinking about another alphanumeric rub—this one with an Asian accent.

AMERICAN 5-4-3-2-1 RUB

YIELD: Makes 1 cup

INGREDIENTS

5 tablespoons sweet or smoked paprika

4 tablespoons brown sugar (light or dark—your choice)

3 tablespoons coarse salt (sea or kosher)

2 tablespoons freshly ground black pepper

1 tablespoon ground cumin

Combine the paprika, sugar, salt, pepper, and cumin in a mixing bowl and mix well, using your fingers to break up any lumps in the sugar.

Transfer to a jar, cover, and store away from heat and light. Keeps for several weeks (not that it will last that long).

TRY THIS!

Use American 5-4-3-2-1 Rub on beef, pork, chicken, and ribs of all persuasions.

ASIAN 5-4-3-2-1 RUB

YIELD: Makes 1 cup

Five-spice powder is a Chinese blend with a smoky anise flavor comprised of star anise, fennel, anise, cinnamon, and white pepper. Look for it in Asian markets or in the spice rack of a well-stocked supermarket.

INGREDIENTS

5 tablespoons turbinado sugar (like Sugar in the Raw) or light brown sugar

4 tablespoons coarse salt (sea or kosher)

3 tablespoons freshly ground black pepper

2 tablespoons Chinese Five-Spice Powder (page 43)

1 tablespoon onion powder

TRY THIS!

Use as a seasoning for barbecued duck and pork tenderloin. Brush the meat with sesame oil, then sprinkle on the rub.

Combine the sugar, salt, pepper, five-spice powder, and onion powder in a mixing bowl and mix well, using your fingers to break up any lumps in the sugar. Transfer to a jar, cover, and store away from heat and light. Keeps for several weeks (not that it will last that long).

LONE STAR STEAK RUB

YIELD: Makes 1¾ cups

If you want a rub with plenty of heat and not a lick of sugar, this lean, mean seasoning is your ticket. There are some foods God never meant to be sweetened, among them the steaks (especially T-bones) and briskets of which Texans are so rightfully proud. Use this rub whenever big flavors are called for and don't use more than you mean to. It burns.

TRY THIS!

Beef is the logical destination for this lip-searing rub, especially steak, roasts, and brisket. But don't overlook its use on chicken, pork, and even seafood. As for grilled vegetables, well, it's great there, too.

INGREDIENTS

½ cup coarse salt (sea or kosher)

½ cup cracked or coarsely ground black pepper

¼ cup sweet or smoked paprika

3 tablespoons pure chile powder (not a blend)

2 tablespoons ground cayenne pepper

2 tablespoons garlic powder

1 tablespoon ground cumin

1 tablespoon dried oregano

1 tablespoon dried thyme

Combine all the ingredients in a bowl and stir or whisk to mix. Transfer to a large jar, cover, and store away from heat and light. The rub will keep for several weeks.

FETTE SAU'S COFFEE RUB

YIELD: Makes about 4 cups

TRY THIS!

Brisket, pork shoulder, chicken, ribs—it's hard to imagine a meat that doesn't excel with this rub. Pair it with another espresso-based condiment: Aaron Franklin's Espresso Barbecue Sauce (page 164).

Musicologist-turned-restaurateur Joe Carroll didn't set out to launch the Brooklyn barbecue revolution when he opened Fette Sau ("Fat Pig," literally) in a dilapidated garage in Williamsburg. But his supernaturally moist brisket and ribs and thoughtfully curated whiskey collection quickly drew line-down-the-block crowds. Carroll uses one rub on all his barbecued meats, but it's a killer—a polymorphic amalgam of espresso, cumin, cinnamon, and brown sugar. You'll love the sweet spicy bark (crust) it creates on any meat. The following recipe was adapted from Joe's book *Feeding the Fire*.

INGREDIENTS

1½ cups packed dark brown sugar

1 cup ground espresso coffee beans

1 cup coarse salt (sea or kosher)

¼ cup freshly ground black pepper

¼ cup granulated garlic

2 tablespoons ground cinnamon

2 tablespoons ground cumin

2 tablespoons ground cayenne pepper

Place all the ingredients in a mixing bowl and mix well, breaking up any lumps in the sugar with your fingers.

Transfer to a jar, cover, and store away from heat and light. The rub will keep for several weeks.

DOUBLE COFFEE SKIRT STEAKS OR VENISON

YIELD: Serves 4 to 6

Coffee has a natural affinity with beef—a combination memorialized by the cowboys of the American West, who brewed coffee over the same campfire they used for grilling steak. (Forget about wine; coffee was the beverage of choice.) These steaks get a double blast of flavor—first from a cumin-scented coffee rub from Brooklyn's Fette Sau, then from a coffee-based barbecue sauce. You have two options for the latter: For a fruitier sauce, try my stepson Jake's Three C's Barbecue Sauce (those three C's are coffee, cocoa, and cherries). Alternatively, try Aaron Franklin's Espresso Barbecue Sauce. By the way, the combination goes amazingly well with venison, elk, and other game.

INGREDIENTS

2 pounds skirt steaks

3 to 4 tablespoons Fette Sau's Coffee Rub (facing page)

2 tablespoons extra-virgin olive oil or melted bacon fat

Jake's Three C's Barbecue Sauce (page 180), or Aaron Franklin's Espresso Barbecue Sauce (page 164)

¼ cup chopped fresh cilantro leaves

1. Arrange the skirt steaks on a sheet pan and generously season both sides with the rub, rubbing it into the meat with your fingertips. Drizzle the steaks on both sides with the olive oil or bacon fat and pat it into the meat with the back of a fork. Let the steaks marinate in the refrigerator while you light your grill.

2. Set up your grill for direct grilling and build a hot fire. Ideally, you'll grill over a wood fire—at the very least, toss some mesquite or other hardwood chunks on the coals or place between the heat diffuser of your gas grill. Brush and oil the grill grate.

3. Arrange the steaks on the grate and grill until sizzling, browned, and cooked to taste, 2 to 3 minutes per side for medium-rare.

4. Transfer the steaks to a platter or plates. Spoon some of the barbecue sauce over each steak and serve the remainder on the side. Sprinkle the steaks with chopped cilantro and you're in business.

FAILPROOF FISH CURE

YIELD: Makes 1½ cups

TRY THIS!

Sprinkle some fish cure on the bottom of a glass baking dish. Place the fish fillets on top and sprinkle more cure over them. Cover the fish with plastic wrap and cure in the refrigerator for 4 hours. Wipe or wash the cure off the fish and blot dry. Smoke the fish, using your preferred method and smoker.

I've probably made this fish cure a thousand times, yet it never fails to amaze me how such a simple concoction can so radically improve the flavor of smoked fish. The sugar and salt impart a sweet briny flavor, with an edge of pepper for heat. The salt also partially dehydrates the fish, firming up its consistency and concentrating its flavor. The most popular fish for smoking is salmon. I cure it for 4 hours, then smoke it in an outdoor or stovetop smoker. The kipper-style salmon that results is some of the best smoked fish you'll ever taste. Even a beginner will have great results.

INGREDIENTS

1 cup packed dark brown sugar

½ cup coarse salt
(sea or kosher)

2 tablespoons cracked or
ground black pepper

1 tablespoon dried dill

1 teaspoon ground coriander

Combine all the ingredients in a bowl and mix with your fingers, breaking up any lumps of brown sugar. Transfer to a large jar, cover, and store away from heat and light. The cure will keep for several weeks.

PASTRAMI RUB

YIELD: Makes 1¼ cups

Remember pastrami? That staple of the delicatessen? Pastrami has gone global these days, as innovators dish up turkey pastrami, duck pastrami, and pastrami shrimp. This isn't quite as strange as it seems, for pastrami originated in Asia Minor, where it's known as *basturma* and where it's still sometimes made with camel or horse meat. As it turns out, what makes pastrami pastrami is less the cut of meat than the seasonings—an invigorating interplay of sweet (sugar), spicy (mustard and peppercorns), perfumed (coriander), and pungent (sweet and hot paprika), with breath-wilting doses of garlic.

INGREDIENTS

3 tablespoons coriander seeds

2 tablespoons black peppercorns

1 tablespoon white peppercorns (or additional black peppercorns)

8 cloves garlic, minced

2 tablespoons yellow mustard seeds

5 tablespoons coarse salt (sea or kosher)

3 tablespoons dark brown sugar

5 tablespoons sweet or smoked paprika

Coarsely crush the coriander seeds and black and white peppercorns in a mortar with a pestle or in a spice mill or in a plastic bag using a heavy mallet. The idea is to crack them rather than pulverize them. Place them in a bowl and stir in the garlic, mustard seeds, salt, sugar, and paprika. You may need to use your fingers to get an even mix. Transfer to a jar, cover, and refrigerate. The rub will keep for at least a week.

TRY THIS!

Sprinkle a layer of rub in the bottom of a baking dish or roasting pan just large enough to hold the meat. Place the meat on top and generously sprinkle more rub on top. Press the rub into the meat with your fingertips, and cover and refrigerate, turning the food several times. The size of the food determines how long you need to flavor it; thus a 1-pound salmon fillet needs 4 hours; a 2-pound turkey breast, 12 hours; an 8-pound brisket flat, 24 hours. (The longer the seasoning time, the more pronounced the pastrami flavor will be.) Once seasoned, the meat should be smoked following the smoker manufacturer's instructions.

PASTRAMI RUB FOR BRINED MEATS

YIELD: Makes about 1 cup

TRY THIS!

Cure a beef brisket or navel, pork belly, or turkey breast with the brine on page 102, then crust it with pastrami rub and slow smoke in your smoker.

Call it America's pastrami moment. Once the province of the delicatessen, pastrami has invaded the barbecue joint. In the past year, I've eaten pastrami brisket, pork shoulder, salmon, shrimp, and bacon, and somewhere out there, someone is surely working on pastrami tofu. Pastrami requires three-step flavoring process: first with a brine, then a rub, and finally a blast of wood smoke. (For classic deli pastrami there's a fourth step—steaming—which is usually omitted at barbecue joints, although wrapping and resting in an insulated cooler produces a similar steaming effect.) Here's a salt-free pastrami rub to use with brined meat. It delivers a one-two punch of aromatic coriander seeds and spicy black peppercorns, with a hint, just a hint of sweetness in the form of ginger, cloves, and brown sugar. For a great pastrami brine recipe, see page 106.

INGREDIENTS

½ cup cracked black peppercorns

½ cup coriander seeds

2 tablespoons mustard seeds

1 tablespoon dark brown sugar

1 teaspoon ground ginger

¼ teaspoon ground cloves

1. Place the peppercorns, coriander, and mustard seeds in a spice mill and quickly and coarsely grind them. Work in the remaining ingredients, running the mill in short bursts.

2. Apply the rub to the meat just prior to smoking, or transfer to a jar, cover, and store away from heat and light. The rub will keep for several weeks.

CAJUN RUB

YIELD: Makes 1⅓ cups

Zydeco. Mardi Gras. Sun-scorched days and steamy nights. No other region in North America has a more soulful spirit or strong culinary sense of place than Louisiana. And no other region makes such extravagant use of spices. Cayenne and black pepper give this Cajun seasoning fire power, but there's more to the rub than heat. Filé powder is ground dried sassafras leaves—often used as a thickener for gumbo. Look for it in gourmet shops and most supermarkets. Don't worry if you can't find it; the rub will still be very tasty without it. So put on some Zydeco music and *laissez les bon temps rouler!*

TRY THIS!

This rub will give a Cajun accent to just about any food you grill or barbecue. It's especially good on seafood, but you can rub it on chicken, turkey, or pork. For that matter, there's no reason not to use Cajun Rub on beef or lamb.

INGREDIENTS

½ cup coarse salt
(sea or kosher)

¼ cup sweet or smoked paprika

3 tablespoons freshly ground
black pepper

1 tablespoon ground cayenne
pepper, or to taste

1 tablespoon dried thyme

1 tablespoon onion powder

1 tablespoon garlic powder

1 tablespoon filé powder
(optional)

2 teaspoons freshly ground
white pepper

1 teaspoon ground bay leaf

Combine all the ingredients in a bowl and stir or whisk to mix. Transfer to a jar, cover, and store away from heat and light. The rub will keep for several weeks.

Variation

For a sweeter rub, add 1 teaspoon fennel seeds. Grind the seeds in a spice mill before adding them to the rub. This fennel variation goes particularly well with fish.

WORLD RUBS

SAZÓN
PUERTO RICAN PIG POWDER

YIELD: Makes ¾ cup

TRY THIS!

Use as you would any seasoned salt. Pork, chicken, and steak are the most predictable choices, but I use it pretty much on everything.

First up in this section is Puerto Rico. Sure it's a US territory, but its food palate is rich with international flavors. Like this pig powder. No pit boss in Puerto Rico would dream of making *lechón asado* (pit-roasted pig) or even grilling steaks or chicken without first sprinkling them with a seasoned salt called *sazón* (sometimes called *adobo*). The basic ingredients include salt, pepper, cumin, and garlic powder; each grill master brings his own twist. You can buy bottled *sazón* at ethnic markets and most supermarkets, but the commercial brands are loaded with MSG. Here's a quick *sazón* that's bursting with Spanish Caribbean flavors, yet versatile enough to season anything.

INGREDIENTS

⅓ cup coarse salt (sea or kosher)

2 tablespoons freshly ground white pepper

2 tablespoons freshly ground black pepper

2 tablespoons dried parsley

1½ tablespoons ground cumin

1 tablespoon dried oregano

1 tablespoon garlic powder

1 tablespoon onion powder

Combine the ingredients in a bowl and stir or whisk to mix. Transfer to a jar, cover, and store away from heat and light. The *sazón* will keep for several weeks.

SPICES AND HOW TO USE THEM

Smoke may be the essence of barbecue, but spices give it soul. A generous hand with spices turns ordinary grilling into barbecue of truly awesome dimensions.

Alas, not all spices are the same. Nor should they be used in the same way. It's fine to buy most spices pre-ground, but some suffer in the processing. Anyone who's ever been on the receiving end of a pepper mill knows the difference between freshly ground and pre-ground black pepper. And, when you buy whole spices, you can roast them in a skillet before grinding, boosting the flavor even more.

You probably have a lot of spices in your spice rack already. Some you may have owned since the Bush administration. This brings us to Raichlen's first rule of spice handling: To become an ace rub maker, the first thing to do is to open all your spices and smell each one. If you aren't greeted with a strong aroma, throw it out. Saffron, coriander, even paprika start to lose their aroma and flavor after six months—even sooner if you store your spices on a rack near the stove. Always store spices away from heat and light.

When you shop for spices, don't buy more than you will use in six months. Turning your inventory frequently ensures freshness. I try to buy my spices at ethnic markets, especially Indian and Middle Eastern. In those cultures, spices are central to the cuisine, so ethnic markets tend to have better quality. They also tend to be cheaper. Another good source for spices is a natural foods store, where you can buy spices in bulk. Besides getting a better deal, you can smell the spices before purchasing to be sure they're fresh and potent.

In many cultures spices are roasted before they're used. In some instances, the spices are actually charred to give them a smoke flavor. Roasting intensifies the flavor by releasing the essential spice oils. The traditional way to roast spices is in a dry heavy skillet. Roast the spices over medium heat, shaking the pan to ensure even roasting. Have a bowl handy and transfer the spices to it when roasted. If you leave them in the skillet, they'll continue to roast, and possibly burn, even once the pan is off the heat. Let the spices cool after roasting, particularly if you are going to grind them.

The final technique for maximizing the flavor of spices is to grind them just before using. I keep a couple of coffee grinders on hand for this purpose. I never use them for coffee. Most spice mixtures stay aromatic for several months when stored in a tightly covered jar, away from heat and light, but the sooner you use them the more flavorful they'll be.

One last bit of advice. Some people believe that if a little is good, more is better. This may be true when it comes to money, but it's definitely not the case with spices. The surest way to ruin a rub or sauce is to overseason it. Too much is too much, no matter how you cut it.

Follow the recommendations above and you'll wind up using less of a particular spice but actually getting more flavor.

Spices that can help make you a barbecue champ include:

ALLSPICE: Small dark round berries native to the Caribbean, which the early explorers mistook for pepper. Sweet and spicy, allspice is one of the defining flavors of Jamaica's Jerk Seasoning (page 85) and it's used throughout the Caribbean and Middle East for flavoring grilled meats and seafood.

ANISE SEED: A tiny light brown seed with a sweet licoricey flavor. Added to sauces and rubs for sweetness.

CARDAMOM: A tan pod the size of a coffee bean with a fragrant scent and haunting flavor. Beloved by grill jockeys in the Near and Far East, from Cairo to Cochin. Adds a sweet exotic accent to marinades, rubs, and sauces. Sold in pod form, as black seeds, and ground. Cardamom is expensive: For the best deal buy it at an Indian or Middle Eastern market.

CINNAMON STICKS: Like its cousin cassia, cinnamon comes from the fragrant bark of a tropical tree. It's used extensively in the grilling of Mexico, Morocco, India, and the Republic of Georgia. Cinnamon sticks most commonly turn up in marinades, but you can also use them as skewers or stuff them into the cavities of spit-roasted ducks and chickens. One great use for cinnamon sticks is the Georgian Tabaka (page 68).

CLOVES: Sweet, fragrant, and highly aromatic, cloves are a key spice in ketchup and many barbecue sauces, as well as in Jamaican jerk seasoning. The clove takes its name from the French word for *nail*, which it resembles.

CORIANDER: The round, ridged seed of the plant that gives us fresh cilantro. Indispensable in pastrami and popular in Asia as well. Highly aromatic with a touch of sweetness.

CUMIN: A sickle-shaped seed with a pungent earthy aroma. Greatly esteemed by Texans, who add it to rubs and barbecue sauces. Also popular in Mexico, South America, the Caribbean, North Africa, the Middle East, and India. Use sparingly: Cumin quickly becomes overpowering.

FENNEL SEED: Another licoricey spice, which you've probably enjoyed in Italian sausage. Used in moderation, it can add a pleasing sweetness to rubs.

GALANGAL (AKA GALANGA): A cousin of ginger used in Southeast Asian spice pastes, galangal looks like ginger, but with zebra-like stripes on the skin. It possesses the peppery hotness of ginger but not the sweetness. Galangal is sold fresh and frozen at Asian markets. Dried galangal is a popular seasoning in Indonesia, where it goes by the name of *laos*. Fresh ginger mixed with black pepper makes an acceptable substitute.

GOCHUGARU: Korean chile flakes used for firing up Korean barbecue and kimchi.

MACE: The lacy membrane surrounding a nutmeg, which it resembles in aroma and flavor, though it's a little sweeter. Mace is sold in blades (twisted orange-tan chips) and powdered. A key ingredient in Chesapeake Bay seafood seasonings, like Old Bay.

MUSTARD SEED: Tiny round seeds that are ground or crushed to make mustard. The three main varieties in ascending order of hotness are white (or yellow), brown, and black. The seeds are often added to rubs.

NUTMEG: A fragrant oval brown nut whose musky aroma hints at cinnamon and vanilla. (Renaissance physicians once prescribed it as a cure for the Plague.) For the best results, buy a whole nutmeg and grate it fresh as you need it. A key ingredient in Jamaican jerk seasoning.

PAPRIKA: This sweet earthy reddish powder is one of the world's most popular spices— an essential ingredient in rubs and barbecue sauces too numerous to mention. Paprika comes mild (sweet), smoked, and hot—the latter with a bite that ranges from pleasantly piquant to incendiary. Paprika is made all over the world: The best comes from Hungary and Spain, so you should make an effort to find an imported brand. Unless I call for hot or smoked paprika in a recipe, you should always use the mild (regular) variety.

PIMENTÓN: Smoked paprika from Spain. Add it in place of paprika to your favorite barbecue rub to reinforce the smoke flavor.

PRAGUE POWDER #1: A curing salt that contains about 6 percent sodium nitrite. Used for curing ham, bacon, jerky, sausages, and so on. Prague Powder #1 (which can be toxic in large quantities) contains pink food coloring to keep you from mistaking it for regular table salt, and is also called pink curing salt #1.

SAFFRON: The fragrant rust-colored stigmas of a crocus that grows in Spain, Iran, and India. It's a popular marinade ingredient in all three countries. Saffron is the world's most expensive spice: It takes 70,000 flowers—picked by hand—to make a single pound. Always buy saffron in threads, not powder—the latter is easier to adulterate. To activate the saffron, soak the threads in a tablespoon of hot water. Try the Persian Saffron-Yogurt Marinade on page 71 and the Saffron Butter Baste on page 117.

SICHUAN PEPPERCORNS: This reddish peppercorn look-alike, with its hair-thin stems and open ends, is native to China. The name is something of a misnomer as it doesn't actually belong to the pepper family, nor is it particularly hot. The flavor is aromatic and piney, with an oddly pleasing quality that numbs the mouth.

STAR ANISE: A star-shaped spice from southwest China and Vietnam. It adds a distinctive smoky, licoricey flavor to the marinades of this region (see the Chinatown Marinade on page 79).

SUMAC: A purplish berry with a tart lemony flavor popular in the Middle and Near East. Ground sumac is a preferred barbecue seasoning in this part of the world: The reddish-purple powder appears in tiny bowls on the table for sprinkling over any type of grilled meat, poultry, or seafood.

TURMERIC: A fragrant orange-fleshed cousin of ginger used widely for seasoning barbecue in Indonesia and Southeast Asia. Turmeric is also a key ingredient in curry powder and a coloring agent for ballpark mustard.

WASABI: This is the hot green paste (it looks like a gob of toothpaste) that accompanies sushi. Often described as Japanese horseradish, wasabi is actually a light green, parsnip-shaped plant known as mountain hollyhock. (The latter is very expensive—most of what passes for wasabi in the United States *is* horseradish.) To reconstitute dry wasabi, combine equal parts powder and water and stir to mix. Let the paste stand for 5 minutes to allow the heat to build. Try it in the Wasabi-Horseradish Butter on page 155.

WORCESTERSHIRE POWDER: If ever there was a "secret" ingredient in barbecue rubs, it's powdered Worcestershire sauce—the powdered form of the popular condiment that owes its sweet-sour aromatic flavor to tamarind. It can be ordered online from Amazon.

JAMAICAN JOLT

YIELD: Makes 2 cups

TRY THIS!

The traditional meat for jerk is pork and this rub will make some of the best Jamaican-style ribs, pork chops, and tenderloins in creation. Don't overlook it as a seasoning for chicken, seafood, or beef and lamb. If you have time, apply the jerk powder 30 to 60 minutes before cooking for greater flavor penetration. This is especially important for pork and poultry. Seafood can be seasoned immediately prior to grilling.

Here's a West Indian spice mix that will light up your mouth like Carnival fireworks. It's based on Jamaica's incendiary Jerk Seasoning (page 85). But sometimes you don't want to wait overnight for your meat to marinate. This knockout blend of allspice, pepper, ginger, onion, garlic, and Scotch bonnet chiles will give you the skull-rattling jolt of traditional jerk seasoning in a rub you can shake on at the last minute. To be strictly authentic, you'll need Scotch bonnet chile powder or its cousin—habanero chile powder. I've given a range for the Scotch bonnet chile powder; don't use more than you mean to.

INGREDIENTS

⅔ cup packed dark brown sugar

½ cup coarse salt (sea or kosher)

¼ cup freeze-dried chives

2 tablespoons freshly ground black pepper

2 tablespoons onion powder

2 tablespoons garlic powder

1 to 4 teaspoons pure Scotch bonnet or habanero chile powder, or to taste

1 tablespoon dried thyme

2 teaspoons ground allspice

2 teaspoons ground coriander

1 teaspoon ground cinnamon

2 teaspoons ground ginger

½ teaspoon ground cloves

½ teaspoon ground nutmeg

Combine all the ingredients in a bowl and whisk to mix. Transfer to a large jar, cover, and store away from heat and light. The rub will keep for several weeks.

HERBES DE PROVENCE

YIELD: Makes 1 cup

The French aren't particularly big on rubs, but there's one seasoning they can't grill without: herbes de Provence. This fragrant blend of rosemary, thyme, basil, oregano, and other herbs has a strong affinity with lamb, pork, and seafood. It's so popular that clay jars and small burlap bags of it turn up at food markets not just in Provence but all over France and the world. Herbes de Provence contain one ingredient you don't normally think of as a seasoning for barbecue—lavender, a purplish flower with a floral aroma that makes it unique in the world of seasoning.

TRY THIS!

Sprinkle the mix on grilled lamb—steaks, chops, rack, and leg. It's also good on seafood, pork, chicken, and beef. To make a wet rub, combine equal parts herbes de Provence and extra-virgin olive oil in a bowl and stir to form a thick paste.

INGREDIENTS

¼ cup dried basil

¼ cup dried rosemary

2 tablespoons dried oregano

2 tablespoons dried summer savory (optional)

2 tablespoons dried thyme

2 teaspoons dried lavender

2 bay leaves, finely crumbled

1 teaspoon freshly ground white pepper

1 teaspoon ground coriander

⅛ teaspoon ground cloves

Combine all the ingredients in a bowl and mix with your fingers, crumbling any large rosemary leaves. Transfer to a jar, cover, and store away from heat and light. The rub will keep for several weeks.

MEDITERRANEAN HERB RUB
ROSEMARY, OREGANO, SAGE, AND MINT

YIELD: Makes about ¾ cup

TRY THIS!

So how do you use this Mediterranean rub? Let me count the ways. On shrimp *a la plancha*, or chicken on the rotisserie, or pork roast in the oven, or steak or fish on the grill.

I've written about hundreds of rubs over the years and I manufacture more than a dozen. But this is the seasoning I use most on a daily basis: a Tuscan-inflected blend of rosemary, sage, oregano, garlic, and hot red pepper flakes, plus a Moroccan touch—dried mint.

INGREDIENTS

3 tablespoons dried rosemary

2 tablespoons dried crushed sage

2 tablespoons dried oregano

2 tablespoons dried mint

1 tablespoon dried garlic flakes

1 tablespoon red pepper flakes

1 tablespoon coarse salt (sea or kosher)

1 tablespoon cracked black peppercorns

Combine the rosemary, sage, oregano, mint, garlic flakes, red pepper flakes, salt, and peppercorns in a bowl and whisk to mix. Transfer to a jar, cover, and store away from heat and light. The rub will keep for several weeks.

PINCHO POWDER

YIELD: Makes 1 cup

inchos is the Spanish term for shish kebabs. These flavor-ful skewers turn up at tapas bars from Majorca to Madrid. An Arabic influence (don't forget, Spain was occupied by the Moors from the eleventh to the fifteenth centuries) is apparent in the presence of cumin, coriander, and saffron. You can buy commercial *pincho* powder in Spain, but it's easy to make your own. Sprinkle it on any kebab meat, especially beef or pork, to give it a Spanish accent. For best results, use an imported Spanish (smoked) or Hungarian paprika. Oh, and have plenty of sangria on hand.

TRY THIS!

To make *pinchos*, sprinkle the rub on cubes of pork, beef, lamb, or chicken and toss to mix in a mixing bowl. Stir in a little olive oil and toss again. Marinate, covered, in the refrigerator for 2 to 4 hours. Thread the meat on skewers and grill over high heat, basting with olive oil. Season with more rub before serving.

INGREDIENTS

½ teaspoon saffron threads

¼ cup smoked paprika

¼ cup dried parsley

¼ cup freeze-dried chives

2 tablespoons coarse salt (sea or kosher)

2 teaspoons dried onion flakes

2 teaspoons dried garlic flakes

2 teaspoons red pepper flakes

2 teaspoons ground cumin

2 teaspoons ground coriander

2 teaspoons dried oregano

2 teaspoons freshly ground black pepper

Crumble the saffron between your fingers into a bowl. Stir or whisk in the remaining ingredients. Transfer to a jar, cover, and store away from heat and light. The powder will keep for several weeks.

BEIJING BLAST

YIELD: Makes 2 cups

TRY THIS!

Sprinkle Beijing Blast on grilled fish, chicken, pork, veal, vegetables, and tofu.

A blast is a rub sprinkled on grilled food just prior to serving to give it a final blast of flavor. (Some blasts can be used for marinating as well.) The Asian roots of the rub are obvious in the sesame seeds, but it's versatile enough to accommodate a wide range of grilled dishes of the West. I developed it when my grandfather had to go on a salt-free diet. The pink peppercorns (see page 18) and black and white sesame seeds make this rub as colorful as it is aromatic. Roasting the sesame seeds intensifies their flavor, so you don't even miss the salt.

INGREDIENTS

1 cup white sesame seeds	½ cup black sesame seeds
¼ cup pink peppercorns	1½ tablespoons poppy seeds
2 tablespoons green peppercorns	1 tablespoon red pepper flakes
	1 tablespoon dried garlic flakes

1. Heat a dry skillet over medium heat. Add half the white sesame seeds and roast, stirring occasionally, until fragrant and golden brown, 2 to 4 minutes. Transfer the sesame seeds to a bowl to cool.

2. Coarsely grind the pink and green peppercorns in a spice mill and add to the sesame seeds. Add the unroasted sesame seeds and remaining ingredients and stir to mix.

3. Transfer to a large jar, cover, and store away from heat and light. The blast will keep for several weeks.

CHINESE FIVE-SPICE POWDER

YIELD: Makes ⅓ cup

Five-spice powder is one of the most alluring seasonings in the Chinese pantry. Star anise and fennel seed give it a licorice flavor; cinnamon and clove provide sweetness; white or Sichuan peppercorns add additional aromatics. Five is something of a mystical number in Chinese culture, representing the five elements: wood, metal, water, fire, and earth. You can buy five-spice powder at Asian markets, natural foods stores, gourmet shops, and many supermarkets, but it's easy to make your own.

TRY THIS!

Five-spice powder is the traditional seasoning for poultry (especially duck and chicken) and pork. Use it to give a Chinese accent to foods or combine it with salt and sugar to make Sweet and Licoricey Duck Rub (page 46).

INGREDIENTS

3 star anise

2 cinnamon sticks
(3 inches each)

3 tablespoons Sichuan peppercorns

2 tablespoons fennel seeds

½ teaspoon whole cloves

1. Heat a dry skillet over medium-low heat. Add the spices and toast until fragrant, 3 to 5 minutes. Transfer the spices to a bowl and let cool completely.

2. Break the star anise and cinnamon sticks into pieces. Grind the spices to a fine powder in a spice mill. Transfer to a jar, cover, and store away from heat and light. The five-spice powder will keep for several weeks.

RUBBING IT IN

Simply defined, a rub is a mixture of herbs and spices used to season meat (or seafood, tofu, or vegetables) before cooking. History is vague about when rubs first came to be used with barbecue. A good place to start might be *Cold Mountain*, Charles Frazier's stunning Civil War novel set in the Smoky Mountains. "When Ruby finally returned, she carried only a small bloody brisket wrapped in paper," writes Frazier. She fetched "salt, sugar, black pepper, and red pepper all mixed together. She opened the paper and rubbed the mixture on the meat to case it, then she buried it in the ashes of the fire." Such are the evocative powers of Frazier's writing that I have tried this recipe, using equal parts salt, sugar, black pepper, and hot paprika. It produces some of the tastiest barbecue in creation.

This simple mixture was the forerunner of the modern American barbecue rub and its ingredients suggest the basic architecture of a well-built spice mix. A good rub will have a sweet component, the sugar. A blast of heat, in this case supplied by black pepper. A fruity or earthy component, provided by the paprika. Most rubs contain salt to make your mouth water—although it's not absolutely mandatory. The passing years have brought considerable refinements to rubs. Pick up a typical Memphis- or Kansas City-style rub today, and you'll detect the presence of onion and garlic powder, mustard, celery seed, bay leaf, oregano, thyme, rosemary, and/or parsley. You may also get a whiff of cumin, turmeric, cinnamon, cloves, nutmeg, and even a shot of citric acid or MSG.

Like barbecue itself, American rubs remain fiercely regional. You'd never confuse a Cajun blackening mix for Chesapeake Bay fish seasoning or a Santa Fe-style chile rub. Cajun blends underscore the Louisiana fondness for onion, garlic, thyme, and cayenne. Chesapeake Bay seasoning has a Teutonic sweetness thanks to the presence of ginger, mace, celery seed, and cardamom. (This isn't as surprising as it sounds: Baltimore's Old Bay Spice Company was founded by a German-Jewish spice merchant.)

As you move West, rubs reveal a Mexican influence—witness the popularity of cumin and chile powders in Tex-Mex and Southwestern rubs. The heat increases to the point where some rubs become almost painfully hot, especially when flavored with ground chipotle (smoked jalapeño) or habanero chiles. But no matter how hot a rub may be, there should be a sense of balance.

Nor do North Americans have a monopoly on rubs. Puerto Ricans season their meats with a lively mixture of salt, pepper, cumin, oregano, and garlic called *sazón* (page 34). The Spanish spice up their *pinchos* (kebabs) with paprika, cumin, coriander, oregano, and saffron (page 41). Herbes de Provence (page 39), that fragrant mixture of rosemary, basil, savory, thyme, and lavender from the south of France, is nothing more than an herb rub with a Mediterranean accent. (And nothing tastes better on lamb.)

Whatever the ingredients, a good rub will play to every taste bud. It should certainly hit the basics: sweet, sour, salty, and bitter. There should be some deep bass tones (offered by such earthy spices as cumin or coriander), some sharp high notes (provided by the chiles and black, white, or Sichuan peppercorns). Above all, the experience should be harmonic: A good rub will remind you of a symphony, not a solo.

So how do you use a rub? There are two ways. First, you can use it as a seasoning, like salt or pepper. Sprinkle the rub on a steak, chop, or chicken breast and grill it right away. For even more flavor, massage it into the meat—that's why it's called a "rub." When you sprinkle the rub on the surface of the meat, it will pretty much taste like it does on its own. There's nothing wrong with this approach, and it's made me look good the times I had to make a meal in a hurry.

The other way to use a rub is similar to the way you'd use a marinade: Apply the rub several hours or even days ahead of time and leave it on to flavor the meat. (Place the rubbed meat in the refrigerator.) With this method, the spice flavor penetrates the meat more deeply and a transformation takes place. The intermingling of seasonings and meat juices alters the original flavor of both the rub and the meat. You wind up with a richer, more dynamic flavor that's greater than the sum of the parts. Rubs also aid in the formation of a savory crust. As you can imagine, this is how I prefer to use rubs.

The length of flavoring time depends on the ingredients in the rub and the size and cut of meat. Rubs that contain lots of salt or chili powder impose their flavor more quickly than rubs that don't. A rub will penetrate a boneless chicken breast faster than it will a whole turkey or pork shoulder. A sturdy cut of meat, like pork shoulder, will stand up to a rub better than a thin cut, like a chop. And salt has a dehydrating effect on meats, which can be good up to a

point (it firms up the flesh and concentrates the flavor). But curing meat or fish with a salt-based rub for too long will make it dry or rubbery. As a rough rule, figure on 2 to 4 teaspoons rub per pound of meat, poultry, or fish.

Here are some guidelines for timing:

- Very small foods, like shrimp: 10 to 20 minutes of marinating.

- Thin cuts of single-serve portions of meat, like boneless chicken breasts and fish fillets: 30 to 60 minutes before cooking.

- Thicker cuts of single-serve portions of meat, like steaks and chops: 1 to 2 hours before cooking.

- Large or tough cuts of meat, like racks of ribs and whole chickens: 4 hours to overnight before cooking.

- Very large or tough cuts of meats, like whole turkeys, briskets, pork shoulders, or fresh hams: overnight to 24 hours before cooking.

SWEET AND LICORICEY DUCK RUB

YIELD: Makes 1½ cups

TRY THIS!

Rub this mixture onto duck, chicken, squab, and pork.

Kansas City meets Canton in this rub. It's a traditional American barbecue rub with a fragrant twist: five-spice powder. Use it on any meat that can benefit from a licoricey sweetness.

INGREDIENTS

½ cup coarse salt (sea or kosher)

½ cup turbinado sugar, such as Sugar in the Raw

⅓ cup Chinese Five-Spice Powder (page 43)

¼ cup freshly ground black pepper

Combine the ingredients in a bowl and whisk to mix. Transfer to a jar, cover, and store away from heat and light. The rub will keep for several weeks.

SINGAPORE SATÉ RUB

YIELD: Makes a generous ½ cup

TRY THIS!

Originally designed for beef, the Singapore Saté Rub works equally well on chicken and pork.

Rubs are relatively rare in Southeast Asia, the preferred method of seasoning being marinating. This Singapore saté rub may remind you of Indian curry thanks to its principal flavorings: coriander, cumin, and turmeric—a nod to the large Indian community in this tiny Asian city-state. The intense fragrant flavor is uniquely Southeast Asian.

INGREDIENTS

3 tablespoons light brown sugar
   (or dark, if that's all you have
   on hand)

2 tablespoons ground coriander

1 tablespoon ground turmeric

1 tablespoon ground cumin

1 tablespoon coarse salt
   (sea or kosher)

1 tablespoon freshly ground
   black pepper

Place the sugar, coriander, turmeric, cumin, salt, and pepper in a bowl and mix well, breaking up any lumps in the sugar with your fingertips. Transfer to a jar, cover, and store away from heat and light. The rub will keep for several weeks.

DESSERT RUB

YIELD: Makes 1 cup

I created this Dessert Rub for grilled peaches and it works equally well on grilled plums, bananas, pineapple, and apple (cut crosswise into ½-inch-thick slices). Turbinado sugar is a coarsely granulated, light brown cane sugar with crunchy crystals. If unavailable, use granulated sugar or demerara.

INGREDIENTS

1 cup turbinado sugar,
   such as Sugar in the Raw

2 teaspoons ground cinnamon

¼ teaspoon ground nutmeg

¼ teaspoon ground allspice

¼ teaspoon ground cloves

Place the sugar in a bowl and whisk in the cinnamon, nutmeg, allspice, and cloves. Transfer to a jar, cover, and store away from heat and light. This rub will keep for several weeks.

TRY THIS!

Brush any sliced juicy fruit with melted butter or coconut milk, then crust it generously with Dessert Rub. Grill over a hot fire. Use the rub on grilled half lemons, limes, oranges, and grapefruit to make an outrageous sangria. Sprinkle on slices of buttered pound cake and grill to make dessert "toast."

SPICE-GRILLED PINEAPPLE
WITH SMOKY WHIPPED CREAM

YIELD: Serves 4 to 8

Pineapple was the first fruit I ever grilled and it remains a Raichlen family favorite. The key is to grill over a hot fire so you caramelize the sugar while leaving the fruit raw and juicy in the center. Mezcal is a tequila-like spirit made with fire-roasted agave cactus hearts. This gives it a smoky flavor—think of it as Mexican liquid smoke.

INGREDIENTS

SPICED SMOKED WHIPPED CREAM:

1 cup heavy (whipping) cream

2 tablespoons Dessert Rub (page 47)

2 tablespoons mezcal or ¼ teaspoon liquid smoke

PINEAPPLE:

1 cup minus 2 tablespoons Dessert Rub (page 47)

1 juicy ripe pineapple, peeled and cut into ½-inch-thick slices (core it or not, your choice)

½ cup coconut milk (use a Thai or Latino brand)

Ground cinnamon or freshly grated nutmeg, for garnish

---

1. Make the whipped cream: Place the cream and Dessert Rub in a chilled metal bowl. Beat to soft peaks with an electric mixer. Add the mezcal or liquid smoke and continue beating to firm peaks. Keep chilled.

2. Set up a grill for direct grilling and preheat it to high. Brush and oil the grill grate.

3. Place the Dessert Rub in a shallow bowl next to the grill. Brush each pineapple slice on both sides with coconut milk, then completely dredge it in the rub, shaking off any excess.

4. Arrange the pineapple slices over the hot fire and grill until darkly browned (the sugar should start to caramelize) on both sides, 2 minutes per side. Transfer to a platter or plates. Top each slice with a dollop of the whipped cream and shake a little ground cinnamon or grate some nutmeg on top.

THE ONLY
MARINADE YOU'LL
EVER NEED

MARINADES, WET RUBS, SPICE PASTES, CURES, AND BRINES

What do Jamaican jerk, Indian tandoori, and Thai saté have in common? Each achieves its bold in-your-face flavor by means of a lengthy soak in a marinade. Marinades, like sauces, are designed to enhance the flavor of simply grilled meats and seafood. The difference is that marinades work their magic before you even light the grill. Of all the flavor-enhancing weapons in a grill jockey's arsenal, none is as powerful as a marinade.

In this chapter I've included the world's great marinades, plus wet rubs and spice pastes—the rubs being somewhat thicker than a conventional marinade, the pastes so thick you spread them on the meat with a spatula. Your grilling will never taste bland again.

MARINADES

THE ONLY MARINADE YOU'LL EVER NEED

YIELD: Makes 1 cup, enough for 1 pound of meat or seafood

TRY THIS!

This marinade goes great with everything, and I mean everything: poultry, seafood, beef, veal, pork, lamb, and vegetables. The larger the piece of meat, the longer you should marinate it (see box, page 54).

I f I could use only one marinade for the rest of my life, it would be this one. Redolent with garlic, piquant with fresh lemon juice, and fragrant with extra virgin olive oil, it instantly transports you to the Mediterranean. I can't think of a single food that doesn't taste better bathed in it. You can use it as both a marinade and a basting sauce. Before marinating poultry, meat, or seafood, simply set a portion aside for basting.

INGREDIENTS

½ teaspoon finely grated lemon zest

¼ cup fresh lemon juice

½ teaspoon coarse salt (sea or kosher), or to taste

½ teaspoon cracked black peppercorns, or to taste

½ teaspoon red pepper flakes (optional)

3 cloves garlic, peeled and crushed with the side of a cleaver or minced

½ cup coarsely chopped fresh herbs, such as parsley, basil, oregano, dill, and/or cilantro

½ cup extra virgin olive oil

Combine the lemon zest, juice, salt, pepper, and red pepper flakes (if using) in a nonreactive (glass, ceramic, or stainless steel) bowl and whisk until the salt crystals are dissolved.

Stir in the garlic and herbs. Stir or whisk in the olive oil. The virtue of this marinade is its freshness: Use it within 2 hours of making. Stir again just before using.

THE LOWDOWN ON LEMONS

Lemons pop up at every stop on the world's barbecue trail—wedges or halves for squeezing over grilled seafood; lemon zest for brightening marinades; lemon juice for souring sauces. Lemon provides two very different types of flavor.

The zest (the oil-rich yellow outer peel) contains aromatic oils that deliver the bright fruity lemon flavor without any acidity. Many recipes in this book call for lemon zest. One easy way to remove lemon zest is in broad thin strips with a vegetable peeler, taking only the yellow peel, not the bitter white pith beneath it. You can also use a Microplane grater or a lemon zester, a tool with a rectangular blade with tiny holes at the leading edge. Drag the holes over the lemon to remove thin strands of zest. You can also grate fresh lemon zest with a box grater. One neat trick is to sandwich a piece of parchment paper between the lemon and grater before grating. The zest will stay on the paper when you lift it off and the grater will be easy to clean.

Before juicing a lemon, roll it on the work surface, pressing the top of the lemon with the palm of your hand. The pressure helps release the juices from the lemon pulp. When you cut the lemon open, the juice will come gushing out. When squeezing lemon halves, do so between your fingers or over a strainer to catch the seeds.

CHAR SIU MARINADE

YIELD: Makes 1½ cups marinade, enough for 2 to 3 pounds meat or seafood

You've seen them hanging in Chinatown restaurant and shop windows: glistening strips of reddish-brown *char siu*, Chinese barbecued pork. (The name literally means "fork roast"—a reference to the barbecue forks traditionally used for roasting the meat over the fire.) Like American barbecue, char siu plays sweet against salty—the former in the form of honey and hoisin sauce; the latter from oyster sauce and soy sauce. What sets char siu apart are the aromatic notes provided by sesame oil and Chinese Five-Spice Powder. (The latter owes its smoky anise flavor to star anise and fennel seed—see page 43.)

TRY THIS!

Char siu is traditionally used to marinate fatty strips of pork shoulder. It also works well with chicken, beef, lamb, seafood, and tofu.

INGREDIENTS

⅓ cup honey

⅓ cup soy sauce

¼ cup oyster sauce

¼ cup rice wine or sake

2 tablespoons Asian (dark) sesame oil

2 tablespoons hoisin sauce

1 teaspoon Chinese Five-Spice Powder, homemade (page 43), or a good commercial brand

1 teaspoon freshly ground white pepper

Place the honey, soy sauce, oyster sauce, rice wine, sesame oil, hoisin sauce, five-spice powder, and pepper in a large bowl and whisk to mix. Use within a few hours of making.

MARINATING TIMES

How long should you marinate a chop or fish fillet before putting it on the grill? It's an easy question with a complicated answer, because the marinating time depends on the strength of the marinade, the particular food to be marinated, and the size and cut of the meat. For example, shrimp and chicken breasts obviously require less marinating than a whole chicken or whole fish. A light herb marinade takes longer to work than a strong marinade fiery with Scotch bonnet chiles and spices.

The following list will provide a rough guide to marinating times. When in doubt, see the instructions in a particular recipe. Note: You can speed up the marinating time by making deep slashes in the sides of whole fish or chicken pieces.

- Very large pieces of meat, such as brisket, prime rib, pork shoulder, leg of lamb, turkey, and capon: 24 hours.

- Large pieces of meat, such as beef and pork tenderloins, pork loins, rack and butterflied leg of lamb, and whole chickens; large whole fish: 6 to 12 hours.

- Medium-size pieces of meat, such as porterhouse steaks, double-cut pork chops, and chicken halves or quarters; small whole fish: 4 to 8 hours.

- Medium-to-small pieces of meat, such as steaks, pork and lamb chops, and bone-in chicken breasts or legs; fish steaks, tofu, portobello mushrooms and other vegetables: 1 to 3 hours.

- Small pieces of meat, such as boneless chicken breasts; fish fillets and shrimp: 15 minutes to 2 hours.

CHAR SIU CHICKEN THIGHS

YIELD: Serves 4

Although traditionally used with pork, the sweet/salty flavor of char siu goes great with chicken—especially the rich fatty meat of the thigh. To avoid flare-ups and the charring associated with sweet marinades, I call for indirect grilling the chicken thighs, with a basting of the reserved marinade and a quick sizzle directly over the fire at the end.

INGREDIENTS

2 pounds bone-in chicken thighs

Char Siu Marinade (page 53)

3 scallions (white and green parts), trimmed and sliced crosswise paper-thin

3 tablespoons toasted sesame seeds

½ cup prepared Chinese mustard in a serving bowl (optional)

1. Marinate the chicken in the Char Siu Marinade in the refrigerator for at least 4 hours, preferably overnight.

2. Set up a grill for indirect grilling and preheat to medium. Brush and oil the grill grate.

3. Drain the chicken thighs well, reserving the marinade. Transfer the marinade to a saucepan and boil it for 3 minutes to sterilize it. Arrange the chicken thighs on the grate skin side up over the drip pan away from the heat. Indirect grill until sizzling, browned, and cooked through, 30 to 40 minutes. The last 3 minutes, brush the chicken thighs with a little reserved marinade and place directly over the fire to sizzle the sauce into the meat, 1 to 2 minutes per side.

4. Transfer the chicken to a platter and pour any remaining reserved marinade over it. Sprinkle with the sliced scallions and sesame seeds. Serve the mustard, if using, on the side for drizzling on the chicken.

JERKY MARINADE

YIELD: Makes about 1½ cups, enough for 2 pounds of beef, venison, bison, or turkey

TRY THIS!

Use this marinade to make beef, venison, or turkey jerky. You need a lean cut of meat to keep the jerky from spoiling.

Jerky is big business. (How big? A whopping 1.5 billion dollar a year business, according to the *Washington Post*.) If you think the store-bought jerky is good, wait until you cure and smoke it at home. That's what my assistant and website editor, Nancy Loseke, has done for 30 years, and her jerky has been known to make vegetarians revert to meat-eating. One advantage of making your own jerky is that you get to customize the flavorings. Another: Your jerky will be free of the artificial flavorings and MSG often found in the commercial stuff. Prague Powder #1 (also known as pink curing salt #1) is a sodium nitrite-based curing salt. It gives the jerky an inviting texture and reddish color and helps prevent spoilage.

INGREDIENTS

¾ cup soy sauce

½ cup cola, beer, or cold-brewed coffee

¼ cup Worcestershire sauce

2 tablespoons brown sugar (light or dark—your choice)

2 teaspoons Prague Powder #1 (see page 37)

1½ teaspoons hot sauce, such as sriracha or Frank's RedHot

1 teaspoon onion powder

1 teaspoon freshly ground black pepper

½ teaspoon liquid smoke

2 cloves garlic, peeled and crushed with the side of a knife or cleaver

Combine the soy sauce, cola, Worcestershire sauce, brown sugar, Prague Powder, hot sauce, onion powder, pepper, and liquid smoke in a bowl. Whisk until the sugar and Prague Powder have dissolved. Stir in the garlic. Use within a few hours of making.

Variation

For a jerky marinade reminiscent of Korean *bul kogi* (thin-sliced grilled rib-eye), substitute pear nectar for the cola and add 2 trimmed, thinly sliced scallions, and 1 tablespoon each minced fresh ginger and Asian (dark) sesame oil.

SMOKED VENISON JERKY

YIELD: Makes 1 pound jerky, enough for 4

Jerky requires lean meat (fat hastens spoilage), and venison meets that need admirably, delivering a superrich beefy taste. If venison isn't available, use bison or lean beef instead.

INGREDIENTS

2 pounds venison

Jerky Marinade (facing page)

1. Partially freeze the meat, 30 to 60 minutes. (This facilitates slicing.) Trim off any fat or silverskin, then cut the meat against the grain into ¼-inch-thick slices using a sharp knife. Or, ask your butcher to do this for you on a meat slicer.

2. Place the meat in a large resealable plastic bag. Add the Jerky Marinade, seal the bag then massage the bag to make sure each strip of meat is coated. Place the bag in a mixing bowl (to contain any potential leaks), and refrigerate for at least 8 hours and up to 24—the longer, the richer the flavor. Turn the bag every few hours to ensure the meat marinates evenly.

3. When ready to cook, drain the meat in a colander, discarding the marinade. Arrange the meat slices on a wire rack over a sheet pan and blot dry with paper towels.

4. Set up your smoker according to the manufacturer's directions and preheat to 200°F. Add the wood as specified by the manufacturer. Lightly oil the smoker racks. Arrange the meat strips in a single layer on the racks. Smoke until the jerky is dry, but still somewhat pliant, 3 to 4 hours. Transfer to a wire rack to cool to room temperature, then place the jerky in a sealed container or resealable plastic bag. The jerky will keep for at least 1 week in the refrigerator—not that it ever lasts that long at Nancy's.

YOU ALSO NEED

Apple, cherry, or your favorite hardwood

CHIPOTLE CHILE MARINADE

YIELD: Makes 2 cups adobo, enough to marinate 2 to 3 pounds of meat or seafood

TRY THIS!

Chipotle Chile Marinade is traditionally used with pork, but it also tastes great on chicken, duck, beef, and dark-fleshed seafood.

This pugnacious marinade belongs to an extended family of Latino seasonings called adobo. Mexican versions contain chiles and this one owes its fiery smoke flavor to chipotle chiles (smoked jalapeños). I prefer canned chipotles over the dried because the juices are loaded with flavor and heat. Traditionally, the marinade would be made with sour orange. To approximate the flavor of this tropical citrus fruit, I combine fresh lime and orange juice.

INGREDIENTS

½ teaspoon cumin seeds

½ teaspoon black peppercorns

3 ripe plum tomatoes

3 cloves garlic, peeled

½ medium-size onion, peeled and cut in half

⅓ cup fresh lime juice

3 tablespoons fresh orange juice

2 tablespoons red wine vinegar

2 to 4 canned chipotle chiles

1 to 2 teaspoons canned chipotle juices

1 teaspoon dried oregano

1 teaspoon coarse salt (sea or kosher)

1. Heat a *comal* or dry skillet over medium heat. Add the cumin and peppercorns and toast until fragrant, 2 minutes. Transfer the spices to a blender or spice mill and grind to a fine powder. Leave the spices in the blender.

2. Place the tomatoes, garlic, and onion on the *comal* and cook until nicely browned on all sides, turning with tongs. This will take 4 to 6 minutes for the garlic, and 10 to 12 minutes for the tomatoes and onion. Coarsely chop the vegetables and transfer them to the blender with the spices.

3. Add the lime and orange juices, the vinegar, chipotle chiles and juices, oregano, and salt. Run the blender in bursts to reduce the ingredients to a thick purée. Transfer to a large jar, cover, and refrigerate. Use within a few hours of making.

SMOKY MARINATED PORK TENDERLOIN
WITH SPICY CORN RELISH

YIELD: Serves 4

Mexico meets Asia in this colorful smoky grilled tenderloin. The pork marinates in a classic Mexican adobo (chipotles provide a smoky flavor). The Asian twist comes from a Spicy Corn Relish. This dish is quick enough to serve as a weeknight dinner (excluding the marinating time, it can be assembled and cooked in 30 minutes). But it's also handsome and sophisticated enough to serve at a party.

YOU ALSO NEED

1½ cups of your favorite wood chips (optional), soaked for 30 minutes, then drained

INGREDIENTS

2 or 3 pork tenderloins (1½ to 2 pounds in all), trimmed

1 recipe Chipotle Chile Marinade (facing page)

1 recipe Spicy Corn Relish (page 302)

3 tablespoons melted salted butter or olive oil

4 sprigs of fresh cilantro, for garnish

1. Arrange the pork tenderloins in a glass baking dish and pour the marinade over them. Cover with plastic wrap and marinate in the refrigerator for at least 6 hours, preferably overnight, turning the tenderloins a few times, so they marinate evenly. Not more than 2 hours before you plan to serve the pork, prepare the Spicy Corn Relish.

2. Set up a grill for direct grilling and preheat it to high. Brush and oil the grill grate. For a smoke flavor, toss wood chips on the coals if using a charcoal grill, or place them in the smoker box if using a gas grill.

3. Remove the pork from the marinade and place on the grate. Grill until cooked to taste, 3 to 4 minutes per side (12 to 16 minutes in all) for medium (160°F on an instant-read thermometer), basting often with melted butter or oil. Transfer the tenderloins to a cutting board and let rest for 5 minutes, then slice on the diagonal. Fan out the pork slices on plates or a platter and mound the relish in the center. Garnish each serving with a sprig of cilantro.

ADOBO
CUBAN GARLIC MARINADE

YIELD: Makes 1 cup, enough for 2 pounds of meat

TRY THIS!

Adobo is a versatile marinade, equally delectable with chicken, pork, beef, lamb, shellfish, and fish. Marinate the food, covered, in the refrigerator for between 1 and 8 hours, depending on the size of the cut. For instance, a fish fillet or chicken breast would marinate 1 to 2 hours, a pork butt, the full 8 hours.

Walk into a Cuban home and this marinade is what you'll smell. Garlic. Cumin. Sour orange juice. Adobo is the very lifeblood of Cuban cuisine. Traditionally, the ingredients are combined in a mortar with a pestle. But acceptable results can be obtained with a blender.

INGREDIENTS

5 cloves garlic, peeled and coarsely chopped

1 teaspoon coarse salt (sea or kosher)

1 teaspoon ground cumin

1 teaspoon dried oregano

½ teaspoon freshly ground black pepper

1 cup fresh sour orange juice (see box, page 194), or ¾ cup fresh lime juice and ¼ cup fresh orange juice

Place the garlic, salt, cumin, oregano, and pepper in a mortar and pound with a pestle to a smooth paste. Gradually work in the sour orange juice. Or place all the ingredients in a blender and blend to a smooth purée. Use within a few hours of making.

ENNOBLED BY ADOBO

Spend time on the barbecue trail in Latin America and you'll hear the word *adobo*. This lively marinade is found throughout the Spanish-speaking barbecue world. I mean this quite literally. Adobo turns up in Spain, the Philippines, the Caribbean, and Central and South America. What's curious is that something that's so delicious should actually be named for a dry medieval legal term—*adobar*, literally to ennoble. (The term survives in English in the word *dub*, as in "I dub thee Sir Knight.") It's meat that's being ennobled in this case, thanks to a bath in a flavorful marinade.

Adobo varies from country to country. In Cuba, it is a refreshingly acidic marinade of sour orange juice, garlic, and cumin. In Mexico, adobos are thick pastes made with chiles, tomatoes, and vinegar. Vinegar and garlic characterize the adobo of the Philippines. You'll find several adobos in this book, including the Cuban adobo on the facing page and a Mexican smoked chile adobo on page 58.

FRENCH WEST INDIAN SCOTCH BONNET-LIME MARINADE

YIELD: Makes 1 cup, enough for 1 cut-up chicken; 2 pounds beef, pork, lamb, goat, or fish steaks; 4 small (1 pound) fish; or use it for grilled lobster

Whenever my wife and I visit Guadeloupe, the first thing we do is head for a roadside shack for grilled chicken. The French of the West Indies do some of the tastiest grilling in the Caribbean. Their secret? A pungent marinade made with garlic, Scotch bonnet chiles, fresh thyme, allspice, and lime juice and/or vinegar.

TRY THIS!

Spoon one third of the marinade over the bottom of a glass baking dish. Arrange the food to be marinated on top. If using chicken pieces or whole fish, make deep slashes in the meat to the bones. Pour the remaining marinade over the food. Cover and marinate in the refrigerator for at least 2 or up to 6 hours, turning the pieces of food a couple of times to ensure even marinating.

INGREDIENTS

4 cloves garlic, peeled and minced

½ to 1 Scotch bonnet chile, seeded and finely chopped (for a spicier marinade leave the seeds in; see box, this page)

1 teaspoon coarse salt (sea or kosher)

½ teaspoon freshly ground black pepper

¾ cup fresh lime juice or white wine vinegar or a mixture of the two

1 bunch chives or 4 scallions (white and green parts), trimmed and finely chopped

2 shallots, peeled and thinly sliced

1 small onion, peeled and thinly sliced

3 tablespoons finely chopped fresh flat-leaf parsley

4 sprigs fresh thyme, stripped, or 1 teaspoon dried thyme

2 bay leaves

4 allspice berries

2 whole cloves

¼ cup peanut or canola oil

Place the garlic, chile, salt, and pepper in a mortar and mash them to a paste with a pestle or place in a bowl and mash with the back of a spoon. Add the lime juice and stir until the salt crystals are dissolved. Stir in the remaining ingredients. Use within a few hours of making.

HOW TO HANDLE SCOTCH BONNET CHILES AND OTHER SCORCHERS

Scotch bonnets and their cousins, Mexican habaneros, rank among the world's hottest chiles—50 times hotter than fresh jalapeños. As you can imagine, handling these scorchers can wreak havoc with the skin on your fingertips and your eyes if you touch them. The easiest way to protect yourself is to wear latex or plastic gloves when handling any chiles. French West Indians use an even simpler method: Hold the chile with the tines of a fork and cut it in half. Scrape out the seeds with the knife tip, then, holding each half with the fork, cut it into thin crosswise slivers, then finely chop.

BRAZILIAN GARLIC MARINADE

YIELD: Makes 1 cup, enough for 2 pounds of meat or seafood

Brazilians use this *tempeiro* (marinade) whenever they grill pork or chicken. (Beef is considered a "noble" meat, so it's grilled in its natural state.) A simple version might contain only lime juice, salt, and garlic—*lots* of garlic. A more elaborate *tempeiro*, like this one, might contain fresh herbs, wine, and even hot sauce.

INGREDIENTS

6 cloves garlic, peeled and finely chopped

2 teaspoons coarse salt (sea or kosher)

¾ cup fresh lime juice

¼ cup dry white wine

1 tablespoon red wine vinegar

1 to 2 teaspoons Piri-Piri Sauce (Brazilian Hot Sauce; page 286), Tabasco sauce, or your favorite hot sauce

3 tablespoons finely chopped fresh flat-leaf parsley

2 scallions (white and green parts), trimmed and finely chopped

1 tablespoon chopped fresh rosemary or mint

Place the garlic and salt in a mortar and mash to a paste with a pestle or place in a bowl and mash with the back of a spoon. Add the lime juice, wine, vinegar, Piri-Piri Sauce, parsley, scallions, and rosemary and stir until all the salt is dissolved. Use within a few hours of making.

TRY THIS!

Use this marinade for pork, chicken, or lamb. Marinate thin cuts of meat (steaks, chops, and chicken breasts), covered, in the refrigerator for 1 to 2 hours; larger cuts of meat, such as pork loins or shoulders, for 6 to 8 hours, or overnight.

THE MYSTIQUE OF MARINADES

When it comes to boosting the flavor of grilled meats, it's hard to top a marinade. This simple truth is appreciated around Planet Barbecue, from the Jamaican jerk master to the Indian tandoori wallah. Marinades bestow on grilled foods their unique ethnic identity. They also help tenderize tough meat fibers and keep foods moist during cooking. The latter function is particularly important for grilling, as the strong heat of live fire tends to dry out the meat.

Most marinades have three components: acids, oils, and aromatics. The acids help break down tough muscle fibers, tenderizing the meat. (In the days before refrigeration, they also served as a preservative.) The oil coats the exterior of the meat, keeping it from drying out during cooking. The aromatics, which can include chopped vegetables, fresh or dried herbs, ground or whole spices, and/or condiments, such as Worcestershire or chile sauce, deliver powerful blasts of flavor. Put them together, and there isn't a food in creation that won't benefit from their transformative powers.

The acids can include vinegars of all kinds (wine, cider, rice, distilled, and balsamic), fruit juices, and cultured milk products, like yogurt. Lemon juice is a popular souring agent in the Mediterranean basin and Central Asia; lime juice in Latin America and the Far East; pomegranate juice in the Middle East. Dairy marinades include the yogurt of India, Iran, Iraq, and Afghanistan.

The oils in a marinade seal in flavor and keep foods moist during grilling. Olive oil is the preferred oil in California and the Mediterranean. (Use a good, fruity cold-pressed olive oil for marinating.) Sesame oil imparts a pleasing nutty flavor to the marinades of the Far East. (Be sure to use a dark fragrant oil made from toasted sesame seeds.) Nut oils, like walnut, hazelnut, and pistachio, work well with poultry, pork, and seafood. If you want the moisturizing benefits of oil without a distinct flavor, use a bland oil, like canola or peanut.

The aromatics are the soul of a marinade. Classic French marinades start with a *mirepoix*—diced onion, celery, and carrot. The Chinese Holy Trinity is ginger, scallion, and garlic. Dried, fresh, and roasted chiles lie at the heart of Mexican marinades, like the Chipotle Chile Marinade on page 58. Herbs and spices add high notes of character and flavor. (On page 88, you'll find a complete discussion of the herbs and on page 35 the spices used in marinades.) As for condiments, they can be as commonplace as soy or Worcestershire sauce or as exotic as fish sauce or shrimp paste.

Marinades are generally liquid, but some can be as thick as paste. These would include wet rubs, like the Island Seasonin' on page 84, and spice pastes, like the Berber mixture on page 95. Pesto makes a delectable marinade for poultry, beef, and fish.

The flavorings for a marinade are limited only by your imagination. Nonetheless, over the course of time, certain flavorings have come to be associated with specific foods. Seafood is well served by the fragrant tartness of lemon juice, olive oil, and fresh herbs. Lamb shines in a marinade of lemon juice, onion, and yogurt. My favorite marinade for beef is an Asian blend of soy sauce, sesame oil, rice wine, fresh ginger, garlic, and scallions.

Most marinades are used raw, but in some instances, they are cooked. The French marinate game in a mixture of boiled red wine and juniper berries. Besides increasing flavor, boiling has the added advantage of muting the taste of alcohol. Mexicans often roast or grill onions and garlic to give their spice pastes a rich smoky flavor. If you cook a marinade, be sure to let it cool to room temperature before using.

Food should be marinated in a nonreactive container—glass, porcelain, ceramic, or stainless steel. Heavy-duty resealable plastic bags work great for marinating. (Place them in a bowl or baking dish to catch any unexpected leaks.) Avoid aluminum and cast iron, which react with the acids in the marinade. (Aluminum foil drip pans are okay.) It is not necessary for the food to be completely submerged in liquid, but it should be turned several times. Cover the pan or bowl with plastic wrap (to keep in smells) and refrigerate the food while it's marinating.

Drain meats well before placing them on the grill: Wet meat tends to stew rather than grill. If you want to use the marinade for basting, bring it to a rapid boil in a saucepan for 3 minutes first to kill any bacteria. Marinades should not be reused.

Be careful not to marinate foods for too long. Meats can become mushy when marinated for longer than 24 hours. In some cases, the acids in a marinade will "cook" the food, particularly a delicate food like fish. On page 54, you'll find a guide to marinating times.

BELGIAN BEER MARINADE

YIELD: Makes 2½ cups, enough for 2 to 3 pounds of meat

TRY THIS!

This marinade goes best with robust meats, like beef, pork, and chicken. You could also use it with rich oily fish, like salmon and kingfish. Marinate large pieces of meat (whole chickens and roasts) overnight; medium-size pieces of meat (steaks, chops, and chicken pieces) for 4 to 6 hours; and smaller cuts (boneless chicken breasts and cubed meat for shish kebabs) for 2 to 4 hours, covered, in the refrigerator.

Barbecue without beer would be like, well, pick your metaphor. Beer is the beverage of choice among many of the world's barbecue cultures and an essential ingredient in innumerable marinades, bastes, and barbecue sauces. There's good reason for its popularity; beer adds a unique malty sweetness, with a pleasantly bitter edge of hops. You can vary the potency of this marinade by your choice of beer: A light ale or pilsner will give you a mild beer flavor; there's no mistaking the presence of a dark beer, like porter or stout.

INGREDIENTS

2 cups of your favorite beer

¼ cup honey mustard

¼ cup canola oil

1 teaspoon coarse salt (sea or kosher)

1 teaspoon freshly ground black pepper

1 medium-size onion, peeled and thinly sliced

½ green or red bell pepper, stemmed, seeded, and finely chopped

4 scallions (white and green parts), trimmed and chopped

4 cloves garlic, peeled and flattened with the side of a cleaver

2 slices fresh ginger (each ¼ inch thick), peeled and flattened with the side of a cleaver

1 tablespoon pickling spice

1 tablespoon sweet or smoked paprika

½ teaspoon caraway seeds

Combine the beer, mustard, oil, salt, and pepper in a nonreactive mixing bowl and stir or whisk until the salt crystals are dissolved. Stir in the remaining ingredients. Use within a few hours of making.

CINNAMON-ORANGE MARINADE

YIELD: Makes 2 cups, enough for 4 Cornish game hens, 1 chicken, or 2 to 3 pounds of meat

This marinade comes from the Caucasus Mountains in the Republic of Georgia, where it's used to flavor a game hen dish called *tabaka*. I first sampled it at an imperial Russian restaurant in the Boston of my youth called The Hermitage and while I've eaten it many times since then, I've never had a *tabaka* I liked quite as much.

INGREDIENTS

3 oranges

2 limes

1 lemon

¼ cup dry white wine

2 cinnamon sticks
(3 inches each)

3 cloves garlic, peeled and
flattened with the side of
a cleaver

3 slices (each ¼ inch thick)
fresh ginger, peeled and
crushed with the side of a
cleaver

½ teaspoon cracked black
peppercorns

1 medium-size onion, peeled and
thinly sliced

3 tablespoons sweet or smoked
paprika

1 tablespoon light brown sugar

½ teaspoon coarse salt
(sea or kosher), or to taste

½ teaspoon red pepper flakes

¼ teaspoon freshly grated
nutmeg

½ cup extra virgin olive oil

TRY THIS!

Arrange the meat or fish in a glass baking dish. Pour the marinade over the meat, cover, and marinate in the refrigerator for as little as 4 hours or as long as overnight (the longer the better), turning once or twice.

1. Using a vegetable peeler, remove 1 strip of orange zest, 1 strip of lime zest, and 1 strip of lemon zest and set aside. Juice the oranges, limes, and lemon. Combined you should have 1¼ to 1½ cups of juice.

2. Place the juices and zests, the wine, cinnamon, garlic, ginger, and pepper in a heavy nonreactive saucepan and bring to a boil over high heat. Reduce the heat to medium and simmer, uncovered, until the mixture is reduced to 1 cup, about 10 minutes.

3. Remove the pan from the heat and cool to room temperature. Stir in the onion, paprika, sugar, salt, red pepper flakes, nutmeg, and oil. Use within a few hours of making.

TABAKA
GRILLED GAME HENS

YIELD: Serves 4

YOU ALSO NEED

A grill press, salt block, or 4 bricks wrapped with aluminum foil

*T*abaka is one of the glories of Georgian gastronomy: butterflied game hens cooked under a weight to compact the meat and crisp the skin. Tradition calls for the birds to be pan-fried, but I like the robust smoke flavor achieved by grilling. To achieve the proper consistency, spatchcock the birds and grill them under a grill press or salt slab.

INGREDIENTS

4 Cornish game hens (1 pound each), rinsed and patted dry

Cinnamon-Orange Marinade (page 67), cooled

6 tablespoons (¾ stick) unsalted butter, melted

Coarse salt (sea or kosher) and freshly ground black pepper

1 onion, peeled and thinly sliced

½ cup coarsely chopped cilantro leaves

Tkemali (page 215), for serving

1. Spatchcock the game hens. To do this, cut out the backbone of each hen, using poultry shears. Open the hens as you would a book and flatten them with the side of a cleaver. Arrange the game hens in a baking dish and pour the marinade over them. Cover with plastic wrap and marinate the hens in the refrigerator for at least 6 hours, preferably overnight. Turn 2 or 3 times to ensure even seasoning.

2. Set up a grill for direct grilling and preheat it to medium. Brush and oil the grill grate.

3. Remove the hens from the marinade, brush with melted butter, and place them on the grate, skin side up. Place a grill press, salt block, or brick on top of each to flatten it. Grill the hens until cooked through, 8 to 10 minutes per side. Baste again with melted butter when you turn the birds. Move birds as needed to prevent flareups. Season with salt and pepper.

4. To serve, arrange the hens on a platter and sprinkle with the onion and cilantro. Serve the *tkemali* on the side.

WILD GAME MARINADE
WITH JUNIPER AND GIN

YIELD: Makes 4 cups, enough for 5 pounds of meat

The year was 1976; the place, the La Varenne cooking school in Paris. A guy who grew up in a decidedly nonhunting family in Baltimore (yours truly) was about to have his first taste of wild game. Our instructor, Chef Fernand Chambrette, had secured a haunch of wild boar, and he prepared a traditional marinade of red wine and juniper berries to heighten its gamy flavor. A shot of gin reinforced the woodsy flavor of the juniper. If I'd known game could be this good, I would have tried it a lot sooner. You'll be amazed by the power of this simple marinade to turn tame supermarket pork, beef, and even lamb into "wild" game.

TRY THIS!

If using a large cut of meat, like a leg of wild boar, haunch or saddle of venison, or a pork shoulder, marinate the meat, covered, in a large earthenware or stainless-steel bowl in the refrigerator for 24 hours, turning several times. If using small cuts of meats, such as steaks or chops, marinate for 2 to 4 hours. The longer you marinate, the stronger the flavor will be.

INGREDIENTS

3 cups dry red wine

½ cup balsamic vinegar

½ cup extra virgin olive oil

2 tablespoons gin

1 medium-size onion, thinly sliced

1 carrot, thinly sliced

1 rib celery, thinly sliced

2 cloves garlic, flattened with the side of a cleaver

3 tablespoons chopped fresh parsley

2 teaspoons juniper berries

2 teaspoons black peppercorns, lightly crushed with the side of a cleaver

2 bay leaves

2 whole cloves

2 sprigs fresh thyme, stripped, or ½ teaspoon dried thyme

Combine all the ingredients in a nonreactive saucepan and bring to a boil over medium-high heat. Boil for 3 minutes. Cool to room temperature. Use right away or transfer to jars, cover, and refrigerate. The marinade will keep for several days.

TURKISH GARLIC-YOGURT MARINADE

YIELD: Makes about 3 cups, enough for 2 to 3 pounds of meat or seafood

TRY THIS!

This garlic-yogurt marinade traditionally goes with lamb—either cubed to make shish kebabs or in chops or a whole rack for grilling—but don't neglect it for chicken or beef. Marinate the meat, covered, in the refrigerator for at least 6 hours, or as long as overnight.

Travel the world's barbecue trail and you'll find yogurt marinades in Greece, Turkey, Iran, Iraq, Afghanistan, and India. As you move east, the spicing becomes more extravagant, reaching its apotheosis in northern India. The idea behind a yogurt marinade is both ancient and practical: The acids in the yogurt served to preserve meat in the age before refrigeration and to break down tough muscle fibers, a function it still serves today. Yogurt marinades give meats an agreeable sourish tang and soft tender texture. Add onion and garlic, as is done throughout the region, and you'll wind up with some of the best kebabs on the planet. Here's a simple, garlicky Turkish yogurt marinade. For best results, use Greek-style whole milk yogurt.

INGREDIENTS

2 cups plain Greek-style whole milk yogurt

½ cup extra virgin olive oil

3 tablespoons fresh lemon juice

1 medium-size onion, peeled and finely chopped

3 cloves garlic, peeled and minced

1 teaspoon coarse salt (sea or kosher)

½ teaspoon freshly ground black pepper

½ teaspoon red pepper flakes, or to taste

Place the yogurt in a bowl and stir in the remaining ingredients. Use within a few hours of making.

PERSIAN SAFFRON-YOGURT MARINADE

YIELD: Makes about 3 cups, enough for 1 cut-up chicken or 2 to 3 pounds of meat or seafood

Iran is one of the great grilling capitals of the world. Indeed, the term *kebab* comes from the ancient Persian word for meat. Iranians use a variety of marinades—some yogurt based, some olive oil based—to make shish kebabs of extraordinary succulence and flavor. To enjoy the full effect of this marinade, you must use whole milk yogurt and saffron in thread form, not powder.

INGREDIENTS

½ teaspoon saffron threads

1 tablespoon hot water

2 cups plain Greek-style whole milk yogurt

2 medium-size onions, peeled and thinly sliced

2 cloves garlic, peeled and finely chopped

2 strips orange zest

½ cup fresh lemon juice

2 teaspoons coarse salt (sea or kosher)

1 teaspoon freshly ground black pepper

1. Crumble the saffron threads between your thumb and forefinger and place in a small bowl with the hot water. Let the saffron infuse for 10 minutes.

2. Place the yogurt in a bowl and stir in the saffron mixture and the remaining ingredients. Use within a few hours of making.

TRY THIS!

This is one of the most compelling marinades I know of for grilled chicken, Cornish game hens, and quail, and it makes terrific lamb or beef shish kebabs. Marinate the meats, covered, in the refrigerator for at least 6 hours and preferably overnight.

PERSIAN SAFFRON LAMB CHOPS

YIELD: Serves 4

Iranians use complex marinades of yogurt and lemon and fragrant basting sauces of butter and saffron to create some of the most spectacular grilled lamb in the world. This recipe works equally well with other foods, including chicken, beef, and seafood.

INGREDIENTS

8 loin lamb chops
(4 to 5 ounces each) or
12 rib lamb chops
(3 ounces each)

Persian Saffron-Yogurt Marinade
(page 71)

Saffron Butter Baste (page 117)

1 small sweet onion, such as
Vidalia or Walla Walla, peeled
and thinly sliced

8 sprigs fresh flat-leaf parsley

1. Arrange the lamb chops in a glass baking dish and pour the yogurt marinade over them. Turn the chops a few times, cover with plastic wrap, and marinate in the refrigerator for 12 to 24 hours, the longer the stay, the richer the flavor.

2. Set up a grill for direct grilling and preheat it to high. Brush and oil the grill grate.

3. Remove the chops from the marinade, drain well, place on the grate, and grill, basting with the Saffron Butter Baste, until cooked to taste, about 4 minutes per side to cook rib chops to medium, about 6 minutes per side to cook loin chops to medium. Place the chops on a platter and arrange the sliced onion on top. Top with parsley and serve.

TANDOORI SHRIMP

YIELD: Serves 6 as an appetizer; 4 as a main course

Tandoori shrimp is one of the glories of Indian gastronomy. To get the full effect you should serve the shrimp with a kaleidoscopic assortment of side dishes. A bare minimum would include raita and tomato chutney, as well as basmati rice. The more people you have, the more elaborate your spread should be. In India, the shrimp would be cooked in a *tandoor*, an urn-shaped clay barbecue pit. A kamado-style ceramic cooker will give you a similar effect, and you can also direct grill the shrimp over a hot fire.

YOU ALSO NEED

8- to 10-inch bamboo skewers

INGREDIENTS

2 pounds jumbo shrimp, peeled and deveined

Indian Tandoori Marinade (see page 76)

4 tablespoons (½ stick) unsalted butter, melted

1 small red onion, peeled and thinly sliced

½ cup fresh cilantro sprigs

1 lemon, cut into wedges

Raita (page 222)

Tomato Chutney (page 327)

Fresh Mango Chutney (page 323)

1. Place the shrimp in a glass baking dish and pour the marinade over them. Cover with plastic wrap and marinate for 2 to 4 hours in the refrigerator. Stir a couple of times to coat evenly.

2. Set up a grill for direct grilling and preheat it to high. Brush and oil the grill grate.

3. Remove the shrimp from the marinade and thread them onto skewers. Place on the grate and grill until firm, pink, and cooked through, 2 to 3 minutes per side, basting with melted butter.

4. Transfer the shrimp to a platter and sprinkle the onion slices and cilantro sprigs on top. Serve with lemon wedges and bowls of raita and the chutneys.

INDIAN TANDOORI MARINADE

YIELD: Makes 2 cups, enough for 1 cut-up chicken or 2 to 3 pounds of lamb or seafood

TRY THIS!

Use skinless chicken pieces to make chicken tandoori. Cover and marinate in the refrigerator for at least 6 hours and preferably overnight. Marinate lamb the same way. Marinate seafood for 2 to 4 hours, depending on the size of the pieces (marinate bigger pieces longer than smaller pieces).

India's contribution to the world of barbecue is tandoori: meats, seafood, or vegetables marinated to a jumpsuit orange in a pungent paste of yogurt, aromatic vegetables, and spices, then grilled on vertical skewers in a blazing clay barbecue pit known as a tandoor.

Good tandoori balances the tartness of the lemon juice with ginger and spices, the fire of chiles with the soothing coolness of yogurt. I've made the food coloring optional, but know that no self-respecting Indian barbecue buff would dream of making tandoori without it.

Indian tandoori wallahs drain yogurt in cheesecloth to remove the excess liquid to make a marinade of incomparable richness. Start with Greek-style yogurt, which comes drained already, and you can omit this step.

INGREDIENTS

2 teaspoons coriander seeds

1 teaspoon black peppercorns

1 teaspoon cumin seeds

1 teaspoon mace blades

½ teaspoon fennel seeds

4 cardamom pods

2 whole cloves

½ cinnamon stick (about 1 inch)

½ teaspoon saffron threads

1 tablespoon hot water

1 small onion, peeled and coarsely chopped

6 cloves garlic, peeled and coarsely chopped

6 slices (each ¼ inch thick) peeled fresh ginger, coarsely chopped

2 jalapeño peppers, preferably red, seeded and coarsely chopped

3 tablespoons fresh lemon juice

3 tablespoons vegetable oil

2 cups plain whole milk yogurt, preferably Greek-style

2 teaspoons coarse salt (sea or kosher)

2 to 4 drops orange food coloring (optional)

1. Heat a dry skillet over medium heat. Add the coriander, peppercorns, cumin, mace, fennel, cardamom, cloves, and cinnamon. Toast, shaking the pan, until fragrant, 3 minutes. Transfer the spices to a bowl to cool. Grind to a fine powder in a spice mill.

2. Crumble the saffron threads between your thumb and forefinger and place in a small bowl with hot water. Let the saffron infuse for 10 minutes.

3. Combine the onion, garlic, ginger, chiles, lemon juice, and oil in a blender or mini processor and purée to a smooth paste. You may need to add a tablespoon or so of water to obtain a paste.

4. Combine the yogurt, spices, saffron mixture, onion paste, salt, and food coloring, if using, in a bowl and stir to mix. Use within a few hours of making.

SWEET SESAME-SOY MARINADE

YIELD: Makes 1½ cups, enough for 2 pounds of food

This marinade mashes up flavorings from several Asian grill cultures: soy sauce and sake from Japan; sesame oil and seeds from Korea; five-spice powder and oyster sauce from China; plus jalapeños from the United States. Put them together and you get a marinade that turns poultry, meat, seafood, and even tofu into championship Asian-style barbecue. To get the full effect, use dark nutty Asian-style sesame oil, made with roasted sesame seeds. Oyster sauce is a thick briny condiment available in Asian markets and many supermarkets.

TRY THIS!

This polymorphic marinade transforms just about everything—shrimp, fish, chicken, beef, pork, lamb, tofu. Marinate small pieces, like shrimp, for 30 minutes; chicken breasts and fish fillets for 2 to 4 hours; ribs and whole chickens for 6 to 8 hours; and large cuts of meat, like leg of lamb, for 1 to 2 days, covered, in the refrigerator.

SESAME GRILLED TOFU

YIELD: Serves 4

NOTE

Black sesame seeds (*kuro goma*) are available at Japanese shops and natural foods markets.

Tofu is hardly the life of the party at a North American barbecue, although, thanks to its health benefits, it's rapidly gaining acceptance. This recipe plays the flavors of soy sauce and honey against the nutty fragrance of sesame oil and sesame seeds. It's guaranteed to turn skeptics into believers.

INGREDIENTS

2 pounds extra firm tofu

Sweet Sesame-Soy Marinade (page 77)

1 tablespoon toasted sesame seeds (see box, page 112)

1 tablespoon black sesame seeds (optional; see Note)

2 scallions (green parts only), trimmed and finely chopped

1. Rinse the tofu under cold water. Place it on a gently sloping cutting board in the sink. Place a heavy plate or frying pan on top of it and let stand for 1 hour. (If you're in a hurry, you can omit this step, but pressing the tofu this way extracts the excess water and firms it up for grilling.)

2. Cut each block of tofu horizontally into 2 broad thin rectangles. Cut each rectangle in half crosswise. Arrange the tofu pieces in a baking dish and pour the marinade over them. Cover with plastic wrap and marinate in the refrigerator for 2 to 4 hours, turning twice.

3. Remove the tofu from the marinade to a platter. Strain the marinade into a saucepan and boil it over high heat until thick and syrupy, 3 to 4 minutes.

4. Set up a grill for direct grilling and preheat it to high. Oil the grate well. Brush the tofu pieces on both sides with vegetable oil, too. (Tofu tends to stick to the grate.)

5. Place the tofu pieces on the grate and grill until nicely browned, 2 to 4 minutes per side, brushing with the boiled marinade and carefully turning with a spatula. Transfer the tofu to a platter and spoon any remaining marinade over it. Sprinkle with the toasted sesame seeds, black sesame seeds, if using, and scallion greens and serve at once.

INGREDIENTS

⅓ cup Asian (dark) sesame oil

⅓ cup sake, rice wine, or dry sherry

⅓ cup soy sauce

3 tablespoons oyster sauce (optional)

3 tablespoons light brown sugar

2 cloves garlic, peeled and minced

1 tablespoon peeled and minced fresh ginger

2 scallions (white and green parts), trimmed and minced

2 strips lemon zest

1 to 2 jalapeño peppers, seeded and chopped

1 tablespoon toasted sesame seeds (see box, page 112)

½ teaspoon Chinese Five-Spice Powder, homemade (page 43) or a good commercial brand

Combine all the ingredients in a bowl and stir or whisk to mix. Use within a few hours of making.

CHINATOWN MARINADE

YIELD: Makes 1½ cups, enough for 2 pounds of seafood, meat, tofu, or vegetables

Grilling plays a relatively minor role in Chinese cuisine, but the Chinese have developed a marinade that lends itself to an endless variety of grilled dishes. At its heart is the basic Asian flavor dialectic of sweet and salty, the former in the form of sugar and cinnamon, the latter in the form of soy sauce. The cool smoky licorice flavor of star anise complements the Asian triad of ginger, garlic, and scallion. Combine them for a marinade that's symphonic in its complexity, but that can be made in a matter of minutes.

This marinade is extremely versatile, working equally well with seafood (especially shrimp and scallops), poultry (chicken, duck, and quail), meat (pork, lamb, and beef), and tofu.

Marinate small pieces (shrimp, diced chicken, etc.) for 30 to 60 minutes; thin cuts of meat (chicken breasts and steaks) for 1 to 2 hours; and large pieces of meat (whole chickens and roasts) for 12 to 24 hours, covered, in the refrigerator.

INGREDIENTS

2 slices fresh ginger (each ¼ inch thick), peeled

2 cloves garlic, peeled

2 scallions (white parts only), trimmed (save the scallion greens for garnish)

½ cup soy sauce

½ cup Chinese rice wine, Japanese sake, or dry sherry

¼ cup honey or sugar

3 tablespoons Asian (dark) sesame oil

½ teaspoon Chinese Five-Spice Powder, either homemade (page 43) or a good commercial brand

2 star anise

2 cinnamon sticks (3 inches each)

Flatten the ginger slices, garlic cloves, and scallion whites with the side of a cleaver. Place them in a bowl with the soy sauce, rice wine, honey, sesame oil, and five-spice powder and stir or whisk to mix. Add the star anise and cinnamon. The marinade tastes best used within a few hours of making.

THAI SATÉ MARINADE

YIELD: Makes ⅔ cup, enough for 1½ pounds of meat or seafood

TRY THIS!

Cut the meat or seafood into strips the size of your pinkie or flat strips the size and shape of tongue depressors—the flat strips work particularly well for beef. Cover and marinate in the refrigerator for 30 to 60 minutes. Then drain, skewer, and grill.

Satés are bite-size kebabs enjoyed throughout Southeast Asia. They likely originated in Indonesia, where literally hundreds of different types are served. As the preparation spread through the region, each culture customized the recipe, using the local spices and seasonings. The Thai version plays the sweetness of sugar against the briny tang of fish sauce or soy sauce, with garlic and coriander for punch.

Note the addition of one ingredient you may not be accustomed to using—cilantro root. The roots of this pungent plant have an earthy aromatic flavor—the sort you might get if you crossed celery root with cilantro. Look for cilantro complete with roots at Asian and Hispanic markets. But don't worry too much if you can't find it; cilantro leaves will get you close to the right flavor. By the way, rinse those roots well; they tend to have dirt still clinging to them.

INGREDIENTS

⅓ cup fish sauce or soy sauce

⅓ cup fresh lime juice

3 tablespoons sugar or honey

3 cloves garlic, peeled and minced

2 tablespoons chopped cilantro roots or leaves

1 teaspoon ground coriander

½ teaspoon ground turmeric

Combine all the ingredients in a bowl and stir or whisk to dissolve the sugar or honey. Use within a few hours of making.

TERIYAKI MARINADE

YIELD: Makes 2 cups, enough for 2 to 3 pounds of meat or seafood

Teriyaki doesn't really exist as a marinade in Japan. Rather, the ingredients are boiled down into a thick syrup that is brushed on the food as it grills. I like to use the mixture as both a marinade and basting sauce. (Be sure to boil the marinade for 3 minutes to sterilize it before you brush it on cooked food.) Mirin is sweetened Japanese rice wine: You can buy it at natural foods stores and many supermarkets. If it's unavailable, use sherry and a little more honey. The traditional sweetener is sugar, but I like the extra flavor provided by honey. Warm the honey jar in a pan of hot water before measuring; this will make it easier to measure and dissolve.

TRY THIS!

Dark in color, this sweet-salty blend of mirin, sesame oil, and soy sauce traditionally accompanies dark meats, such as chicken thighs and drumsticks, pork, beef, and dark fish, like mackerel or bluefish. You can also use it on light meats (chicken breasts, white fish, shrimp, and so on), of course, but expect a little discoloration.

Marinate large cuts of meat (whole chickens and flank steaks) for 8 hours (or overnight); smaller pieces of meat (fish steaks and chicken breasts) for 1 to 2 hours; very small pieces of meat (shrimp or diced chicken) for 30 to 60 minutes, covered, in the refrigerator.

INGREDIENTS

½ cup tamari or other Japanese soy sauce

½ cup mirin

¼ cup honey or sugar

¼ cup Asian (dark) sesame oil

4 slices fresh ginger (each ¼ inch thick), peeled and lightly flattened with the side of a cleaver

3 cloves garlic, peeled and lightly flattened with the side of a cleaver

3 scallions, trimmed, white parts flattened with the side of a cleaver, green parts finely chopped

Combine the tamari, mirin, and honey in a bowl and whisk until the honey is dissolved. Whisk in the remaining ingredients. Use within a few hours of making.

Variation

Orange or Tangerine Teriyaki: Add ½ cup orange or tangerine juice when you add the tamari.

KOREAN HONEY-SESAME MARINADE

YIELD: Makes 2 cups, enough for 2 pounds of meat or seafood

F ew flavorings are as beguiling as the dark, nutty, sweet-salty marinade Koreans use on butterflied beef ribs and rib eye steak. Generally, the meats are thinly sliced, so the marinating and cooking times are brief.

INGREDIENTS

½ cup soy sauce

¼ cup Asian (dark) sesame oil

¼ cup sugar

¼ cup sake or dry sherry

4 cloves garlic, peeled and minced

4 scallions (white and green parts), trimmed and finely chopped

2 tablespoons toasted sesame seeds (see box, page 112)

1 tablespoon minced fresh ginger

1 teaspoon gochugaru (Korean hot pepper powder), or hot paprika

½ teaspoon freshly ground black pepper

1 small Asian pear or regular pear, peeled, cored, and diced

Combine all the ingredients for the marinade in a blender or food processor and blend to a smooth purée. The marinade tastes best used within a few of hours of making.

TRY THIS!

This is the classic marinade for *bul kogi* (grilled thinly sliced beef) and *kalbi kui* (grilled butterflied short ribs), but it also delivers for chicken, seafood, tofu, and vegetables, like shiitake mushrooms. Marinate butterflied beef ribs for 4 to 6 hours; steaks or chicken breasts for 1 to 2 hours, covered, in the refrigerator.

WET RUBS AND SPICE PASTES

ISLAND SEASONIN'

YIELD: Makes 2½ to 3 cups, enough for 3 to 4 pounds of meat, poultry, or seafood

TRY THIS!

Place chicken pieces, pork or beef tenderloin, rack or butterflied leg of lamb, lobsters or shrimp, fish fillets or whole fish (if using the latter, make deep slashes in both sides with a knife) in a baking dish and spread the Island Seasonin' on top with a spatula, turning the food a few times to ensure even marinating. Marinate large pieces of meat 12 to 24 hours, medium-size (chicken pieces, for example) for 4 to 6 hours, small pieces (chicken breasts or fish fillets, for example) for 2 hours, covered, in the refrigerator.

Every island in the Caribbean has its version of seasoning, from Cuba's tangy adobo (page 60) to Jamaica's fiery jerk (facing page) to a pungent green herb and pepper paste used in the southern Caribbean. Always flavorful, the blend contains bell peppers and often chiles, but the latter are used more for their aroma than their heat. Use seasonin' to flavor all manner of grilled fare, from chicken to pork to seafood. Here's how it's made in Barbados.

INGREDIENTS

1 green bell pepper, stemmed, seeded, and coarsely chopped

½ red bell pepper, stemmed, seeded, and coarsely chopped

2 jalapeño peppers, or ½ Scotch bonnet chile, seeded and chopped

2 ribs celery, finely chopped

1 medium-size onion, peeled and coarsely chopped

6 cloves garlic, peeled and coarsely chopped

3 bunches fresh chives, or 2 bunches scallions (white and green parts), trimmed and chopped

1 bunch fresh flat-leaf parsley, stemmed, leaves coarsely chopped (about 1 cup)

1 tablespoon fresh thyme, or 1½ teaspoons dried thyme

2 tablespoons chopped fresh oregano, or 2 teaspoons dried oregano

2 tablespoons chopped fresh marjoram, or 2 teaspoons dried marjoram

⅓ cup vegetable oil

⅓ cup fresh lime juice

2 tablespoons soy sauce

1 tablespoon coarse salt (sea or kosher)

½ teaspoon freshly ground black pepper

½ teaspoon ground allspice

Combine the green and red bell peppers, the jalapeños, celery, onion, garlic, chives, parsley, thyme, oregano, and marjoram in a food processor and purée to a coarse paste. Add the oil, lime juice, soy sauce, salt, pepper, and allspice and purée until smooth. The seasonin' tastes best used within a few hours of making.

Variation

Paramin Seasonin' from Trinidad: Trinidad's seasonin' owes its invigorating flavor to fresh cilantro and mint—herbs that grow in profusion on the Paramin Hills outside Port of Spain. Prepare the recipe, adding 1 bunch each of rinsed, stemmed, chopped cilantro and spearmint or peppermint.

JAMAICAN JERK SEASONING

YIELD: Makes 2 cups, enough for 3 to 4 pounds meat, chicken, or seafood

Around the time that reggae music began rocking America's airwaves, a new dish began blasting our taste buds: jerk. Invented by the Maroons (runaway slaves who lived in the hills of north-central Jamaica in the eighteenth century), this fiery Jamaican barbecue combines local seasonings (allspice, fresh thyme, Caribbean chives, and prodigious quantities of Scotch bonnet chiles) in a fiery paste that's rubbed on pork and chicken. The pit master would "jook" the meat (poke holes in it with a sharp stick) to hasten the absorption of the seasonings—the process that gives us our word jerk. The other remarkable thing about Jamaican jerk is the cooking method: open-pit barbecuing over a low smoky fire made of burning allspice wood. You may be aghast by the amount of chiles and salt in this recipe, but that's how Jamaicans make it. (The salt helped preserve the meat without refrigeration.) I've given a range for the Scotch bonnet chiles—to be authentic you'd use the full twelve. For a less fiery jerk seasoning, seed the chiles or use as few as two Scotch bonnets.

TRY THIS!

Place the food in a baking dish and spread the jerk seasoning over it, turning to ensure an even coating. Marinate large pieces of meat 12 to 24 hours; medium-size pieces for 4 to 6 hours; and small pieces, like shrimp or fish fillets, for 1 to 2 hours, covered, in the refrigerator. Barbecue or indirect grill the meat using moderate heat and plenty of wood smoke.

INGREDIENTS

4 to 12 Scotch bonnet chiles, stemmed and cut in half

1 medium-size onion, peeled and coarsely chopped

½ cup coarsely chopped shallots

2 bunches chives or scallions (white and green parts), trimmed and coarsely chopped

4 cloves garlic, peeled and coarsely chopped

½ cup coarsely chopped fresh flat-leaf parsley

½ cup chopped fresh cilantro leaves

1 tablespoon peeled and chopped fresh ginger

1 tablespoon coarse salt (sea or kosher), or to taste

1 tablespoon fresh thyme, or 1½ teaspoons dried thyme

2 teaspoons ground allspice

1 teaspoon freshly ground black pepper

½ teaspoon ground cinnamon

½ teaspoon freshly grated nutmeg

¼ teaspoon ground cloves

¼ cup fresh lime juice

¼ cup vegetable oil

¼ cup packed dark brown sugar

2 tablespoons soy sauce

¼ cup cold water, or as needed

Combine the chiles, onion, shallots, chives, garlic, parsley, cilantro, ginger, salt, thyme, allspice, pepper, cinnamon, nutmeg, and cloves in a food processor and process to a coarse paste. Add the remaining ingredients, including the water, 1 tablespoon at a time, processing to mix to a thick but spreadable paste. Use within a few hours of making.

JERK LEG OF LAMB

YIELD: Serves 8 to 10

The traditional meat for jerk is pork, with chicken coming in a close second. But fiery jerk seasoning goes great with an unexpected meat: leg of lamb. This recipe requires only a few minutes of actual preparation time, but you should marinate the lamb for 12 to 24 hours to achieve the maximum flavor. The rum rids the lamb of any gamy flavor and puts you in the right mood for jerk.

YOU ALSO NEED

2 cups fruitwood chips, soaked for 30 minutes, then drained

INGREDIENTS

½ bone-in leg of lamb
    (3 to 4 pounds)

½ cup rum

Jamaican Jerk Seasoning
    (page 85)

¼ cup allspice berries

1. Using the tip of a paring knife, make 24 small holes in the lamb, each about ¼ inch deep. Place the lamb in a roasting pan and rinse it on all sides with the rum. Let marinate in the refrigerator for 30 minutes. Pour off and discard the rum and let the lamb air-dry for 5 minutes.

2. Smear the jerk seasoning on the lamb on all sides with a spatula or your fingers, forcing it into the holes in the meat. Cover with plastic wrap and marinate in the refrigerator for 12 to 24 hours.

3. Set up the grill for indirect grilling and preheat to 350°F. Brush and oil the grill grate. If using a charcoal grill, toss the wood chips and allspice berries on the coals. If using gas, place the wood chips and allspice berries in the smoker box and preheat until you see smoke.

4. Place the lamb on the grate and indirect grill until cooked to taste, 1 to 1½ hours for medium. Transfer the lamb to a platter, loosely tent with aluminum foil, let rest for 10 minutes, then carve and serve.

HOMAGE TO FRESH HERBS

"**W**hat is an herb?" a scholar once asked Charlemagne. "The friend of physicians and the praise of cooks," the emperor replied. You don't need to be a ruler or a sage to know that fresh herbs make all the difference between ordinary grilling and electrifying live-fire cooking. The fact is that fresh herbs will give your sauces and marinades a Technicolor brightness.

Fresh herbs add a distinct ethnic character to whatever you're grilling. Fresh cilantro is, of course, one of the defining flavors of Mexican barbecue. Fresh basil, rosemary, and sage evoke Italy and the south of France. Greek grill masters would be lost without oregano; Moroccans, without mint; Thais, without lemongrass and kaffir lime leaves. The truth is that it's hard to think of a grilled dish that doesn't taste better with fresh herbs.

Fresh herbs serve the grill master in several ways. First, as an aromatic flavor enhancer to marinades and spice pastes. Second, as a surface flavoring for spit-roasted meats. Tuscan grillers, for example, place sprigs of fresh rosemary under the trussing strings when roasting chicken. Malaysian grillers use lemongrass stalks as a basting brush. You can also use the slender stalks of many herbs, such as lemongrass and rosemary, as flavorful skewers on which to grill kebabs. Bunches of fresh herbs can be tossed on the coals just prior to grilling to create fragrant clouds of smoke. (This is a good use for wilted herbs.)

Don't worry too much if you can't find the particular herb a recipe calls for. Lacking cilantro, I once made a spectacular salsa with fresh mint. Another aborted shopping mission led me to the discovery of rosemary pesto.

Before talking about specific herbs, here are a few general observations about rinsing and storing fresh herbs: To rinse cilantro, basil, parsley, and other bushy herbs, fill a bowl with cold water. Holding the herbs by the stems, plunge the leaves in the water and gently agitate up and down. Pour off the dirty water, add fresh water, and continue this process until the water runs clean.

Fresh herbs will keep for longer than you might think, provided they are stored properly. Loosely wrap the herbs in a damp paper towel and place in an *unsealed* plastic bag in the refrigerator; don't seal the bag or you'll get a funky smell. Check the paper towel every few days, moistening it as needed. It should be damp, not soaking wet. Stored this way, the herbs will keep for a week to ten days.

So what about dried herbs? Contrary to what you may have been led to believe, they're not inherently evil. In fact, drying intensifies or even reconfigures the flavor of many herbs and grill jockeys from Buenos Aires to Baku would be lost without them. What you need to know is which herbs dry well and which don't. The good dryers include basil, bay leaf, dill seed (but not the leaves), marjoram, mint, oregano, rosemary, and thyme. Herbs that lose their flavor in drying include cilantro, dill, parsley, and tarragon—avoid them. To freshen up the flavor of any dried herb, mince it with a little fresh parsley.

Specific herbs that can help the griller include:

BASIL: Lends a decided Mediterranean accent. Purée the leaves in oils and spice pastes, like the Sweet Basil Oil on page 139. Place whole basil leaves between the various ingredients on shish kebabs. Basil goes particularly well with poultry and seafood.

BAY LEAF: A popular ingredient in marinades, especially for game and beef. On the Portuguese island of Madeira, bay leaf branches are used as skewers and whole fresh bay leaves are placed between chunks of beef on shish kebabs.

CHIVES: Chop and sprinkle on grilled seafood, poultry, and vegetables when a delicate onion flavor is desired.

CILANTRO: One of the world's most popular barbecue herbs, used in marinades and for sprinkling chopped over grilled meats in countries as diverse as Mexico, India, and Thailand. Cilantro roots are used in Southeast Asian spice pastes and barbecue sauces.

DILL: A popular flavoring in Greek, Georgian, and Central Asian grilling. The signature flavoring of the Georgian Rhubarb sauce Tkemali (page 215).

KAFFIR LIME LEAF: The fragrant leaf of a Southeast Asian lime tree. Adds a wonderfully perfumey lime flavor to spice pastes, marinades, and grilled fish.

LEMONGRASS: Has the herbal flavor of lemon without the tartness. Used throughout Southeast Asia as an ingredient in marinades, spice pastes, and even as skewers. (Fish mousse grilled on lemongrass skewers is a classic Indonesian saté.)

MARJORAM: A traditional ingredient in French herbes de Provence and in central European grilling. Used in Mediterranean marinades.

MINT: A popular barbecue seasoning in Afghanistan and Morocco. Fresh mint is also a key ingredient in Paramin Seasonin' from Trinidad (page 85) and in Indian and Afghan chutneys. Great with lamb.

OREGANO: One of the defining flavors of Greek and Mexican grilling. Great with pork and lamb.

PARSLEY: Grillers can't seem to live without this commonplace herb. Argentineans use it to make Chimichurri (page 192). Turks add it to onion relish. Parsley is often paired with onion and garlic with good reason—it helps neutralize their pungency. Think of it as nature's mouthwash. Use the flat-leaf variety.

ROSEMARY: One of the quintessential flavors of the Mediterranean and an essential seasoning for lamb, beef, and poultry. Rosemary stalks make fragrant skewers for kebabs.

TARRAGON: Its licoricey flavor goes well with seafood, poultry, and beef.

THYME: Popular on much of the world's barbecue trail. You taste it strongly in Jamaica's jerk, Barbados's seasonin', and French herbes de Provence. Also used in wild game marinades.

THREE RECADOS
YUCATÁN SPICE PASTES

TRY THIS!

When cooking chicken breasts, fish fillets or steaks, pork chops or pork loins, rub the *recado* on the outside. For chicken quarters and halves and whole fish, make slashes in the sides to the bone and force a little of the *recado* mixture into the slits, then spread the remainder on the outside. For whole chickens, spread half the *recado* in the cavity. Force half of the rest under the skin and the remainder over it. Marinate thin pieces of meat for 1 to 2 hours; medium-size pieces for 4 to 6 hours; large pieces overnight, covered, in the refrigerator.

Americans call them wet rubs. Mexicans call them *recados*; and in the Yucatán, no one would dream of grilling a steak, spit-roasting a fish, or pit-roasting a turkey without seasoning it first with one of these pungent pastes of chiles, herbs, and spices. Yucatán grill jockeys have it easier than their North American counterparts, for they can buy *recados* ready-made at any market. If you want to enjoy their robust flavor in the United States, you'll have to make your own. This takes a little work, but the results are eminently worth it.

The classic Yucatecan *recados* include: *rojo* (red), *verde* (green), *recado de bistec* (steak *recado*), and the most prized of all, *recado negro* (black *recado*). The first owes its bright color and taste to a rust-colored Caribbean spice called annatto (aka achiote). Green *recado*, made with *pepitas* (pumpkin seeds), serves more as a sauce base than as a seasoning, and so I have not included a recipe for it. Steak *recado* is a salty fragrant greenish-brown paste used, as the name suggests, as a seasoning for beef. Black *recado* owes its color to burnt chiles de árbol and tortillas. It is used as a seasoning for turkey and suckling pig.

The following recipes have been modified so that you can make them in a food processor or blender, but I've tried to keep the flavors as authentic as possible.

RECADO ROJO
YUCATÁN RED SPICE PASTE

YIELD: Makes about 1⅓ cups; use 2 to 4 tablespoons per pound of meat

This recipe comes from Carlos Cavich, owner of a spice stall at the central market in Mérida in the Yucatán. Normally, the *recado* would be purchased as a paste and thinned to pourable consistency at home with sour orange juice and vinegar. I've incorporated that step here.

Annatto is a pungent, rust-colored Caribbean seed, sometimes called poor man's saffron. It gives the sauce a vivid orange color and a flavor reminiscent of iodine (but in a good way). Masa harina is a kind of cornmeal made from hulled cooked corn. (It's the main ingredient in tortillas.) Both annatto and masa harina are available in most large supermarkets. If you can't find masa, substitute cornmeal.

Traditionally, the onion and garlic are roasted until brown and soft on an ungreased *comal*, or griddle, or a cast-iron skillet, but you could also thread them onto bamboo skewers and grill them over a medium fire until soft and brown.

INGREDIENTS

- 2 plum tomatoes
- 1 medium-size onion, peeled and quartered
- 1 head garlic, broken into cloves and peeled
- 1 tablespoon annatto seeds
- 1 teaspoon black peppercorns
- 6 allspice berries, or ¼ teaspoon ground allspice
- 4 whole cloves, or ¼ teaspoon ground cloves
- 1 teaspoon cumin seeds or ground cumin
- 1 cinnamon stick (1 inch), or ½ teaspoon ground cinnamon
- 2 teaspoons pure chile powder (not a blend) or paprika
- 1 teaspoon dried oregano
- 2 tablespoons masa harina or cornmeal
- 1½ teaspoons coarse salt (sea or kosher)
- 1 teaspoon sugar
- ⅔ cup sour orange juice (see box, page 194) or lime juice
- 2 tablespoons distilled white vinegar
- 2 tablespoons vegetable oil

1. Heat a *comal* or cast-iron skillet over medium heat. Add the tomatoes, onion, and garlic and cook, turning with tongs, until browned on all sides and soft, 4 to 6 minutes for the garlic, 10 to 12 minutes for the tomatoes and onion pieces. Do not let the vegetables burn. Transfer the vegetables to a plate to cool as they are done.

2. Combine the annatto, peppercorns, allspice, cloves, cumin, cinnamon, chile powder, and oregano in a spice mill and grind to a fine powder.

3. Place the ground spices, masa harina, salt, sugar, sour orange juice, vinegar, oil, and roasted vegetables in a food processor or blender. Purée to a thick paste—stopping the processor and scraping down the side of the bowl with a spatula several times. Use right away or transfer to a large jar, cover, and refrigerate. The *recado* will keep for at least a week.

RECADO DE BISTEC
STEAK RECADO

YIELD: Makes about 1 cup; use 2 to 4 tablespoons per pound of meat

Oregano and pepper give this *recado* its dark-green color and distinctive aroma. It's not too sweet, which makes it perfect for seasoning grilled steak. This recipe comes from Evaristo Escamillo, a veteran spice seller at the Central Food Market in Mérida.

INGREDIENTS

1 medium-size onion, peeled and quartered

2 heads garlic, broken into cloves and peeled

2 tablespoons dried oregano, preferably Mexican

2 teaspoons black peppercorns or freshly ground black pepper

1 teaspoon cumin seeds or ground cumin

2 whole cloves, or ⅛ teaspoon ground cloves

3 tablespoons minced fresh flat-leaf parsley

1 tablespoon masa harina or cornmeal

2 teaspoons coarse salt (sea or kosher)

¼ cup distilled white vinegar

¼ cup sour orange juice (see box, page 194) or lime juice

¼ cup vegetable oil

TRY THIS!

Rub a little of the *recado* on both sides of the steaks and marinate, covered, in the refrigerator for 1 to 2 hours. Grill as you would any steak and serve with the Smoky Two Chile Salsa on page 295.

1. Heat a *comal* or cast-iron skillet over medium heat. Add the onion and garlic and cook, turning with tongs, until browned on all sides and soft, 4 to 6 minutes for the garlic, 10 to 12 minutes for the onion pieces. Do not let the vegetables burn. Transfer the onions and garlic to a plate to cool as they are done.

2. Combine the oregano, peppercorns, cumin, and cloves in a spice mill and grind to a fine powder.

3. Place the parsley, masa harina, salt, vinegar, sour orange juice, oil, onion, garlic, and spices in a food processor or blender. Purée to a smooth paste—stopping the processor and scraping down the side of the bowl with a spatula several times. Use right away or transfer to a large jar, cover, and refrigerate. The *recado* will keep for at least a week.

RECADO NEGRO
BLACK RECADO

YIELD: Makes about 2¼ cups; use 2 to 4 tablespoons per pound of meat

This dark, shiny, intensely aromatic paste is the most venerated *recado* of all. Like many blackened dishes, it probably began as an accident. My guess is that someone burned the chiles and tortillas and, rather than waste them, pounded them into a spice paste. The broad outline of this recipe comes from Carmita Uicap, a tiny woman whose hands are jet-black from kneading and packaging spice pastes at her stall at the Mérida market. Her recipe may seem a little involved. It *is* involved, but it produces one of the most electrifying seasonings in Mexico, and is definitely worth the time it takes to make. Charring the chiles produces a virulent smoke, so you should cook them outdoors on your grill. (Not that you need urging.)

Note: To be strictly authentic, you'd use only chiles de árbol, but the resulting *recado* would be incendiary. To make a milder black *recado*, replace two-thirds of the chiles de árbol with milder guajillo or New Mexican red chiles.

TRY THIS!

This *recado* is the traditional seasoning for pit-roasted turkey or suckling pig. These are fiesta foods in the Yucatán, served at weddings or on the anniversary of a loved one's death. To prepare a 12-pound turkey in this fashion, use 1½ to 2 cups black *recado* to season the bird, spreading some in the neck and main cavity, some under the skin, and rubbing the remainder over the skin. Marinate the turkey, covered, in the refrigerator overnight. The next day, set up the grill for indirect grilling. Roast the turkey until cooked, 2½ to 3 hours, replenishing the coals every hour, or as needed.

Otherwise, rub the *recado* on pork, chicken, or steak; marinate, covered, in the refrigerator, for several hours, then grill.

INGREDIENTS

3 ounces dried chiles de árbol, stemmed, or 1 ounce chile de árbol and 2 ounces guajillo or New Mexican red chiles

Cold water for soaking the chiles

2 corn tortillas

1 head garlic, broken into cloves and peeled

1 medium-size onion, peeled and quartered

4 teaspoons dried oregano

2 teaspoons annatto seeds

2 teaspoons black peppercorns

1 teaspoon cumin seeds

1 teaspoon allspice berries

½ teaspoon whole cloves

2 bay leaves

1 tablespoon coarse salt (sea or kosher)

1 teaspoon sugar

¾ cup distilled white vinegar

¼ cup vegetable oil

1. Set up a grill for direct grilling and preheat to high. Place a dry *comal*, or griddle, or a cast-iron skillet over the hottest part of the fire.

2. Add the chiles and cook, turning with tongs, until black, 1 to 2 minutes. Don't burn the chiles, but come close to it. Keep your face away from the *comal* to protect your eyes from the virulent smoke. Transfer the chiles to a large bowl and add cold water to cover.

3. Place the tortillas on the *comal* and cook, turning with tongs, until very dark, 4 to 6 minutes per side. Transfer to a plate. Place the garlic and onion on the *comal* and cook, turning with tongs, until darkly browned on all sides and soft, 4 to 6 minutes for the garlic, 10 to 12 minutes for the onion pieces.

Transfer to the plate with the tortillas as they are done.

4. Grind the oregano, annatto, peppercorns, cumin, allspice, cloves, and bay leaves to a fine powder in a spice mill.

5. Drain the chiles and snip in half lengthwise. Rinse the chiles under cold water to remove the seeds. Shake off the excess water and place the chiles in a food processor or blender.

6. Break the tortillas into 1-inch pieces and add to the processor. Add the salt, sugar, vinegar, oil, onion, garlic, and spices and purée to a smooth paste—stopping the processor and scraping down the side of the bowl several times. Use right away or transfer to a large jar, cover, and refrigerate. The *recado* will keep at least a week.

BERBER SPICE PASTE

YIELD: Makes 1 cup, enough for 2 pounds of meat

I first encountered this pungent rust-red Berber seasoning at the spice market in Marrakech. It's piquant without being pushy; hot without being unpleasant; perfumed but robust. Fenugreek is a rectangular seed with a pleasantly bitter flavor. I've made it optional; the spice paste will still be plenty tasty without it. Fenugreek and cardamom seeds can be purchased at Indian and Middle Eastern markets.

INGREDIENTS

2 teaspoons cracked black peppercorns

1 teaspoon coriander seeds

1 teaspoon cardamom seeds

1 teaspoon fenugreek seeds (optional)

1 cinnamon stick (1 inch)

4 allspice berries

3 whole cloves

1 small onion, peeled and cut into 1-inch pieces

2 cloves garlic, peeled and coarsely chopped

1 piece fresh ginger (1 inch), peeled and thinly sliced

⅓ cup sweet or hot paprika

1 tablespoon coarse salt (sea or kosher)

1 to 2 teaspoons red pepper flakes

½ cup extra-virgin olive oil

3 tablespoons fresh lemon juice

1. Heat a dry skillet over medium heat. Add the cracked pepper, coriander, cardamom, fenugreek (if using), cinnamon, allspice, and cloves and toast, stirring occasionally, until fragrant, about 3 minutes. Transfer the spices to a bowl and cool. Grind to a powder in a spice mill.

2. Place the onion, garlic, and ginger in a food processor and finely chop. Add the toasted spices and remaining ingredients and process the mixture to a fine paste. Use right away or transfer to a jar, cover, and refrigerate. The spice paste will keep for at least a week.

TRY THIS!

Smear or spread the paste on chicken breasts (or under the skin of a whole chicken), lamb chops, a beef tenderloin, or steak. For whole grilled fish, make slashes in both sides and spread with paste, forcing it into the slashes. For a quick weeknight dinner, spread it on tuna or salmon steaks and grill. Marinate all, covered, in the refrigerator, 1 to 2 hours for smaller cuts (chops and chicken breasts), 4 to 6 hours for larger cuts (tenderloins and whole fish).

GREEN TANDOORI SPICE PASTE

YIELD: Makes 1 cup, enough for 1 cut-up chicken or 2 pounds of lamb or seafood

TRY THIS!

Green tandoori spice paste is traditionally used for seasoning chicken, but it also works wonders with lamb and seafood. Marinate meats for 6 to 8 hours, seafood for 3 to 6 hours, covered, in the refrigerator. You can also serve this spice paste as a relish.

I like to think of this pungent chile paste as an Indian pesto. It produces some of the tastiest grilled chicken I know that's spicy without being unbearably fiery. Traditionally, the meat to be grilled would be marinated twice, first in yogurt, then in the green chile spice paste. You can certainly do this if you want, but even a single dip in the chile mixture produces exceptionally flavorful barbecue. The Indian green bell pepper is hotter than ours. A poblano makes a good substitute.

INGREDIENTS

1 cup cold water

1½ teaspoons coarse salt (sea or kosher), or to taste

4 ounces fresh spinach, stemmed and rinsed

2 tablespoons unsalted butter

3 tablespoons vegetable oil

1 medium-size onion, peeled and finely chopped

3 cloves garlic, peeled and minced

1 tablespoon peeled and minced fresh ginger

1 poblano chile, or ½ green bell pepper, stemmed, seeded, and diced

4 jalapeño peppers, seeded and diced

¼ cup chopped fresh cilantro leaves

½ cup plain whole milk Greek-style yogurt

3 tablespoons fresh lemon juice, or more to taste

1 teaspoon ground coriander

½ teaspoon ground turmeric

½ teaspoon freshly ground black pepper

1. Bring the water and ½ teaspoon of the salt to a boil in a saucepan. Add the spinach and cook until limp, 2 minutes. Drain in a colander, rinse under cold water, and drain again. Squeeze the spinach between your fingers to wring out the water. Transfer the spinach to a food processor.

2. Melt the butter in the oil in a skillet over medium heat. Add the onion and cook until softened, about 2 minutes, stirring with a wooden spoon.

Add the garlic and ginger and cook until the onions are golden brown, 2 to 4 minutes more. Lower the heat as needed so the vegetables don't burn. Transfer the onion mixture to the food processor.

3. Add the remaining ingredients (including the remaining 1 teaspoon salt) to the processor and purée to a smooth paste. Correct the seasoning, adding salt or lemon juice; the paste should be highly seasoned. Use right away or transfer to a jar, cover, and refrigerate. This spice paste tastes best if used within a few hours of making.

BALINESE SPICE PASTE

YIELD: Makes about 2 cups; enough for 3 to 4 pounds of pork or fish or 2 chickens or ducks

The Balinese make some of the most flavorful barbecue in the world. Their secret? A tongue-blasting *base* (spice paste) perfumed with garlic, galangal, lemongrass, and fresh turmeric. Like many of the great spice pastes and basting mixtures of Southeast Asia, the flavorings are pounded to a paste in a mortar with a pestle, then fried in a wok. This softens the harsh flavors of garlic and galangal, adding color and complexity. *Base* is the starting point of two of Bali's most famous grilled dishes: *babi guling* (spit-roasted suckling pig) and *bebek betutu* (duck barbecued in banana leaves).

Because some of the called-for ingredients are not easy to find, I've noted readily available substitutes. Galangal and turmeric are members of the ginger family. Galangal is a striped rhizome with peppery tan flesh. Imagine ginger without the sweetness but with the bite of freshly ground black pepper. If you can't find it, use fresh ginger instead. You're probably familiar with ground turmeric, which is an ingredient in ballpark mustard; fresh turmeric (a small tan rhizome) can be found at Whole Foods. Candlenuts are oily round nuts added for texture; macadamias or cashews make acceptable substitutes. Shrimp paste is a malodorous paste of fermented

Use this spice paste to season a suckling pig or pork shoulder or poultry. Marinate, covered, in the refrigerator for the length of time noted.

- For suckling pig, spread some of the paste in the cavity and rub the remainder over the skin. Marinate for 24 hours.
- For pork shoulder, make a few deep holes in the meat with a knife and force some of the paste into the holes. Spread the remaining rub over the pork. Marinate overnight.
- For a whole duck or chicken, spread some of the paste in the cavities and some under the skin. Spread the remainder over the bird. Marinate for 8 hours.

shrimp and salt, which tastes a lot better than it sounds. You can approximate the flavor by substituting anchovy fillets or fish sauce. The recipe sounds more complicated than it really is. Using a food processor and a wok, you can prepare the spice paste in about 15 minutes.

INGREDIENTS

4 to 6 shallots, peeled and quartered

6 cloves garlic, peeled and cut in half

6 candlenuts or macadamia nuts

3 to 8 Thai chiles, or 2 to 4 jalapeños (depending on your tolerance for heat)

3 to 4 stalks lemongrass, trimmed and finely chopped (¼ cup), or 4 strips lemon zest

2 tablespoons coarsely chopped fresh ginger

1 tablespoon coarsely chopped fresh galangal (or use more ginger)

1 tablespoon coarsely chopped fresh turmeric, or 1 teaspoon ground turmeric

1 teaspoon shrimp paste, or 2 anchovy fillets or 1 tablespoon fish sauce

1 tablespoon light brown sugar

2 teaspoons coarse salt (sea or kosher)

2 teaspoons ground coriander

1 teaspoon freshly ground black pepper

2 tablespoons fresh lime juice

⅓ cup vegetable oil

1. If you have a large mortar and pestle, place the shallots, garlic, candlenuts, chiles, lemongrass, ginger, galangal (if using), turmeric, shrimp paste, brown sugar, salt, coriander, and pepper in the mortar and pound to a smooth paste with the pestle. Work in the lime juice. Or purée the ingredients through the pepper in a food processor—stopping it and scraping down the work bowl several times with a spatula. Add the lime juice at the end.

2. Heat a wok or skillet over high heat to smoking. Reduce the heat to medium and swirl in the oil. Add the spice paste and fry until fragrant and shiny and the oil starts to separate out, 5 minutes. Cool to room temperature. This spice paste tastes best used within a few hours of making.

Variation

Substitute tamarind purée for the lime juice when making this paste for seafood.

LEMONGRASS

This tall grass-like herb is one of the defining flavors of Southeast Asia. Fresh lemongrass has an herbal lemon flavor, but no tartness. Lemon zest will give you some of the lemony flavor of fresh lemongrass, but not its haunting aroma.

When buying lemongrass, choose fat heavy stalks. Examine the stalks closely: There should be a bulbous base. Some misguided merchants sell only the leafy tops, which are useless. If you press your fingernail into the core, it should feel moist. Fresh lemongrass is available at Asian markets and at an increasing number of supermarkets.

To prepare lemongrass for cooking, cut off the green leaves, leaving a firm, 3-to-4-inch-long slightly bulbous stalk. (You can save the leaves and tie them together to use as a basting brush.) Cut off the root end and strip off the outside leaves to expose the cream-colored core. This is the edible part of lemongrass, but even so it's quite fibrous, so mince it very fine or leave the pieces large enough that you can fish them out before serving.

CURES AND BRINES

HONEY CURE

YIELD: Makes 4 cups; enough for 2 pounds of fish, poultry, or pork

TRY THIS!

This cure is traditionally used with fish, but don't dismiss it for chicken or turkey breast. Cover and marinate fish steaks for 1 to 2 hours, larger fish fillets for 2 to 4 hours, and whole fish overnight in the refrigerator. Chicken breasts need 2 to 4 hours; a whole bird, overnight.

A brine is used for salting; a marinade for flavoring. Somewhere between lies a mixture that both salts and flavors—a cure. Cures are used for curing seafood, chicken, or pork before smoking. This one works especially well with salmon and turkey. The salt partially dehydrates the meat, while the spicing and seasoning provide extra flavor. The honey adds a floral sweetness that's offset by the tang of the lemon zest.

INGREDIENTS

4 cups cold water

¾ cup honey (warmed so it pours more easily)

½ cup coarse salt (sea or kosher)

4 strips lemon zest

10 whole cloves

10 allspice berries

10 peppercorns

2 bay leaves

Combine all the ingredients in a bowl and whisk until the salt and honey are dissolved. Use right away.

BRINING

Quick: What do bacon, ham, pastrami, and kippered salmon have in common? All owe their distinctive succulence and flavor to brine. Brining, along with a related salting technique called salt curing, was one of the world's first methods of preserving food for extended storage, and although this function is no longer needed in today's world of ubiquitous refrigeration, we still prize brined foods for their soulful, salty, umami flavors.

Brine, simply defined, is a saline solution—a mixture of salt and water—and often other seasonings, such as spices like cloves and peppercorns and herbs like bay leaves and thyme. Many brines contain sugar, producing the pleasing sweet-salty flavor contrast in country ham and smoked salmon. Brines also often contain another salt-like preservative—sodium nitrite or sodium nitrate—the former also called Prague Powder #1 or pink salt. (Sodium nitrite can be toxic in large quantities, so pink food coloring is added to it to prevent you from confusing it with table salt.) This is pink *curing* salt, not the pink salt from the Himalayas, which is used as a table salt for seasoning.

But if brine is simple, there's nothing simple about the way it works to preserve food and keep it moist. First, the salt slows bacterial development and retards spoilage. According to food science professor Robert Lindsay, it does so by creating an osmotic effect that dries out microbes and by tying up water molecules so that they're not available to foster bacterial growth.

Brines serve another important function: adding moisture to foods that tend to dry out on the grill or in the smoker. Here, the mechanism is a little more complicated. Two elements comprise salt: sodium and chloride. When you dissolve salt in water, it breaks down into positively charged sodium ions and negatively charged chloride ions. During the brining process, these ions diffuse through and attach to the muscle fibers in the meat. The sodium ions impart the pleasant salty flavor. The negatively charged chloride ions repel each other, like two magnets placed face to face, creating gaps in the muscle fibers. The liquid flows into those gaps—and stays there—adding as much as 10 percent to the weight of the meat.

Brining is a great way to keep intrinsically dry meats, like pork chops, chicken breasts, and turkey, moist during smoking or grilling. It also adds flavor to any meat, from Canadian bacon and ham to smoked bluefish and kippered salmon.

Brine formulas vary from cook to cook and region to region, but the basic ratio is about 7 ounces (200 grams) of salt to 1 gallon (3.78 liters) of water. This gives you a salt concentration of about 7 percent. For a sweet brine, add about the same amount of sugar (or honey, maple syrup, or the like) as salt. When adding sodium nitrite, you'll need 1 tablespoon per gallon of water.

To help the salt and sugar dissolve more quickly, I like to bring half the water to a boil, then whisk in the salt and other dry flavorings. Have the remaining water ice cold so it chills the mixture to room temperature. If the brine is still warm, let it cool to room temperature before adding the meat.

Brining should be done in the refrigerator in a deep bowl or large heavy-duty resealable bag. (Place the latter in a baking dish to catch any unforeseen leaks.) It's common to rinse brined foods with cold water to remove any surface salt before smoking or grilling, then drying that food on a wire rack over a sheet pan in the refrigerator until the surface feels tacky.

On page 102, you'll find a recipe for the basic brine with optional flavorings, followed by special brines.

OPTIONAL FLAVORINGS FOR ALL-PURPOSE BRINE

- Sugar, honey, agave, or other sweetener (up to ¾ cup)

- Bourbon, brandy, rum, mezcal, tequila, gin, or other spirit (up to 1 cup)

- Sweet onion (1 medium), quartered

- Garlic (up to 6 cloves), peeled and lightly crushed with the side of a cleaver

- Lemon, orange, grapefruit, tangerine, or lime zest (grated or in strips)

- Bay leaves (up to 4)

- Whole star anise (up to 4)

- Cinnamon sticks (up to 4)

- Black or white peppercorns (up to 1 tablespoon)

- Allspice berries or juniper berries (up to 8—for extra flavor, lightly crush with the side of a cleaver)

- Whole cloves (up to 1 teaspoon)

- Fennel seeds (up to 1 teaspoon)

ALL-PURPOSE BRINE

YIELD: Makes 1 gallon brine, enough for 2 pork shoulders or one 12-pound turkey—in short, 8 to 12 pounds of meat

TRY THIS!

Use this simple brine for curing pork loins and shoulders, pork chops, turkey breasts, chicken breasts, shrimp—any lean protein that tends to dry out on the grill.

Brining is one of the core elements of smoking and grilling—used for everything from smoked turkey to pastrami to ham. It's also useful for keeping lean foods, like chicken breasts and pork chops, moist when exposed to the high heat of the grill. Note the use of both hot and ice water—the former to help dissolve the seasonings; the latter to cool the brine to room temperature so you can add the meat and refrigerate safely. Prague Powder is available from Barbecuebible.com and Amazon.com.

INGREDIENTS

2 quarts boiling water

¾ cup coarse salt (sea or kosher)

2 teaspoons Prague Powder #1 (aka pink curing salt; optional)

2 quarts ice water

Optional flavorings (see box, this page)

Place the boiling water and salt(s) and optional sweetener in a stockpot or large mixing bowl and whisk until the salts and sugar (if using) are dissolved. Whisk in the ice water and any other seasonings. Let the brine cool to room temperature before adding the meat. Cover and refrigerate.

BEER BRINE

YIELD: Makes 6 cups, enough for 3 to 4 pounds of meat

Beer gives brine a malty hops flavor that anticipates the beer you'll serve with the barbecue. Use a light beer, like pilsner or wheat beer, with light foods, like shrimp or chicken wings. A dark beer, like porter or stout, goes great with pork or beef. Tip o' the hat to Barbecue University alum and craft cutting board maker Paul Kukonis for the idea.

INGREDIENTS

3 cups water

½ cup coarse salt (sea or kosher)

½ cup packed dark brown sugar

1 tablespoon black peppercorns

1 tablespoon red pepper flakes, or to taste

2 bottles or cans (12 ounces each) of your favorite beer, chilled

Place the water, salt, sugar, peppercorns, and red pepper flakes in a large saucepan and bring to a boil, whisking until the salt and sugar dissolve.

Remove the pan from the heat and whisk in the beer. Let cool to room temperature before adding the meat or seafood to the brine. Cover and refrigerate.

LEMON-GINGER CIDER BRINE

YIELD: Makes 6 cups, enough for 3 to 4 pounds of meat

TRY THIS!

Originally created for pork chops, cider brine works well with all cuts of pork and poultry.

How do you grill a pork chop without drying it out? The new super-lean breeds of pork have made this challenge even tougher. My Australian barbecue writer friend, Bob Hart, has a simple solution: Brine it. More specifically, soak the pork in a fruity mixture of apple cider, sea salt, lemon, and ginger. Two options for cider: For a sweet brine, use fresh apple cider. For a less sweet brine, use a hard cider, like Strongbow or Woodchuck.

INGREDIENTS

3 cups water

¼ cup coarse salt (sea or kosher)

3 cups cold apple cider

4 strips lemon zest (remove it with a vegetable peeler)

1 piece fresh ginger (2 inches), peeled and cut crosswise into ¼-inch-thick slices and lightly crushed with the side of a cleaver

1 teaspoon freshly ground black pepper

Bring the water and salt to a boil in a large saucepan. Remove the pan from the heat and stir in the cider, lemon zest, ginger, and pepper. Let cool to room temperature before adding the meat to the brine. Cover and refrigerate.

CIDER-BRINED PORK CHOPS

YEILD: Serves 4

Pork possesses a natural affinity for apples. Consider the following cider-brined pork chops, inspired by *Heat & Smoke* from Australian barbecue writer Bob Hart. An apple calvados glaze stands in for a sauce.

YOU ALSO NEED

Hardwood chunks or chips, soaked in cold water for 30 minutes and drained (optional)

INGREDIENTS

4 pork porterhouses, or pork rib chops (12 to 16 ounces each), cut 1 inch thick

Lemon-Ginger Cider Brine (facing page), at room temperature

2 tablespoons melted butter or vegetable oil

Fruit + Booze Glaze (page 133; optional)

1. Arrange the chops in a large baking dish or place them in a large resealable plastic bag. Pour the brine over them. If using a plastic bag, lay it in a baking dish to catch any leaks. Brine the pork in the refrigerator for 6 hours, turning several times so they brine uniformly. Drain the chops well, discarding the brine. Blot dry with paper towels.

2. Set up your grill for direct grilling and preheat to medium-high. For a smoke flavor, toss wood chunks or chips on the coals or place them in the grill's smoker box.

3. Brush the pork chops on both sides with melted butter. Direct grill until cooked to taste, about 4 minutes per side for medium (150°F on an instant-read thermometer). Give each chop a quarter turn after 2 minutes to lay on a crosshatch of grill marks. After you turn the chops, baste with any remaining butter.

4. Two minutes before they're done, brush the chops with the glaze on both sides, if using. Sizzle the glaze into the meat over a hot fire. Brush once more before serving and serve any extra glaze on the side.

PASTRAMI BRINE AND INJECTOR SAUCE

YIELD: Makes 1 gallon, enough for 12 pounds of meat

Billy Durney embodies the new generation of American pit master—versed in traditional American barbecue, but forward thinking enough to bring Jamaican, Thai, and Vietnamese flavors into the food he serves at his wildly popular Hometown Bar-B-Que in Red Hook, Brooklyn, New York. Or, in his own words, "I'm a street kid from Brooklyn; I work with the flavor profiles popular with the people in the neighborhood where I grew up." Durney has taken the pastrami mania sweeping America to new heights, using pastrami brine and pastrami rub on pork belly to make a first for this food writer: pastrami bacon. His brine contains just the right ratio of garlic to salt to spice to sweetness. And because we live in a hurried age, he injects the pork belly with pastrami brine, shortening a two-week curing process to five days.

INGREDIENTS

1 gallon (4 quarts) water

⅔ cup coarse salt (sea or kosher)

1 tablespoon Prague Powder #1 (pink curing salt)

⅔ cup sugar

2 teaspoons whole black peppercorns

2 teaspoons ground coriander

1 teaspoon juniper berries, lightly crushed with the side of a knife

1 teaspoon garlic powder

1 teaspoon mustard powder

1 teaspoon dill seed

½ teaspoon celery seed

Combine the water, salt, Prague Powder, sugar, peppercorns, coriander, juniper berries, garlic powder, mustard powder, dill seed, and celery seed in a stockpot and bring to a boil. Boil until the salts and sugar are dissolved, whisking as needed. Remove the pot from the heat. Let cool to room temperature, then use for brining pastrami.

PASTRAMI BACON

YIELD: Makes 5 pounds bacon

Turkey pastrami? Been there. Salmon and shrimp pastrami? Done that. This insanely luscious pastrami bacon from Hometown Bar-B-Que in Red Hook, Brooklyn, takes this brine-cured, spice-rubbed smoked meat from Eastern Europe to its ultimate extreme. Of course, you can also use the spice- and garlic-scented brine to cure more conventional beef navel or brisket.

YOU ALSO NEED

Hardwood of choice (Hometown uses oak) in the quantity required by your smoker

INGREDIENTS

1 piece pork belly (5 pounds)

1 batch Pastrami Brine and Injector Sauce (facing page), cooled to room temperature

Pastrami Rub for Brined Meats (page 32)

1. Skin the pork belly, or better yet, ask your butcher to do it. Place the pork belly in a nonreactive roasting pan or jumbo heavy-duty resealable plastic bag. Using a meat injector (and following the instructions on page 126), inject the pork belly all over with pastrami brine. (You'll use 1 to 2 cups.) Pour the remaining brine over the pork belly (or add it to the resealable bag). If using a plastic bag, lay it in a baking dish to catch any leaks. Brine the pork belly in the refrigerator for 5 days, turning it over daily. Re-inject it with the brine after 3 days.

2. Drain the pork belly well, rinse with cold water, and drain again. Place the pork belly on a wire rack over a sheet pan and let dry in the refrigerator until it feels tacky, 1 to 2 hours.

3. Thickly crust the pork belly on the top, bottom, and sides with the pastrami rub.

4. Set up your smoker following the manufacturer's instructions and preheat to 200°F. Add the wood as specified by the manufacturer.

5. Smoke the pork belly (former skin side up) to an internal temperature of 160°F, 4 to 5 hours, adding wood as needed.

6. Transfer the pastrami bacon to a clean wire rack over a sheet pan and let it cool to room temperature, then refrigerate until serving.

7. To serve, slice the pastrami bacon widthwise as thickly or thinly as you like. (I like ¼-inch-thick slices.) Sear on a hot grill or in a skillet until browned on both sides, 1 to 2 minutes per side.

BASTES, MOPS, BUTTERS, AND SO MUCH MORE

For many people, barbecue is the true religion. Like any good faith, it has its holy water and its unguents—the bastes, mops, glazes, flavored oils, finishing sauces, and compound butters that will help you turn out righteous barbecue every time.

Bastes are designed to keep foods moist and flavorful during grilling. The Garlic Butter Baste on page 111 or Saffron Butter Baste on page 117 will turn apostates into believers. The same holds true for those flavorful liquids called mops, which are traditionally applied to large quantities of ribs and pork shoulders with a clean cotton floor mop. Check out the fiery Buffalo Mop (page 124) and Cider Squirt (page 125). You'll also meet up with the new injector sauces, which you squirt into roasts and turkeys using an oversize hypodermic needle.

Glazes and finishing sauces are used to give grilled meats an inviting sheen before serving. Some even have a kick, such as the Fruit + Booze Glaze (page 133). This brings us to the last unction of an expertly seared steak or chop: flavored oils and butters. A golden disk of Tarragon-Lemon Butter (page 151) or Mustard-Beer Butter (page 153) can turn a piece of grilled meat or fish into a religious experience. Keep a selection of these flavorful butters in your freezer and you're only a slice away from barbecue heaven.

BASTES

GARLIC BUTTER BASTE

YIELD: Makes ½ cup plus, enough for 2 to 3 pounds of seafood or meat

This aromatic butter may be the world's most popular baste. During my travels on the world's barbecue trail, I enjoyed variations of this garlicky butter in places as diverse as Brazil, India, Malaysia, France, and Turkey. Its virtue lies in its simplicity—the pungency of garlic and the moisturizing sweetness of butter—yet within these simple parameters, a host of variations exist. Add parsley, or cilantro, or hot pepper flakes, or paprika, or lemon juice. Or brown the butter to achieve the golden brown color and nutty flavor that the French call *beurre noisette*, "hazelnut butter." (Why not make a real hazelnut butter by adding chopped toasted hazelnuts and a shot of Frangelico liqueur?) Use the following recipe as a starting point, customizing the flavorings to suit your taste. The baste can be made ahead of time, but it's so quick and easy to prepare, you might as well make it as you need it.

TRY THIS!

Everything is fair game for this baste, including bread (grilling is the best way I know to make garlic bread), mushrooms, corn, and other vegetables, all types of seafood, poultry, meats, sweetbreads, and starches, such as grilled polenta or grits.

Brush the baste on the food while it's grilling, using a long-handled basting brush. Take care to brush just enough baste on the meat to coat it. Don't slop it on, or the dripping butter will catch fire, resulting in flare-ups and giving a sooty taste to your food.

INGREDIENTS

BASIC BASTE

8 tablespoons (1 stick) salted butter

3 cloves garlic, minced

½ teaspoon freshly ground or cracked black peppercorns

OPTIONAL FLAVORINGS

¼ cup finely chopped fresh flat-leaf parsley or cilantro

1 teaspoon sweet, smoked, or hot paprika

½ to 1 teaspoon red pepper flakes

1 tablespoon drained capers

1 tablespoon chopped toasted hazelnuts or almonds (see box, page 112)

1 to 2 tablespoons fresh lemon juice

½ teaspoon grated lemon zest

Melt the butter in a heavy saucepan over medium heat. Add the garlic and pepper and any of the optional flavorings (except the lemon juice), if using, and cook until the garlic pieces turn golden (but not quite brown), 2 minutes. Remove the pan from the heat. Add the lemon juice, if using. If storing, transfer to a jar, cover, cool to room temperature, and refrigerate. The baste will keep for at least a week. Reheat to melt the butter before using.

Variations

- For a milder garlic flavor, peel the cloves and gently crush them with the side of a cleaver, but do not chop. Cook them in the butter until fragrant and just beginning to brown, then remove.

- For *beurre noisette* flavor, cook the butter over medium heat until it starts to brown. Add the garlic and continue cooking until the garlic is fragrant and golden and the butter is golden brown.

- For a Mediterranean baste, substitute extra-virgin olive oil for the butter. For extra flavor, add a sprig of rosemary.

TOASTING SESAME SEEDS AND NUTS

In many recipes in this book you'll be instructed to toast sesame seeds or nuts in a dry skillet. The reason is simple: Toasting intensifies their flavor, adding a smoky taste as well. To toast sesame seeds or nuts, preheat a dry heavy skillet over medium heat. Add the seeds or nuts and toast, shaking the pan to ensure even toasting, until lightly colored and fragrant, 2 to 4 minutes. Immediately transfer the seeds or nuts to a bowl. (If you leave them in the pan, they'll continue to cook, and possibly burn, even after the pan is off the heat.) If you've never toasted sesame seeds or nuts, you'll be amazed at how much this simple procedure boosts the flavor.

SESAME SOY BUTTER BASTE

YIELD: Makes ¾ cup, for 2 to 3 pounds of seafood, poultry, meat, or vegetables

I first tasted this savory baste at a grilled fish house in Jakarta. It's one of those preparations that transcend national borders, offering the richness of butter, the salty tang of soy sauce, nutty sesame, plus the irresistible aroma of garlic. Seldom do so few ingredients pack such a wallop of flavor.

TRY THIS!

Brush this baste on hot-off-the grill chicken, pork, seafood, vegetables, or tofu. Serve any extra baste as a sauce.

INGREDIENTS

- 8 tablespoons (1 stick) unsalted butter
- 2 tablespoons toasted sesame seeds (see box, facing page)
- 2 cloves garlic, peeled and minced
- 2 scallions (white and green parts), trimmed and finely chopped
- 2 tablespoons soy sauce
- ½ teaspoon freshly ground black pepper

Melt the butter in a saucepan over medium heat. Add the sesame seeds, garlic, and scallions and cook until the garlic and scallions are aromatic but not brown, 3 minutes. Stir in the soy sauce and pepper. Simmer for 2 minutes. This is so quick and easy to prepare, there's no reason not to make it right before using. However, you can make it in advance. If storing, transfer to a jar, cover, cool to room temperature, and refrigerate. The baste will keep for at least 1 week. Reheat to melt the butter before using.

GRILLED CORN
WITH SESAME SOY BUTTER BASTE

YIELD: Serves 2 to 4

YOU ALSO NEED

12-inch bamboo skewers (optional)

Grilled corn turns up across Planet Barbecue—slathered with mayonnaise and grated cheese in Mexico, for example, or doused with lime juice and cayenne in India. Here's the Japanese version, basted with sesame soy butter. Black sesame seeds are available at Japanese markets; use toasted sesame seeds (see page 112) as an alternate.

INGREDIENTS

4 ears of sweet corn

Sesame Soy Butter Baste
   (page 113)

3 tablespoons black or toasted
   sesame seeds

1. Set up your grill for direct grilling and preheat to high.

2. Husk the corn, stripping the husks back as though you were peeling a banana, leaving them attached at the base. Tie the husks back below the corn to make a handle, using a strip of husk or a string. (Alternatively, strip off the husks altogether and impale the grilled corn on wooden skewers.)

3. Lightly brush the ears of corn with the butter baste. Grill the corn until nicely browned on all sides, 2 to 3 minutes per side, 8 to 12 minutes in all, rotating the ears so they grill evenly. Position the corn so that the tied husks hang over the edge of the grill or away from the hot coals, or slide a folded sheet of aluminum foil under them so they won't burn. Continue to baste the corn on all sides with the butter as it grills.

4. Transfer the corn to a platter. Sprinkle with the black sesame seeds and serve.

SECRET WEAPON BASTING SAUCE

YIELD: Makes ¾ cup, enough for 2 to 3 pounds of meat

TRY THIS!

Brush Secret Weapon Basting Sauce on any meat or seafood (or vegetable, for that matter) that needs additional smoke flavor. Terrific on grilled steak.

Desperate times call for desperate measures. Some years ago, I found myself on a television set in Tokyo—about to battle Iron Chef Rokusaburo Michiba. There was one major problem: I planned to barbecue chicken and ribs, but I didn't have a smoker. I did have a grill and I did have Scotch whisky. So I came up with this smoky basting sauce, which used butter for richness and whisky and liquid smoke to provide the smoke. Scotch is made with smoked barley—use a single malt for maximum smoke flavor. As for liquid smoke, it may have a bum rap among purists, but it is a natural product, made by burning hardwood in a pit. While it's no substitute for true wood smoke, a splash applied judiciously can give you an authentic barbecue flavor when burning wood just isn't possible. Does it work? Well, let's just say the American beat the Japanese Iron Chef on his home turf.

INGREDIENTS

8 tablespoonns (1 stick) salted
   butter

2 tablespoons Scotch whisky

½ teaspoon liquid smoke

Melt the butter in a heavy
nonreactive saucepan. Stir in
the whisky and liquid smoke
and simmer for 30 seconds.

SAFFRON BUTTER BASTE

YIELD: Makes ¾ cup, enough for 2 to 3 pounds of meat

What makes Persian barbecue so extraordinary? First, there's the marinade—Iranians give their meats a tenderizing bath in a yogurt or lemon juice-based marinade for a full day or even two. Then, there's the basting mixture, and here, butter, lemon juice, and saffron conspire to make one of the most succulent anointments ever brushed on grilled chicken, lamb or shish kebab. Note: When buying saffron, look for threads, not powder. The threads (the stigmas of the saffron crocus) are harder to adulterate than saffron powder, so you're more likely to get the real McCoy.

TRY THIS!

Brush this fragrant butter on grilled chicken, game hen, quail, lamb, beef, pork, and shish kebab. It also makes a surprising bruschetta.

INGREDIENTS

½ teaspoon saffron threads

1 tablespoon hot water

8 tablespoons (1 stick) salted
   butter, melted

3 tablespoons fresh lemon juice

1 clove garlic, peeled and
   minced

½ teaspoon freshly ground
   black pepper

1. Crumble the saffron threads between your thumb and forefinger and place in a small bowl with the water. Let the saffron infuse for 10 minutes.

2. Combine the saffron and the remaining ingredients in a saucepan and cook over low heat for a few minutes to warm the garlic. Use right away.

COCONUT CURRY BASTE

YIELD: Makes 1¼ cups, enough for 2 to 3 pounds of meat

TRY THIS!

Traditionally, this baste would be brushed on Asian-style grilled fish and satés. Also great on grilled pork loin and chicken.

Gurney Road in Penang, Malaysia, is one of the meccas of the world's barbecue trail—a broad bayfront avenue lined with hundreds of open-air food stalls that serve some of the tastiest satés in Asia. The following basting sauce is part of what makes Malaysian barbecue so succulent.

Be sure to buy unsweetened coconut milk (not coconut cream).

INGREDIENTS

2 tablespoons vegetable oil

3 cloves garlic, peeled and minced

1 large shallot, peeled and minced

1 stalk lemongrass, trimmed and minced, or ½ teaspoon grated lemon zest

1 tablespoon curry powder

1 cup unsweetened coconut milk

1 tablespoon fish sauce or soy sauce

1. Heat the oil in a wok or saucepan over medium heat. Add the garlic, shallot, and lemongrass and cook, stirring with a wooden spoon, until softened, 3 minutes. Add the curry powder and cook until the vegetables are golden brown, 1 to 2 minutes more. Do not burn.

2. Stir in the coconut milk and bring to a boil. Stir in the fish sauce. The baste can be made ahead and refrigerated, but it's so quick and easy, I usually make it as I need it. If made ahead, transfer to a jar, cover, cool, and refrigerate. The baste will keep for up to 5 days. Reheat before using.

GREEK LEMON-GARLIC BASTE

YIELD: Makes 1½ cups, enough for 2 to 3 pounds of meat or seafood

Wherever Greeks gather, you'll find a fire for grilling, and wherever you find Greeks grilling, you'll find this simple flavorful baste. For when you combine fragrant dark Greek olive oil with fresh garlic and lemon juice, you wind up with a taste that's as ancient and soulful as Greek civilization itself. Greek oregano has a different flavor—more minty and aromatic—than the familiar Italian style. Look for it at Greek or Middle Eastern markets.

INGREDIENTS

½ cup fresh lemon juice

3 cloves garlic, peeled and minced or crushed

1 teaspoon coarse salt (sea or kosher)

1 teaspoon cracked black peppercorns

1 tablespoon dried oregano, preferably Greek

1 cup extra-virgin olive oil

Combine the lemon juice, garlic, salt, pepper, and oregano in a bowl and stir or whisk until the salt crystals are dissolved.

Stir in the oil. This baste tastes best used within a few hours of making. Stir, again, before using.

TRY THIS!

Brush this baste on spit-roasted lamb, or beef kebabs, grilled chicken (the high oil content makes it especially welcome for chicken breasts), and seafood, from shrimp to fish to octopus. For even more flavor, make a basting brush with a bunch of rosemary. You'll need to stir the baste each time you use it to mix the oil and lemon juice (which tend to separate as they sit). Note that the dripping oil may cause flare-ups. For this reason, don't overcrowd the grill grate. You want to have room to move the food to dodge any flames. This baste works especially well for spit-roasting.

NASHVILLE HOT CHICKEN BASTE

YIELD: Makes 1 cup

TRY THIS!

Use not just on wings, but on any grilled or smoked chicken. It's also pretty awesome brushed on barbecued ribs, steak, and shrimp.

What happens when Buffalo wings meet Nashville hot chicken? Smoke and fire in two of America's favorite fried chickens. My stepson, Jake Klein, created this basting sauce for his Nashville hot chicken sausage at his Brooklyn gastropub, Jake's Handcrafted. Yes, 4 tablespoons of cayenne sounds like a *lot* of hot pepper (Jake gives you a range), but the cayenne mellows somewhat when cooked and you need this much to get the requisite bite.

INGREDIENTS

2 to 4 tablespoons ground cayenne pepper

2 tablespoons dark brown sugar

1 tablespoon garlic powder

1 tablespoon smoked paprika

1 tablespoon celery salt

1 tablespoon coarse salt (sea or kosher)

1 cup vegetable oil, such as peanut or canola

Place the cayenne, sugar, garlic powder, paprika, and salts in a heavy saucepan and whisk to mix. Cook over medium heat until the sugar starts to melt and the spices smell fragrant, 3 minutes. Whisk in the oil and simmer, 2 to 3 minutes. Remove the pan from the heat and let the mixture cool to room temperature. Use immediately for basting, or transfer to an airtight container, cover, and refrigerate. Nashville Hot Chicken Baste will keep for up to 1 month and just gets better with age.

NASHVILLE HOT WINGS

YIELD: Makes 32 pieces; serves 6 to 8 as an appetizer

Okay, I know: Nashville chicken is supposed to be fried. But smoke-roasting gives you soulful wings with great depth of flavor and a lot less fat.

YOU ALSO NEED
(OPTIONAL)

1½ cups hardwood chips, soaked in water for 30 minutes, then drained

INGREDIENTS

16 whole chicken wings (about 3½ pounds)

2 teaspoons coarse salt (sea or kosher)

2 teaspoons freshly ground black pepper

2 teaspoons onion powder

2 teaspoons ground oregano

1 to 2 teaspoons red pepper flakes

2 tablespoons extra-virgin olive oil or vegetable oil

Nashville Hot Chicken Baste (facing page)

3 tablespoons chopped fresh chives or cilantro

1. Rinse the chicken wings under cold running water, then blot dry with paper towels. Cut the tips off the wings and discard or save them for stock (page 160). Cut each wing into 2 pieces through the joint—the drumette and the flat.

2. Place the chicken wings in a large bowl and sprinkle with the salt, pepper, onion powder, oregano, and red pepper flakes. Stir so the spices coat the wings evenly. Stir in the olive oil. You can grill the wings right away, but you'll get a better flavor if you marinate them for 2 hours in the refrigerator before smoking.

3. Set up your grill for indirect grilling and build a medium-hot fire (400°F). Brush and oil the grill grate.

4. Arrange the wings skin side up on the grate away from the heat over the drip pan. If you want a smoke flavor, add the chips to the coals if using a charcoal grill or place in the smoker box of your gas grill. Set aside ¼ cup of baste.

5. Indirect grill until the skin is browned and the meat cooked through, 30 minutes. After 15 minutes, start brushing the wings with the ¾ cup chicken baste. Continue basting every 5 minutes or so. To test for doneness, make a slit in the thickest part of the meat of the largest wing. There should be no trace of red or pink at the bone.

6. Pile the wings on a platter. Pour the ¼ cup baste over them and sprinkle with chives or cilantro. Serve with plenty of napkins.

MOP SAUCES/SPRAY SAUCES

Mop sauces are applied to keep meats moist and add an extra layer of flavor during smoking. The name comes from the traditional cotton mop used to apply the sauce. You can also apply a mop sauce with a food-safe spray bottle, but in this case omit the pepper, which could clog up the spray nozzle. Unlike barbecue sauces, mop sauces are thin and not particularly sweet. (Excess sugar in a mop sauce would burn before the meat is fully cooked.) Use the following as guidelines—for a sweeter mop sauce (for pork and poultry), use apple cider or pineapple juice. For a savory sauce, use brewed coffee.

BASIC MOP SAUCE

YIELD: Makes about 2 cups

TRY THIS!

Swab this mop sauce on ribs, pork shoulder, spatchcocked chickens, and more—whenever an extra layer of moisture and flavor is needed.

Mop sauces take their name from the utensil used to apply them: a clean mop—miniature-size for home use, or a full-size floor mop for swabbing barbecue to feed a large crowd. Many companies manufacture barbecue mops; my Best of Barbecue mop, for example, has a detachable head so you can put it in the dishwasher. I hope it goes without saying: Wash the mop between active duties.

INGREDIENTS

4 tablespoons (½ stick)
   unsalted butter

1 cup beef or chicken stock,
   preferably homemade

¼ cup Worcestershire sauce

¼ cup whiskey, brandy, or rum

2 tablespoons soy sauce

Freshly ground black pepper

**OPTIONAL FLAVORINGS
(USE ONE OF THE FOLLOWING)**

¼ cup apple cider or pineapple
   juice

¼ cup tomato sauce

¼ cup brewed coffee

Coarse salt (sea or kosher)

TABASCO SAUCE

Tabasco sauce ranks among the world's most famous hot sauces. If you had a nickel for every bottle sold in a day, you'd have a small fortune. If you made the same deal for a year, you could buy an island.

Tabasco sauce takes its name from the Mexican state of Tabasco—itself named for an Indian word meaning "humid soil." The name aptly describes the place where Tabasco sauce is produced: Avery Island, Louisiana. Located off the coast, 140 miles west of New Orleans, Avery Island has a hot humid climate that's perfect for growing the fiery small red chiles—members of the cayenne family—that give Tabasco sauce its distinctive hue and heat. As for the flavor, it comes from a unique process in which the chiles are mashed to a pulp, mixed with vinegar and local salt, placed in white oak barrels to ferment, then aged for up to 36 months. What results is a hot sauce with a lot more going for it than mere heat. Tabasco sauce is hot, tart, salty, and intensely aromatic. The barrel aging gives it a complexity unique among hot sauces.

Tabasco sauce was invented by Edmund McIlhenny, who planted his first red pepper on Avery Island in the 1860s. By 1868, he was making and selling his sauce, which he packaged in perfume bottles. The sauce is still made by the McIlhenny family and sold in more than 100 countries.

1. Melt the butter in a saucepan over medium heat. Add the stock, Worcestershire sauce, whiskey, soy sauce, pepper, and one of the optional flavorings, and whisk to combine. Simmer the ingredients to blend the flavors, 5 minutes. Add salt as needed.

2. Apply the mop sauce during smoking with a barbecue mop, basting brush, or spray bottle. Start applying it *after* the first hour of smoking so the outside of the meat is partially cooked. This keeps you from cross-contaminating the mop sauce with juices from raw meat. Once the meat is cooked, boil any remaining mop sauce for 3 minutes to sterilize it, then store it in a covered jar in the refrigerator. It will keep for at least 3 days. Warm it before reusing.

BUFFALO MOP

YIELD: Makes 1½ cups, enough for 2 pounds of meat

TRY THIS!

The obvious use for Buffalo Mop is on grilled or smoked chicken wings. Marinate the wings in half the mop in a covered baking dish in the refrigerator for at least 4 hours, preferably overnight. Use the remainder of the mop for basting, but don't start mopping until the outside of the chicken is cooked. This mop works equally well on chicken breasts and thighs, turkey, pork, and shrimp.

October 30, 1964, was no red-letter day in history. No rocket ship blasted off for the moon, no landmark presidential speech was made, no internet stock went public. But human happiness was immeasurably enriched on that fateful day, when Teressa Belissimo, owner of the Anchor Bar in Buffalo, New York, invented buffalo wings. Faced with an extra shipment of chicken wings and a houseful of teenagers, she had the inspiration to deep-fry the wings, then slather them with melted butter and hot sauce. Here's my version of that sauce. I suppose you could make this mop ahead, but why bother? It takes 5 minutes to assemble on the spot. Note: Tradition calls for Tabasco sauce; for an Asian twist, try Thai-inspired sriracha.

INGREDIENTS

8 tablespoons (1 stick) salted butter, cut into 1-inch pieces

2 cloves garlic, peeled and minced

2 tablespoons tomato paste

¼ cup dry white wine

2 tablespoons distilled white vinegar

¼ to ½ cup of your favorite hot sauce, such as Tabasco or sriracha (depending on your tolerance for heat)

Melt 2 tablespoons of the butter in a saucepan over medium heat. Add the garlic and cook until golden, 3 minutes. Stir in the tomato paste and cook for 1 minute. Add the wine and vinegar and bring to a boil, whisking to dissolve the tomato paste. Add the hot sauce and remaining butter and simmer for 2 minutes.

CIDER SQUIRT

YIELD: Makes 4¼ cups, enough for 4 pounds of meat

One of the secrets of world-class barbecue is consistent and conscientious basting while the meat is cooking. The traditional tool for basting is literally a kitchen mop (hence the term mop sauce), but more and more pit masters use spray bottles or misters. Here's a simple baste that's short on preparation time but long on flavor.

INGREDIENTS

2 cups apple cider

¾ cup cider vinegar

½ cup bourbon

½ cup water

¼ cup Worcestershire sauce

¼ cup fresh lemon juice

½ teaspoon coarse salt (sea or kosher)

Combine all the ingredients in a heavy saucepan and bring to a boil over high heat. Reduce the heat and simmer the sauce for 5 minutes. Let cool to room temperature. Transfer the squirt to a spray bottle and use right away or refrigerate. Use within 2 days of making.

TRY THIS!

You wouldn't want to eat this stuff straight, but spray it on roasting or smoking meat and it adds a world of flavor. I put the sauce in a spray bottle and spray it right on the meat. Or you can brush it on with a mop or basting brush. When cooking chicken or ribs, apply every 30 minutes. When cooking a large cut of meat, like a brisket or pork shoulder, apply every hour.

INJECTOR SAUCES

The theory is simple enough: Use an oversize hypodermic needle to shoot a flavorful liquid deep into chickens, turkeys, pork loins and shoulders, hams, and other meats to keep them moist during grilling or smoking. Injector sauces are simple, but you should avoid chopped garlic and large flakes of herbs and spices, which risk clogging the holes in the needle. Many companies make meat injectors, including my own Best of Barbecue. Here are four injector sauces that guarantee a succulent turkey or roast every time.

BUTTER-BROTH INJECTOR SAUCE

YIELD: Makes 1½ cups, enough for 3 chickens or 1 to 2 turkeys or roasts

TRY THIS!

Place the sauce in the injector and inject it in several places into the deepest part of the meat.

Here's my homemade version of what makes a commercial butter-injected turkey. Ideally, you'll use homemade chicken broth. Canned broth can be quite salty, so if you use it, the butter should be unsalted.

INGREDIENTS

1 cup unsalted or low-sodium chicken broth, preferably homemade, or Smoked Stock (page 146)

4 tablespoons (½ stick) salted butter

2 tablespoons fresh lemon juice

½ teaspoon garlic powder (must be powder, not granulated garlic)

½ teaspoon freshly ground white pepper

Fine salt (sea or kosher), to taste

Combine all the ingredients in a nonreactive saucepan and warm over medium heat until the butter melts. Correct the seasoning, adding salt if needed. Cool to room temperature (the butter should remain liquid), then draw it into the injector and fire away.

NOTE: If your injector has a slender needle, strain this sauce through a fine-mesh strainer to remove any spice pieces that could clog it.

BEER-BUTTER BEEF INJECTOR SAUCE

YIELD: Make 2½ cups, enough for an 8- to 12-pound brisket

Brisket is the high holy beef of barbecue—simultaneously the easiest and most difficult dish to achieve. So what does it take to nail first prize in the brisket category at the world's largest barbecue contest, the Kansas City Royal? Ask Andy Husbands. Chef, pit master, and author, Husbands and his barbecue team IQUE won top honors for brisket at the American Royal, the Jack Daniel's Invitational, and dozens of other contests. To be sure, Husbands and crew owe their success to a rub, sauce, and slow smoking technique honed over years of competition and practice. A lot of teams do. But the secret weapon might just be an injector sauce concocted from beef broth and Worcestershire sauce. I also like to add butter and beer.

TRY THIS!

Inject this sauce deep into the brisket flat and point before it goes in the smoker. Also excellent for beef sirloin, tenderloin, and shoulder clod.

INGREDIENTS

2 tablespoons unsalted butter

¼ cup beer (your choice what kind)

2 cups Smoked Stock (page 146) or beef broth, preferably homemade (if using commercial broth, select a low-sodium brand)

2 tablespoons Worcestershire sauce, or to taste

Melt the butter in a large saucepan. Add the beer and bring to a boil. Remove the pan from the heat and stir in the stock and Worcestershire sauce. Let cool to room temperature, then draw it into the injector and fire away.

HOW TO USE AN INJECTOR

Pour the injector sauce into a slender container. Fully depress the injector plunger and insert the needle in the injector sauce. (Some needles are closed at the end but have holes along the sides. Make sure the perforations are fully submerged in the sauce.) Pull the plunger back to fill the syringe with liquid. Plunge the needle deep in the meat following the direction of the grain (the needle should be parallel to the meat fibers to the extent possible), then depress the plunger slowly and steadily. (A quick plunge may send streams of injector sauce squirting in the opposite direction.)

Withdraw the needle gradually. Minimize the number of holes you put in the meat by angling the needle in two or three directions using the same entry hole. Continue injecting until liquid begins leaking from the holes, indicating the meat cannot hold any more. For easier cleanup, work over a rimmed baking sheet.

ASIAN INJECTOR SAUCE

YIELD: Makes 1½ cups, enough for 3 chickens or 1 to 2 turkeys or roasts

TRY THIS!

Use as described in the box on this page. This sauce goes especially well with chicken or pork.

Based on a traditional Chinese dish called master sauce chicken, this sauce plays salty soy sauce against nutty sesame oil and sweet anise-y five-spice powder.

INGREDIENTS

1 cup unsalted chicken broth, preferably homemade, or Smoked Stock (page 146)

3 tablespoons Asian (dark) sesame oil

2 tablespoons rice wine or dry sherry

2 tablespoons soy sauce

½ teaspoon Chinese Five-Spice Powder (page 43) or a good commercial brand

2 tablespoons honey

½ teaspoon garlic powder

½ teaspoon onion powder

½ teaspoon freshly ground white pepper

½ ground cinnamon

Fine salt (sea or kosher; optional)

Combine all the ingredients, except the salt, in a nonreactive saucepan and warm over medium heat. Correct the seasoning, adding salt if needed. Cool to room temperature, then draw into the injector and fire away.

NOTE: If your injector has a slender needle, strain this sauce through a fine-mesh strainer to remove any spice pieces that could clog it.

CAJUN INJECTOR SAUCE

YIELD: Makes 1½ cups, enough for 3 chickens or 1 to 2 turkeys or roasts

Many commercial injector sauces are manufactured in Louisiana, so I thought it fitting to offer a recipe for a Cajun variation. Use the Cajun Rub from this book or your favorite commercial brand.

INGREDIENTS

1 cup unsalted chicken broth, preferably homemade, or Smoked Stock (page 146)

4 tablespoons (½ stick) salted butter

2 tablespoons white wine or dry vermouth

¼ cup Cajun Rub (page 33), or a good commercial brand

½ teaspoon freshly ground white pepper

Fine salt (sea or kosher; optional)

TRY THIS!

Use as described on the facing page. The injector sauce goes particularly well with turkey or chicken.

Combine all the ingredients, except the salt, in a nonreactive saucepan and cook over medium heat just until the butter melts. Correct the seasoning, adding salt if needed. Cool to room temperature (the butter should remain liquid), then draw it into the injector and fire away.

NOTE: If your injector has a slender needle, strain this sauce through a fine-mesh strainer to remove any spice pieces that could clog it.

GLAZES AND OILS

NOT-JUST-FOR-HAM GLAZE

YIELD: Makes 1¼ cups

TRY THIS!

The first logical use for this glaze is ham, either a whole fresh or cooked ham or a ham steak grilled directly over the coals. Pork loin or chops benefit from the clove-scented sweetness of this glaze; so do chicken, turkey, and quail. It's pretty darned grand on grilled sweet potatoes, too.

This sweet-spicy glaze is inspired by an American classic: mustard-painted, brown sugar-crusted, clove-studded smoked ham. I combined these ingredients with just enough butter and rum to make a glaze.

INGREDIENTS

½ cup packed dark brown sugar

8 tablespoons (1 stick) unsalted butter, cut into 1-inch pieces

½ cup dark rum

3 tablespoons Dijon mustard

1 tablespoon cider vinegar

Scant ½ teaspoon ground cloves, or to taste

¼ teaspoon freshly ground black pepper

Place all the ingredients in a heavy nonreactive saucepan and bring to a boil over high heat, whisking steadily.

Reduce the heat to medium and simmer the mixture until thick and syrupy, about 5 minutes. Use right away.

PINEAPPLE GARLIC GLAZE

YIELD: Makes 2 cups

We don't normally link pineapple and garlic in North America, but elsewhere in the world, especially in Southeast Asia, these flavorings are often combined to make a barbecue sauce or relish that plays the acidity of fruit against the pungency of the fried garlic. A shot of Scotch whisky reinforces the smoke flavor.

TRY THIS!

This glaze works equally well with poultry, pork, and seafood. Start brushing it on during the last 10 minutes of cooking.

INGREDIENTS

4 tablespoons (½ stick) unsalted butter

4 cloves garlic, peeled and thinly sliced crosswise

1 cup packed dark brown sugar

1 cup Scotch whisky

½ cup pineapple juice

½ cup ketchup

3 tablespoons fresh lemon juice

½ teaspoon freshly ground black pepper

1. Melt the butter in a heavy nonreactive saucepan over medium heat. Add the garlic and cook until golden brown, 1 to 2 minutes.

2. Stir in the remaining ingredients and simmer over medium heat until thick and flavorful, about 5 minutes. Use right away.

TANGERINE LACQUER GLAZE

YIELD: Makes 1½ cups

TRY THIS!

This glaze goes great on anything you decide to grill. Because of the relatively high sugar content, brush it on the meat during the last 5 to 10 minutes of cooking.

This sauce was inspired by the culinary lacquers of Japan and China—those sweet-salty glazes traditionally brushed on chicken and duck to give them a glossy lacquered finish. This one contrasts the sweetness of honey and tangerines with the salty tang of soy sauce. When tangerines aren't in season, use oranges.

The easiest way to zest the tangerines is with a vegetable peeler or Microplane. Star anise is described on page 37.

INGREDIENTS

½ cup soy sauce

½ cup fresh tangerine juice

⅓ cup honey

3 tablespoons Asian (dark) sesame oil

5 strips (½ inch each) tangerine zest

3 cloves garlic, peeled and lightly crushed with the side of a cleaver

3 scallions (white parts only), trimmed, lightly crushed with the side of a cleaver

3 slices fresh ginger (¼ inch thick each), peeled and lightly crushed with the side of a cleaver

1 cinnamon stick (3 inches)

1 star anise (optional)

Place all the ingredients in a heavy saucepan and bring to a boil over medium heat. Reduce the heat slightly and simmer, uncovered, until the mixture is thick and syrupy, 6 to 8 minutes. Strain the glaze into a bowl. Use right away.

FRUIT + BOOZE GLAZE

YIELD: Makes 1½ cups

Like mop sauces, glazes are flavorful liquids applied to meats or seafood during smoking or grilling. They tend to be thicker and sweeter than mop sauces and are applied toward the end of cooking. (If applied too early, the sugar in the glaze burns.) You can customize this glaze by varying the fruit juices and spirits.

TRY THIS!

Brush the glaze on grilled or smoked pork loin, chops, or ribs, grilled or smoked chicken, turkey, and all manner of game.

INGREDIENTS

2 cups fresh apple cider, pineapple juice, passion fruit juice, or pomegranate juice

½ cup bourbon, whiskey, rum, brandy, or other spirit

½ cup packed light or dark brown sugar, granulated sugar, honey, or cane syrup, or to taste

1 cinnamon stick (3 inches)

4 allspice berries

4 whole cloves

1 teaspoon red pepper flakes

3 tablespoons butter

Coarse salt (sea or kosher) and freshly ground black pepper, to taste

Place the fruit juice, booze, sugar, cinnamon, allspice, cloves, and red pepper flakes in a nonreactive saucepan. Bring to a boil over high heat and boil, whisking often, until thick, syrupy, and reduced by half, about 10 minutes. Whisk in the butter and salt and pepper. The glaze should be fruity and sweet, with just a hint of salt to balance the sugar. Strain the glaze into a heatproof bowl. Use immediately or store in a clean jar in the refrigerator, where it will keep for at least a week.

BRANDY-BRINED TURKEY BREAST
WITH TANGERINE LACQUER GLAZE

YIELD: Serves 8 to 10

Turkey—especially the breast—tends to dry out when smoked or grilled. Enter this brandy brine—which pumps moistness into the lean meat and keeps it there, imparting luscious salty-fruity Cognac flavors. The tangerine lacquer glaze adds a lustrous sheen and Asian-inflected sweetness.

YOU ALSO NEED

1½ cups cherry or other hardwood chips, soaked for 30 minutes, then drained

INGREDIENTS

1 whole turkey breast (5 to 6 pounds), skin on, boned, rolled, and tied

All-Purpose Brine (page 102) flavored with ½ cup brandy or Cognac, 2 cinnamon sticks, and 2 strips tangerine or orange zest

Extra-virgin olive oil

Tangerine Lacquer Glaze (page 132)

1. Rinse the turkey breast and blot dry with paper towels. Place the turkey in a jumbo resealable plastic bag.

2. Add the brine, seal the bag, and place in a large bowl (to catch any unexpected leaks). Brine the turkey breast for at least 12 hours or as long as 24 in the refrigerator, turning it several times so it brines evenly.

3. Rinse off the turkey breast and blot dry. Let dry on a wire rack in the refrigerator until the surface feels tacky, 1 to 2 hours. Lightly brush the outside of the turkey with oil.

4. TO GRILL THE TURKEY BREAST:
Set up the grill for indirect grilling and preheat to 350°F. Brush and oil the grill grate. Add the wood chips to the coals. Indirect grill the turkey until the outside is golden brown and the internal temperature in the thickest part of the meat reaches 165°F. This will take

1 to 1½ hours. Start basting the turkey with extra-virgin olive oil after 30 minutes, and continue basting every 15 minutes.

TO SMOKE YOUR TURKEY BREAST: Light your smoker according to the manufacturer's instructions and preheat to 250°F. Add the wood as specified by the manufacturer. Place the bird in the smoker. Smoke until the outside is bronzed with smoke and the internal temperature of the meat reaches 165°F. This will take 2½ to 3 hours. Start basting the turkey with extra-virgin olive oil after 1 hour and continue basting every 45 minutes.

5. Whichever cooking method you use, during the last 5 minutes, baste the turkey with Tangerine Lacquer Glaze. Baste once more before carving. Let rest on the cutting board loosely draped with aluminum foil for 5 to 10 minutes. Remove the string and carve into slices. Serve the remaining glaze on the side.

THREE VARIATIONS ON A THEME OF GARLIC OIL

There are three ways to make garlic oil. The first gives you a robust fresh garlic taste, but it's the most perishable. The second, fried garlic oil, delivers a soulful fried garlic flavor; while the third—roasted garlic oil—emphasizes the bulb's earthy sweetness. Whichever oil you make, start with whole fresh heads of garlic, not commercial pre-peeled or pre-chopped.

FRESH GARLIC OIL

YIELD: Makes 1 cup

This oil delivers the strongest garlic flavor. Great for basting.

TRY THIS!

Brush this pungent oil on anything—bread, seafood, poultry, vegetables, beef. Use it before or during grilling. It's too strong to serve as a sauce.

INGREDIENTS

3 cloves garlic, peeled and chopped

1 cup extra-virgin olive oil or canola oil

Combine the ingredients in a blender or food processor. Process until the garlic is puréed. This oil tastes best used within a few hours of making.

Variations

Add other flavorings to this oil, such as fresh basil; black pepper and cumin seeds; fresh or dried chiles; lemon or lime zest; or even a cool combination of these flavorings.

FRIED GARLIC OIL

YIELD: Makes 1 cup

This aromatic oil turns up at opposite sides of the globe. The Portuguese spoon it over grilled seafood; in Southeast Asia, fried garlic oil is a popular condiment for grilled chicken, fish, and saté.

INGREDIENTS

1 head garlic, broken into cloves and peeled

1 cup extra-virgin olive oil, preferably Portuguese

1. Finely chop the garlic by hand or in a mini processor.

2. Heat the oil in a heavy saucepan over medium heat. Add the garlic and cook until light golden brown, 4 to 6 minutes. Don't burn the garlic; it will become bitter.

Immediately, transfer the garlic and oil to a heatproof bowl to cool.

3. Use right away or transfer to a jar, cover, and store in the refrigerator. The oil will keep for at least 3 days. Bring it to room temperature before using.

TRY THIS!

Great for marinating and basting, but even better served as a condiment. Spoon it over grilled meats, seafood, and vegetables.

ROASTED GARLIC OIL

YIELD: Makes 1 cup

TRY THIS!

Use this fragrant oil as a baste for grilled poultry and seafood. Drizzle or spoon it over grilled food at the table.

Roasting garlic in oil blunts its nose-jarring pungency, bringing out an earthy aromatic sweetness.

INGREDIENTS

1 head garlic, broken into cloves and peeled

1 cup extra-virgin olive oil

1. Place the garlic and oil in a heavy saucepan over medium-low heat. Gently simmer until the garlic cloves are soft and golden, 10 to 15 minutes. Do not let burn. Transfer the garlic and oil to a heatproof bowl and let cool to room temperature.

2. Use right away or transfer the garlic cloves and oil to a jar, cover, and refrigerate. The oil will keep for at least 3 days. Bring it to room temperature before using.

HOW TO PEEL AND SMASH GARLIC

Lightly flatten each clove with the side of a chef's knife or cleaver. Once cracked, the skin will slip off easily. To smash the garlic, cut it crosswise into ¼-inch-thick slices. Stand each slice on end on a cutting board near the edge. Place the side of the knife or cleaver on top of it, blade angled downward slightly, and slam the top of the blade with the heel of your hand. The garlic will be reduced instantly to an aromatic paste.

SWEET BASIL OIL
WITH GARLIC

I like to think of this oil as Provence in a bottle. Use basil oil for marinating and basting, and drizzle it over grilled food the moment you're ready to serve it. When the cool oil hits the hot meat or fish, it's pure olfactory magic. Even if you miss the food, the oil looks cool in telegraphic dashes or dots on the white part of the plate. I give two methods for making basil oil.

FRESH BASIL OIL

YIELD: Makes 2 cups

The uncooked version of this oil gives you the most intense basil taste, but the flavor fades fairly quickly.

INGREDIENTS

1 bunch fresh basil, stemmed
(2 cups loosely packed basil
leaves)

½ cup loosely packed fresh
spinach leaves, stemmed

1 clove garlic, peeled and
chopped

2 cups extra-virgin olive oil

1. Rinse the basil and spinach in cold water and blot or spin the leaves dry. Place the basil, spinach, garlic, and oil in a blender and blend until very finely chopped. Transfer the oil to a bowl and let steep for 4 hours at room temperature.

2. Strain the oil through a fine-mesh strainer into a large jar. The oil tastes best used within 2 hours of making. Cover and refrigerate, but let it come to room temperature before serving.

TRY THIS!

Use this emerald oil as a marinade, baste, or drizzle on everything from grilled meats to seafood to vegetables to polenta. To make a simple marinade, combine 2 parts basil oil with 1 part fresh lemon juice.

BLANCHED BASIL OIL

YIELD: Makes 2 cups

TRY THIS!

Use as described in the recipe for Fresh Basil Oil (page 139).

Blanching the basil (shock by boiling in salted water) delivers a brighter, longer-lasting oil. Make a batch as the summer basil season winds down so that you have enough to take you through the fall.

INGREDIENTS

1 tablespoon coarse salt (sea or kosher)

1 bunch fresh basil, stemmed (2 cups loosely packed basil leaves), rinsed

½ cup packed fresh spinach leaves, stemmed and rinsed

2 cups extra-virgin olive oil

3 cloves garlic, peeled and crushed with the side of a cleaver

1. Bring 3 quarts water and the salt to a rapid boil in a large saucepan. Have ready a large bowl of ice water.

2. Add the basil and spinach to the boiling water and blanch for 15 seconds. Drain in a colander, then plunge the greens into the ice water. Drain well, then squeeze the greens in the palm of your hand to wring out all the water.

3. Heat ¼ cup of the oil in a small frying pan over medium heat. Add the garlic and cook until golden brown, about 4 minutes. Remove the pan from the heat.

4. Transfer the garlic and oil to a blender with the blanched basil and spinach and the remaining oil and purée well. Transfer the oil to a bowl and let steep for 4 hours at room temperature. Strain the oil through a fine-mesh strainer into a large jar. Use right away or cover and refrigerate, but let it warm to room temperature before serving. The oil will keep for at least a week.

LEMON PEPPER OIL

YIELD: Makes 2 cups

This aromatic oil brings together three of my favorite flavors for grilling: lemon, black pepper, and extra-virgin olive oil. You can buy pre-cracked black peppercorns, but you'll get more flavor if you crack whole peppercorns fresh yourself (see page 21).

INGREDIENTS

2 large lemons, scrubbed and dried

3 tablespoons cracked black peppercorns

1 cup grapeseed or canola oil

1 cup extra-virgin olive oil

1. Using a vegetable peeler, remove the zest (oil-rich outer peel) of the lemon in broad, thin strips. Place these strips in a small frying pan with the peppercorns and grapeseed oil. Place the pan over medium-low heat and cook until the peppercorns sizzle and the lemon zest strips just begin to brown, 3 to 5 minutes. Transfer the mixture to a heatproof bowl and let cool to room temperature.

2. Add the olive oil, then churn the mixture in a blender. Let stand at room temperature for 4 hours. Strain the oil through a fine-mesh strainer into a large jar. Use right away or cover, away from heat and light. The oil will keep for at least a week. Bring it to room temperature before using.

Variation

Combine the uncooked ingredients in a blender and blend well. Infuse and strain as described above. This gives you a great-tasting lemon pepper oil without any cooking. Refrigerate as described above.

TRY THIS!

Lemon pepper oil works well with delicate grilled foods, such as shellfish (especially shrimp and scallops), fish, and poultry. It's fantastic on grilled vegetables, from asparagus to zucchini. Use it as a marinade, baste, or sauce.

CURRY OIL

YIELD: Makes 2 cups

TRY THIS!

Curry oil works equally well as a marinade, baste, or sauce for seafood, poultry and meat. Drizzle it over grilled vegetables, especially eggplant and corn, not to mention over grilled tofu.

You'll love this aromatic oil—its golden color, fragrant scent, and complex flavor. Cooking mellows the taste of the curry powder, so even if you don't normally care for curry, you may like it.

INGREDIENTS

2 cups canola oil

1 medium-size onion, peeled and minced

3 cloves garlic, minced

1 tablespoon minced fresh ginger

2 tablespoons curry powder

1. Heat the oil in a skillet over medium heat. Add the onion, garlic, ginger, and curry powder and cook until the ingredients are golden and fragrant, 2 to 3 minutes. Remove the pan from the heat and let cool.

2. Transfer the mixture to a blender and blend until very finely chopped. Transfer to a bowl and let stand for 4 hours at room temperature. Strain the oil through a fine-mesh strainer into a large jar or bottle. Use right away or cover and refrigerate. The oil will keep for at least a week. Bring it to room temperature before using.

CHINESE FIRE OIL

YIELD: Makes 2 cups

Preparation of this oil is something of a baptism by fire. You toss Chinese dried chiles into hot oil. The ensuing smoke will burn your eyes, savage your gullet, and make your teeth clench with discomfort. Over the years, I've used this oil to electrify everything from smoked spareribs to grilled tofu, and I've varied the chiles and flavorings, adding black or Sichuan peppercorns, or garlic, ginger, and scallions. Which is to say that you should consider the following recipe as a broad guideline, not a formula to be followed to the letter. Prepare this fiery oil outdoors on your grill's side burner. If you make it indoors, run the exhaust fan on high.

INGREDIENTS

1 cup peanut oil

½ to 1 cup small dried Chinese chiles or other dried chiles (the more you use, the hotter the oil will be)

2 tablespoons Sichuan peppercorns or black peppercorns

4 scallions (white parts only), trimmed and crushed with the side of a cleaver

4 slices fresh ginger (each ¼ inch thick), peeled and crushed with the side of a cleaver

4 cloves garlic, peeled and crushed with the side of a cleaver

4 strips tangerine zest or orange zest (see Note)

1 cup Asian (dark) sesame oil

1. Heat the peanut oil in a wok or deep heavy saucepan to 375°F on a deep-fry thermometer. Add the chiles, peppercorns, scallions, ginger, garlic, and zest and fry for 10 seconds, then remove the wok or pan from the heat. Pour into a heatproof bowl and let cool for 10 minutes, then stir in the sesame oil. Let the ingredients steep at room temperature for 2 hours.

2. Pour the oil through a fine-mesh strainer into a jar or bottle. Use right away or cover and refrigerate. The oil will keep for several weeks. Bring it to room temperature before using.

NOTE: The best way to remove the zest from the tangerines is to use a vegetable peeler.

TRY THIS!

The Chinese use this fiery oil the way we would a good hot sauce. A few teaspoons will invigorate any marinade. The oil is probably too fiery to use for basting, but that doesn't mean that some chile head out there won't try it.

To make an interesting dipping sauce, combine equal parts fire oil, soy sauce, rice wine, and rice vinegar, adding sugar or honey to taste for sweetness.

MEXICAN CHILE OIL

YIELD: Makes 2 cups

TRY THIS!

Use this oil in Mexican or Tex-Mex marinades. Drizzle it over carnitas, fajitas, and quesadillas.

*C*hiles pequines or de árbol deliver a strong back-of-the-throat heat. Dried chipotles will give you an interesting smoke flavor. For a milder chile oil, you could use guajillo or dried New Mexican red chiles. Prepare this one outdoors on your grill's side burner.

INGREDIENTS

2 cups canola or peanut oil

½ to 1 cup dried Mexican chiles or other dried chiles (the more you use, the hotter the oil will be)

1 tablespoon black peppercorns

1 teaspoon cumin seeds

½ medium-size onion, peeled and finely chopped

2 cloves garlic, peeled and crushed with the side of a cleaver

4 strips orange zest

1. Place the oil in a wok or deep, heavy saucepan and heat over high heat to 375°F on a deep-fry thermometer. Add the remaining ingredients, fry for 10 seconds, then remove the wok or pan from the heat. Transfer to a heatproof bowl and let stand at room temperature for 1 to 2 hours.

2. Pour the oil through a fine-mesh strainer into a large jar. Use right away or cover and refrigerate. The oil will keep for at least a week. Bring it to room temperature before using.

TRUFFLE OIL

YIELD: Makes 2 cups

This will be the most expensive flavored oil you've ever made. Why bother? Can't you buy truffle oil in every high-end supermarket? The fact is, most of what's sold as truffle oil is concocted from a chemical approximation of the exquisitely aromatic fungus that grows at the foot of oak trees in Italy's Piedmont region. You know the story: how truffle hunters use specially trained dogs or pigs to find them, often hunting truffles at night to keep their location secret from competitors. Once found, truffles aren't particularly handsome to look at: misshapen tan or brown lumps with a haunting musky aroma. But as with Asian fish sauce or aged cheese, what initially seems off-putting becomes addictive. Truffle oil is a great way to capture the flavor of fresh truffle; it's also a way of making a little go a long way. Fresh white truffles are in season from October through January.

TRY THIS!

During truffle season in the Italian truffle city of Alba, I ate one of the most memorable meals of my life—a simple grilled veal chop drizzled with truffle oil and sprinkled with shavings of fresh white truffle. Keep the protein simple: grilled chicken, shellfish, steak. Equally awesome on simply grilled vegetables and polenta. Remember—it's all about the truffle oil.

INGREDIENTS

1 cup extra-virgin olive oil

1 cup grapeseed or canola oil

½ ounce fresh white truffle

Place the oils in a large jar and shake to mix. Cut the truffle into paper-thin slices (see Note). Add the truffle slices to the oil. Cover and let the truffle oil stand at room temperature for 1 day. At that point, it's ready to use. The oil will keep, covered in the refrigerator, for at least a week. However, the flavor will fade as time passes.

NOTE: Cookware shops sell special truffle cutters for this purpose. If you're investing in truffles, you might as well invest in a cutter. They're worth buying, for the thinner a slice of truffle, the more aromatic it will be.

FINISHING SAUCES AND BUTTERS

SMOKED STOCK

YIELD: Makes 2 to 4 quarts

TRY THIS!

Use smoked stock to make the Texas Bar-B-Que Sauce, Kansas City Style on page 176 or the injector sauces on pages 126 to 129. Add it to chili, stews, baked beans, and gravies.

Stock is a liquid essence of meat, bones, aromatic vegetables, and herbs, not to mention a building block in the world's great cuisines, both East and West. It reflects two of a chef's guiding principles: Think flavor and don't waste food. Homemade stock makes your kitchen smell good and immeasurably improves soups, stews—almost anything that calls for a liquid. It's about to get a lot better, because you're going to use the bones from smoked chicken, beef, and spareribs or baby backs. (Lamb bones are too strong unless you're making lamb stock.)

Store smoked bones, vegetable trimmings, herb stems, and so on in a bag in your freezer. When you have enough, pull out your stockpot. Store smoked stock in cup and pint containers in your freezer so you always have pre-measured amounts on hand. Here's a general guide you can customize based on the ingredients you have on hand.

INGREDIENTS

MEAT

1 smoked chicken or turkey
   carcass

Beef, veal, or pork bones,
   steak or roast trimmings
   (up to 3 pounds; optional)

VEGETABLES

1 unpeeled medium-size onion
   (the skin adds color),
   quartered

1 to 2 carrots, unpeeled, cut into
   1-inch pieces

1 rib celery, cut into 1-inch pieces

1 leek, trimmed, rinsed, and cut
   into 1-inch pieces

1 clove garlic, peeled and lightly
   crushed with the side of a
   cleaver

HERBS AND SPICES (ANY OR ALL OF THE FOLLOWING)

Bay leaf

Sprigs of thyme

Sprigs or stems of parsley, basil,
   or rosemary

Whole black peppercorns
   (up to 1 teaspoon)

1 or 2 whole cloves (stick in one
   of the onion quarters)

1. Place all the ingredients in a large stockpot and add water to cover by 1 inch. Bring the mixture to a boil over medium-high heat. This is important for bringing any impurities to the surface. Immediately reduce the heat to a gentle simmer (bubbles should barely break the surface). Repeatedly and carefully skim off any foam or fat on the surface of the stock and discard it. Do not let the stock boil again or it will turn cloudy.

2. Simmer the stock until reduced to the level of the bones and richly flavored: 1 hour for a single chicken carcass, 1½ to 2 hours for multiple birds or a large turkey carcass. Again, skim the stock often and cook it at a gentle simmer: This is the secret to a clean, appetizing stock.

3. Strain the stock through a fine-mesh strainer into plastic containers (for clearer stock, strain through a coffee filter). Discard the solids. Let cool to room temperature, then chill. The stock will keep for at least 3 days in the refrigerator or 6 months in the freezer.

MERLOT-SOY FINISHING SAUCE

YIELD: Makes 2 cups; use 2 to 3 tablespoons per pound of meat

TRY THIS!

Spray or squirt this sauce on steaks, chops, and roasts toward the end of grilling, and continue grilling until all the sauce evaporates: The flavor will pass right through to the meat.

Like mops and bastes, finishing sauces go on the meat while it grills. This one sets the piquancy of red wine and vinegar against the salty tang of soy and Worcestershire sauce. Apply it after the meat has been browned by the fire for the last 5 minutes of cooking.

INGREDIENTS

1 cup soy sauce or tamari

½ cup merlot or other dry red wine

¼ cup wine vinegar or rice vinegar

¼ cup Worcestershire sauce

Combine all the ingredients in a bowl and stir to mix. Transfer to a mister or squirt bottle and spray or squirt on grilled meats. Store any extra in the refrigerator; it will keep for several weeks.

MONROE COUNTY VINEGAR DIP

YIELD: Makes 2½ cups

TRY THIS!

Originally designed for pork shoulder steak, this vinegar dip invigorates any grilled or smoked meat, from chicken to lamb to pork chops.

Monroe County vinegar dip may be the best barbecue condiment you've never heard of. Pulled pork smoked low and slow over hickory is king in western Kentucky. But not in the tiny town of Tompkinsville. According to my friend, *Project Smoke* fire wrangler and Kentucky resident Rob Baas, in Tompkinsville "barbecue" means thin pork shoulder steaks grilled (notice I said grilled) over blazing hickory embers. The steaks are first basted with, then immersed in a fiery vinegar-butter-pepper-cayenne dip. "They flip often and mop often," explains Rob, "and the meat is dipped just prior to serving. If you're a glutton for punishment, you ask for it double-dipped."

Count me in. Vinegar slaw (page 317) is served on the side, says Rob, which helps blunt the peppery bite of the dip. This vinegar dip definitely belongs in your arsenal—consider it your secret weapon for flavor.

INGREDIENTS

8 tablespoons (1 stick) unsalted butter

2 cups distilled white vinegar

2 tablespoons freshly ground black pepper

2 tablespoons granulated white sugar or brown sugar

1 tablespoon ground cayenne pepper

1 tablespoon coarse salt (sea or kosher)

1 tablespoon hot sauce (Rob uses Frank's RedHot)

Melt the butter in a heavy nonreactive saucepan over medium-high heat. Add the vinegar, pepper, sugar, cayenne, salt, and hot sauce. Reduce the heat and gently simmer for 3 minutes, whisking to dissolve the sugar and salt. Remove the dip from the heat and let cool slightly. Use right away for dipping. Let any extra dip cool to room temperature, then cover and refrigerate. It will keep for at least 3 days. Reheat to melt the butter before serving.

VINEGAR-DIPPED PORK STEAKS

YIELD: Serves 4 to 6

If you come from Tompkinsville, Kentucky, or St. Louis, Missouri, you know and love pork steak. If you come from anywhere else, this thin, generously marbled, crosscut slice of pork shoulder may take you by surprise. If not available in your area (which means virtually the rest of the United States), ask your butcher to custom-cut a pork shoulder crosswise with a meat saw into ½-inch-thick slices. Thin-cut pork chops or sliced pork loin will get you in the ballpark, but neither has the luscious marbling of a true pork shoulder steak.

INGREDIENTS

2 pounds pork shoulder steaks or thin-cut pork chops

Coarse salt (sea or kosher) and cracked or coarsely ground black peppercorns

Monroe County Vinegar Dip (page 148)

1. Generously season the pork steaks on both sides with salt and pepper. Keep the vinegar dip warm in a large saucepan.

2. Set up a grill for direct grilling and preheat to high. Brush and oil the grill grate.

3. Arrange the pork steaks on the grate and grill until sizzling, browned, and cooked through, about 4 minutes per side. Start basting or mopping the steaks with vinegar dip once you turn the meat. When the pork steaks are cooked, hold them one at a time with tongs and plunge them into the vinegar dip, turning to coat both sides. Gluttons for punishment can dip twice, spooning a little extra dip on top before serving.

TARRAGON-LEMON BUTTER

YIELD: Makes ½ cup, enough for 8 servings

Here's a twist on the classic French *maître d'hôtel* butter (lemon-herb butter). The bright licorice tang of fresh tarragon goes equally well with beef, poultry, and seafood.

TRY THIS!

Cut the butter cylinder crosswise into ½-inch-thick slices. Place these slices on steaks, chops (especially veal and lamb), fish fillets, or vegetables hot off the grill and watch the butter melt over and into the food.

INGREDIENTS

- 8 tablespoons (1 stick) salted butter, at room temperature
- 3 tablespoons finely chopped fresh tarragon leaves
- 1 clove garlic, peeled and minced
- ½ teaspoon finely grated lemon zest
- Several drops of fresh lemon juice
- Freshly ground white or black pepper, to taste

Place the butter, tarragon, garlic, lemon zest, lemon juice, and pepper in a mixing bowl and stir or whisk until light and fluffy. Or do the stirring with a mixer or in a food processor. Wrap, roll, store, and use the butter as described in the box on this page.

MAKING AND STORING COMPOUND BUTTERS

Arrange a 12-inch square piece of plastic wrap or parchment paper on your work surface and mound the butter in the center. Roll it up into a cylinder 1½ inches in diameter, twisting the ends of the wrap to compact the butter. Store the butter in the refrigerator for up to 5 days or in the freezer for up to 3 months.

GRILLED BREAD
WITH WALNUT-ROQUEFORT BUTTER

YIELD: Serves 10 to 12

Grilling is the best way I know to make garlic bread. The fire crisps the bread and imparts an irresistible smoke flavor, especially when coupled with the salty tang of Roquefort cheese.

INGREDIENTS

1 baguette

Walnut-Roquefort Butter (facing page), at room temperature

1. Set up a grill for direct grilling and preheat the grill to high.

2. Cut the bread sharply on the diagonal into ½-inch-thick slices. Arrange the slices on a baking sheet. Using a spatula, lightly spread the Walnut-Roquefort Butter on both sides of the bread slices.

3. Transfer the bread to the grill grate and grill until golden brown on both sides, 1 to 2 minutes per side. Don't take your eyes off the grill for a second, as the bread will burn quickly. Serve at once.

WALNUT-ROQUEFORT BUTTER

YIELD: Makes ¾ cup, enough for 10 to 12 servings

Walnuts and Roquefort cheese are a classic combination of southwestern France. The salty tang of the Roquefort goes particularly well with grilled meats.

INGREDIENTS

¼ cup toasted walnut pieces (see box, page 112)

8 tablespoons (1 stick) salted butter, at room temperature

2 ounces Roquefort cheese, at room temperature

½ teaspoon freshly ground black pepper, or to taste

1. Place the nuts in a food processor and coarsely chop, running the machine in short bursts. Add the butter, Roquefort, and pepper and process until creamy and smooth.

2. Wrap, roll, store, and use the butter as described in the box on page 151.

TRY THIS!

Roquefort cheese has a natural affinity for beef, lamb, and veal. Tuck disks of the tangy butter into hamburgers. Serve it on a grilled salmon steak or on a plate of grilled vegetables. Unwrap the roll and cut it crosswise into ½-inch-thick slices. Place the slices on the hot grilled food.

MUSTARD-BEER BUTTER

YIELD: Makes ¾ cup, enough for 10 to 12 servings

This Mustard-Beer Butter was inspired by a classic Wisconsin barbecue combination: bratwurst, mustard, and beer. To reinforce the mustard flavor, we use three types: seed, powder, and prepared. Black mustard seeds are available at Indian and other ethnic and natural food markets. If unavailable, use more yellow mustard seeds.

TRY THIS!

Mustard-Beer Butter goes well with grilled pork. Be sure to cut nice thick—½ inch— slices as a topping.

INGREDIENTS

2 teaspoons yellow mustard
 seeds

2 teaspoons black mustard
 seeds, or additional yellow
 mustard seeds

¼ cup finely chopped shallots

½ cup dark beer

2 teaspoons white wine vinegar
 or distilled white vinegar, or
 to taste

2 teaspoons mustard powder

2 tablespoons prepared
 mustard, or more to taste

8 tablespoons (1 stick) salted
 butter, at room temperature

1. Place both mustard seeds, the shallots, beer, and vinegar in a small saucepan and bring to a boil over high heat. Reduce the heat to medium and simmer until most of the beer has evaporated and the mixture is syrupy, 6 to 8 minutes. Remove the pan from the heat and let cool to room temperature.

2. Place the mustard powder, prepared mustard, and butter in a mixing bowl and stir or whisk until light and fluffy. Stir in the mustard-beer mixture. Correct the seasoning, adding more prepared mustard or vinegar if needed.

3. Wrap, roll, store, and use the butter as described on page 151.

BACON-ONION BUTTER

YIELD: Makes ½ cup, enough for 8 servings

TRY THIS!

This smoky oniony butter screams hamburger. Place slices atop well-charred burgers. Alternatively, tuck disks of it into the center of the raw patties. Close the meat around the butter and grill. You could also serve this butter on steaks, chicken, and grilled mushrooms.

I f you like bacon, you'll love the smoky flavors of this compound butter, which also contains caramelized onions for sweetness and a touch of mustard for bite.

INGREDIENTS

8 tablespoons (1 stick) salted
 butter, at room temperature

3 strips lean bacon, cut into
 ¼-inch-wide slivers

1 medium-size onion, peeled and
 very finely chopped

2 teaspoons prepared mustard,
 preferably brown or
 Dusseldorf-style, or more
 to taste

½ teaspoon freshly ground black
 pepper, or more to taste

1. Melt 1 tablespoon of the butter in a skillet over medium heat. Add the bacon and cook until the fat begins to render. Add the onion and sauté until the bacon crisps and the onions are golden brown, about 5 minutes. Do not let the bacon burn. Transfer the bacon mixture to a mixing bowl and cool to room temperature.

2. Add the remaining butter, the mustard, and pepper to the bowl and beat the mixture with a wooden spoon until light and fluffy. Correct the seasoning, adding more pepper or mustard if needed.

3. Wrap, roll, store, and use the butter as described in the box on page 151.

WASABI-HORSERADISH BUTTER

YIELD: Makes ½ cup, enough for 8 servings

The English fondness for horseradish with beef is well documented, as is the Japanese love for a fiery, pale-green, horseradish-like plant called wasabi with tuna. Put them together and you get a butter that fires a double-barrel blast of heat.

INGREDIENTS

1 tablespoon wasabi powder

1 tablespoon rice wine vinegar or distilled white vinegar

8 tablespoons (1 stick) salted butter, at room temperature

1 tablespoon prepared white horseradish

½ teaspoon freshly ground black pepper

1. Place the wasabi powder and vinegar in a small bowl and stir to mix into a paste. Let stand for 5 minutes.

2. Place the butter in a mixing bowl and stir or whisk until light and fluffy. Stir in the wasabi paste, horseradish, and pepper.

3. Wrap, roll, store, and use the butter as described in the box on page 151.

TRY THIS!

Imagine a whole roast beef, the outside dark and crusty, the center sanguine and juicy. Or a bible-thick tuna steak, charred on the outside and sushi-rare in the center. Those are two great uses for Wasabi-Horseradish Butter, but don't overlook grilled chicken, veal, or trout. Unwrap the roll and cut it into ½-inch-thick slices. Place a slice on each portion of meat or fish.

SWEET & SMOKY
BBQ SAUCE

AMERICAN BARBECUE SAUCES

Smoke may be the soul of barbecue, but the sauce gives it personality. However, what you mean by barbecue sauce depends on where you live or grew up. In Kansas City, barbecue sauce typically means a thick, red, sweet, smoke-scented condiment typified by the commercial brand, KC Masterpiece. (And, even in Kansas City there are variations.)

In North Carolina, that sauce would be a watery amalgam of vinegar, salt, pepper, and hot red pepper flakes—with nary a drop of molasses in sight. South Carolinians favor yellow mustard-based barbecue sauces, while in Alabama, you might get a white sauce comprised of mayonnaise and vinegar that leaves you wondering if it's barbecue sauce or salad dressing. The truth is that while we Americans love barbecue sauce, we don't agree on what it is.

HOW TO BUILD A GREAT BARBECUE SAUCE

Barbecue sauces can contain literally dozens of different ingredients. I've seen sauces flavored with everything from coffee to cranberry sauce to cough syrup. But whether you're making a simple North Carolina-style vinegar sauce or a Kansas City-style everything-but-the-kitchen-sink sauce, there's one component you can't do without: balance. The goal of any good sauce is to meld the contrasting elements—sweet, sour, salty, aromatic, hot—into a harmonious whole.

Here's a look at the essential building blocks you need to construct a great barbecue sauce.

THE BASE: The base provides the foundation for a barbecue sauce. Common bases for barbecue sauce include:

Ketchup
Tomato sauce/tomato purée/tomato paste
Fresh tomatoes
Chili sauce
Mustard
Vinegar
Chicken or beef stock
Mayonnaise

THE SWEETENERS: Most barbecue sauces have an element of sweetness. Kansas City-style sauces are the sweetest, but even a western North Carolina vinegar sauce contains a little sugar to blunt the edge of the vinegar. Here are some common sweeteners:

Granulated sugar: The common white sugar you use to sweeten your coffee.

Turbinado sugar (Sugar in the Raw brand): A granulated light brown sugar that owes its color to an added trace of molasses. I like its gritty texture.

Light or dark brown sugar: Sweet with a molasses flavor.

Piloncillo: Unrefined Mexican brown sugar; sold in pyramids or cones. Sweet with an earthy, malty molasses flavor.

Sucanat: Freeze-dried sugarcane juice; sold in natural foods stores. Sweet with a malty flavor.

Honey: Sweet with a floral flavor.

Molasses: Sweet and earthy.

Cane syrup: Sweet with a rich mouthfeel.

Corn syrup (light or dark): Less sweet than cane sugar, with a rich mouthfeel.

Maple sugar/maple syrup: Less sweet than cane sugar, with a musky maple flavor.

Rice syrup: Sold in natural foods stores. Less sweet than cane sugar, with earthy malt flavors.

Jams and jellies: Sweet, fruity flavor.

THE SOURING AGENTS: Every great barbecue sauce contains a souring agent to help keep the sweetness in check. Here are the most commonly used souring agents:

Distilled vinegar: Just plain sour.

Cider vinegar: Acidic with a fruity finish.

Wine vinegar: Acidic with a wine flavor.

Balsamic vinegar: Acidic with a fruity sweetness.

Lemon juice: Tart with a fruity flavor; sometimes whole lemons are added to a sauce, contributing a bitter element as well as acidic.

Lime juice and sour orange juice: Work in the same way as lemon juice.

Tamarind: Sour-sweet smoky flavor.

Pickle juice: Need I say more?

THE SEASONINGS: Every barbecue sauce needs a touch of salt to balance the acidity and sweetness:

Salt: In particular, sea salt or kosher salt (see page 14).

Soy sauce: Salt with an Asian accent.

Fish sauce: Salt with a Southeast Asian accent.

Miso: Cultured soybean paste; available in many colors and flavors. Salt with a luscious umami finish.

Hoisin sauce: A thick Chinese condiment that's both salty and sweet.

Anchovy fillets/paste: An ingredient in many steak sauces.

Capers: The pickled buds of a Mediterranean flowering shrub; salty and tangy.

Olives: Especially salty olives, like Kalamata or Sicilian.

Sun-dried tomatoes: Dried or oil-packed, your choice.

THE HEAT: A defining element in many barbecue sauces (particularly those from Texas and the American Southwest). Here are some of the ingredients that can help set your sauce on fire:

Hot sauce: Tabasco, for example, owes its distinctive flavor to lengthy aging in barrels. Other favorites are Crystal Hot Sauce and Texas Pete, made here in the United States; Cholula, from Mexico; for a fiery Caribbean-style hot sauce, try Scotch bonnet-based Matouk's from Trinidad.

Fresh chile peppers: Range from the relatively mild jalapeño to the tongue-torturing ghost peppers and scorpion peppers; pickled chiles, such as pickled jalapeños, which add an acidic element as well.

Black and white pepper: Grind it fresh for extra flavor.

Ground cayenne pepper and red pepper flakes: Their heat builds gradually—start easy.

Fresh ginger: Minced or grated.

Mustard: Either prepared or powder.

Horseradish: Either freshly grated or prepared; add it at the last minute, as cooking diminishes its heat and makes it sweet.

Wasabi: A green horseradish-like condiment from Japan (see page 37). Dissolve the powder in a little cold water to form a thick paste and add it at the last minute, as cooking diminishes its heat.

THE AROMATICS: Aromatics give barbecue sauce its personality. Use with restraint; some people—especially guys—think that if a little is good, more is better. But too much is too much, no matter how you cut it:

Onions: Fresh (either raw or sautéed), dried flakes, powder, or onion salt.

Garlic: Fresh (either raw or sautéed), dried flakes, powder, or garlic salt.

Celery: Fresh, also celery seed and celery salt.

Bell peppers and poblano chiles: Fresh.

Chili powder: Indispensable in Texas.

Herbs: Both fresh and dried. Common barbecue sauce herbs include basil, bay leaf, chives, cilantro, dill, marjoram, mint, oregano, parsley, rosemary, and thyme.

Spices: Common barbecue sauce seasonings include both sweet spices (such as allspice, anise seeds, cardamom, cinnamon, cloves, fennel seed, ginger, mace, nutmeg, and star anise) and savory spices (such as caraway seed, coriander, cumin, curry, dill seed, mustard seed, paprika, pepper, saffron, sage, Sichuan peppercorns, and turmeric).

Liquid smoke: Dallas's legendary barbecue emporium, Sonny Bryan's, actually smokes its barbecue sauce in the pit; the rest of us can add a few drops of this natural product to give barbecue sauce the flavor of wood smoke.

Worcestershire sauce: Salty-sweet and aromatic; contains tamarind and anchovies. Also available in powdered form (page 37).

Steak sauce: Salty and tomatoey, with a touch of raisin and orange.

ENRICHERS: A well-conceived barbecue sauce not only tastes good, it feels good on your palate. That's where enrichers come in. Animal and vegetable fats will give your sauce a properly luscious mouthfeel.

Butter: Salted or unsalted.

Oil: Olive, sesame, walnut, and hazelnut add flavor as well as richness; vegetable oil is merely rich.

Lard: Traditional fat used for frying Mexican salsas.

Bacon/bacon fat: Adds a rich smoky flavor.

Meat drippings: The secret ingredient in many sauces, including the lip-smacking sauce served at Shorty's in Miami.

Beef stock/chicken stock: Adds a rich meaty flavor without fat.

WILD CARDS: To be a great sauce master, you need two attributes of creative genius: inspiration and fearlessness. The former leads to the juxtaposition of unexpected flavors. The latter allows you to try adding anything. Some of the stranger sauce ingredients I've seen include:

Coffee: Brewed coffee wakes up a barbecue sauce the way a cup of Joe gets you going in the morning.

Soda: Cola, root beer, ginger ale, lemon-lime, and orange soda, to name a few options.

Wine: Lends a pleasing acidity.

Spirits: Popular spirits for barbecue sauce include bourbon, rye, Scotch, brandy, rum, and tequila.

Peanut butter: Sounds strange and this is the primary ingredient for Thai and Indonesian saté sauce.

Vanilla extract: Adds an exotic but familiar sweetness.

Water: Despite its lack of flavor, it can help mellow strong flavors and knit disparate flavors into a harmonious whole.

PUTTING IT ALL TOGETHER: Simply put the ingredients in a pot and bring to a boil. Then, reduce the heat and simmer, stirring just enough to keep it from burning. That's the beauty of barbecue sauce: You can't curdle it, scramble it, or break it.

SWEET-AND-SMOKY BARBECUE SAUCE

YIELD: Makes 5 cups

Ask most Americans to describe the perfect barbecue sauce and they'll invoke a thick sweet red ketchup-based sauce with a zing of vinegar and a whiff of liquid smoke. In short, the sort of sauce Kansas City barbecue buffs have slathered on ribs and briskets for decades. The following recipe comes from the Kansas City Barbecue Society. (Motto: "Barbecue—it's not just for breakfast.")

TRY THIS!

Use as you would any barbecue sauce, that is to say, brushed on pork, ribs, and chicken toward the end of cooking and poured freely at the table.

INGREDIENTS

6 tablespoons packed dark brown sugar

½ cup cider vinegar

¼ cup molasses

¼ cup honey

¼ cup Worcestershire sauce

2 tablespoons dark rum

2 tablespoons yellow mustard

1 tablespoon liquid smoke

1 tablespoon chile powder

2 teaspoons freshly ground black pepper

2 teaspoons garlic powder

1 teaspoon ground allspice

¼ teaspoon ground cloves

4 cups ketchup

Coarse salt (sea or kosher) and freshly ground black pepper

1. Combine all the ingredients through the cloves in a large, deep, heavy, nonreactive saucepan and bring to a simmer over medium heat. Cook, uncovered, until all the ingredients are dissolved, stirring constantly, about 5 minutes. Stir in the ketchup and bring to a boil, stirring well, as the ketchup has a tendency to spatter. Add salt and pepper to taste.

2. Reduce the heat and gently simmer, uncovered, until dark, thick, and richly flavored, 15 to 20 minutes, stirring often. Use right away or transfer to jars, cover, cool to room temperature, and refrigerate. The sauce will keep for several weeks.

RIGHTEOUS RIBS

YIELD: Serves 4 really hungry people, 6 to 8 as part of a full meal

Eating these ribs can be almost a religious experience, especially when coupled with Sweet-and-Smoky Barbecue Sauce. I like the succulence and tenderness of baby back ribs, but you could certainly use spare ribs if you prefer. You'd need to increase the amount of rub and sauce for the latter.

INGREDIENTS

4 racks baby back ribs
(8 to 12 pounds)

¾ cup Basic Barbecue Rub
(page 19)

1 cup Cider Squirt (page 125;
optional), in a spray bottle

2 cups Sweet-and-Smoky
Barbecue Sauce (page 161)

YOU ALSO NEED

4 to 5 cups hardwood chips, preferably apple or hickory, soaked in water for 30 minutes, then drained

1. Remove the papery skin on the back of each rack of ribs by pulling it off in a sheet with your fingers (using a corner of a dish towel to secure your grip), or ask your butcher to do it. Sprinkle the ribs on both sides with the rub, rubbing it in with your fingers. Cover and marinate in the refrigerator for 1 hour.

2. Set up a smoker following the manufacturer's instructions, and preheat to 250°F. Add the wood as specified by the manufacturer.

3. Place the ribs, rounded side up, in the smoker. Smoke until cooked, 3 to 4 hours. After 1 hour, spray the ribs with Cider Squirt, and spray again every hour. The last half hour, brush the ribs with half the barbecue sauce. (Omit this step if you opt for Step 4.) When the ribs are ready, the meat will have shrunk back from the ends of the bones by about ½ inch. The meat will be so tender, you can pull the ribs apart with your fingers.

4. This is optional: Set up a grill for direct grilling and preheat to high. Brush and oil the grill grate. Brush the smoked ribs with half the barbecue sauce and direct grill for 2 to 4 minutes per side to sear the sauce into the meat.

5. Serve the ribs on a platter, with the remaining sauce on the side.

AARON FRANKLIN'S ESPRESSO BARBECUE SAUCE

YIELD: Makes 3 cups

TRY THIS!

Obviously, you'll want to try this with brisket (see facing page), but it also works nicely with pork, lamb, and poultry.

Aaron Franklin is surely one of the most famous pit masters in America today. Even if you haven't waited in line for three hours to gain access to his bare-bones Austin barbecue restaurant and taste his wondrous brisket, you may have read his illuminating cookbook and know that Franklin's Barbecue is the only barbecue joint to have won a James Beard Award for Best Regional American Restaurant. Franklin's brisket is so juicy, so smoky, so luscious, it doesn't really need a barbecue sauce. But any condiment created by Aaron deserves your attention—especially if it contains an invigorating shot of espresso. Brisket drippings make an amazing sauce even better.

INGREDIENTS

1½ cups ketchup

½ cup cider vinegar

½ cup distilled white vinegar

¼ cup soy sauce

1 tablespoon garlic powder

1 tablespoon onion powder

¼ cup packed dark brown sugar

2 to 3 tablespoons brisket drippings or bacon drippings

3 tablespoons freshly brewed espresso

1. Place the ketchup, vinegars, soy sauce, garlic and onion powders, brown sugar, and brisket drippings in a heavy nonreactive saucepan. Gradually bring to a boil over medium-high heat. Reduce the heat and simmer the sauce, uncovered, until thick and richly flavored, 15 to 20 minutes.

2. Remove the pan from the heat and whisk in the espresso. Use right away or transfer to clean jars, cover, cool to room temperature, and refrigerate. The sauce will keep for several weeks.

BBQ TITANS' BRISKET

YIELD: Serves 12 to 14

This awesome brisket features the coffee rub from Brooklyn BBQ landmark, Fette Sau, combined with Austin 'cue legend Aaron Franklin's Espresso Barbecue Sauce. Need I say more?

INGREDIENTS

1 packer brisket (with both flat and point), 12 to 14 pounds

1 cup Fette Sau's Coffee Rub (page 28)

1 cup distilled white vinegar in a food-safe spray bottle

3 cups Aaron Franklin's Espresso Barbecue Sauce (facing page)

YOU ALSO NEED

Unlined butcher paper; a large insulated cooler; wood for the smoker: oak, or hardwood

1. Trim the brisket, leaving a fat cap on top at least ½ inch deep. Place the brisket on a rimmed baking sheet. Very generously season on all sides with the coffee rub.

2. Set up a smoker following the manufacturer's instructions and preheat to 250°F. Add the wood as specified by the manufacturer.

3. Place the brisket fat side up in your smoker. Cook until the outside is darkly browned and the internal temperature is about 170°F, 10 to 12 hours, replenishing the charcoal and wood as needed. Start spraying the brisket with vinegar after 1 hour and spray with vinegar every hour for the first 5 hours.

4. Tightly wrap the brisket in unlined butcher paper. Return it to the smoker. Continue cooking until the internal temperature is 205°F and the meat is tender enough to pierce with a gloved finger or wooden spoon handle, an additional 2 hours or so. (You'll need to unwrap the brisket to check it. If it needs additional cooking, rewrap it.)

5. Transfer the wrapped brisket to an insulated cooler. Let rest for 1 to 2 hours. Unwrap the brisket and transfer it to a cutting board, reserving any juices that accumulate in the butcher paper.

6. To serve, trim off any large lumps of fat and slice the brisket across the grain as thick or thin as you desire. Spoon the brisket juices over the slices. Serve Aaron Franklin's Espresso Barbecue Sauce on the side.

B.B.'S LAWNSIDE SPICY APPLE BARBECUE SAUCE

YIELD: Makes about 3 cups

TRY THIS!

I've served this sauce with everything from barbecued chicken to brisket. But I especially love it with pork, which has a natural affinity for apples. Slather it on ribs or rib tips, which are a B.B.'s specialty. Brush it on grilled pork chops. You could even serve it with pulled pork—although that might get you arrested in North Carolina.

A rough-and-tumble roadhouse on the outskirts of the city, B.B.'s Lawnside specializes in the three Bs of the Kansas City good life: blues, beer, and barbecue. The barbecue cooks in an ancient brick pit fueled with hickory. Rib tips (the meaty trimmings of spareribs) are the house specialty and the gumbo (made with home-smoked meats) would be at home in Louisiana. B.B.'s proprietor, Lindsey Shannon, is a die-hard blues buff and his club/restaurant hosts some of best blues acts in the Midwest. As for his sweet-suave barbecue sauce, it owes its fruity finish to apple cider.

INGREDIENTS

1 bottle (14 ounces) ketchup (Lindsey uses Hunt's)	1½ tablespoons dark brown sugar
1 cup apple cider	1 tablespoon granulated sugar
2 tablespoons Worcestershire sauce	1 teaspoon ground cayenne pepper
1 tablespoon molasses	½ teaspoon freshly ground black pepper
1 tablespoon cider vinegar	½ teaspoon celery seed
1 tablespoon soy sauce	½ teaspoon ground cinnamon
½ teaspoon liquid smoke	⅛ teaspoon ground cloves

Combine all the ingredients in a large, heavy, nonreactive saucepan and stir or whisk to mix. Bring the sauce to a boil over medium heat. Reduce the heat to low and gently simmer the sauce, uncovered, until thick and richly flavored, stirring often to prevent scorching, 15 to 20 minutes. Use right away or transfer to jars, cover, cool to room temperature, and refrigerate. The sauce will keep for several weeks.

LEAN-AND-MEAN TEXAS BARBECUE SAUCE

YIELD: Makes about 6 cups

Texans take the same bold no-nonsense approach to barbecue sauce that they do to beef. Little or no sugar and plenty of vinegar and chile hellfire. Consider this sauce—inspired by the original Sonny Bryan's in Dallas. (It isn't the sauce served today at Sonny Bryan's, but you can taste a family resemblance.) For an added measure of authenticity, serve it warm in a clean beer bottle.

INGREDIENTS

1 bottle (14 ounces) ketchup

3 cups water

1 cup cider vinegar

½ cup Worcestershire sauce

⅓ cup brisket or bacon drippings (optional)

2 tablespoons yellow mustard

2 tablespoons fresh lemon juice

½ teaspoon liquid smoke

¼ cup chile powder

2 tablespoons sweet or smoked paprika

1 teaspoon red pepper flakes, or to taste

1 teaspoon freshly ground black pepper

1 teaspoon dark brown sugar (optional)

Combine all the ingredients in a large, heavy, nonreactive saucepan and stir or whisk to mix. Bring the sauce to a rolling boil over high heat. Reduce the heat slightly and briskly simmer the sauce, uncovered, until thick and richly flavored, stirring often to prevent scorching, 15 to 20 minutes. Use right away or transfer to jars, cover, cool to room temperature, and let ripen for 2 to 3 days in the refrigerator before serving. The sauce will keep for several weeks.

TRY THIS!

It's customary to serve Texas-style barbecue sauce warm. The obvious meat for this sauce is brisket, especially Texas-style brisket, smoked dark and tender in an oak- or mesquite-fired pit. Friends swear by it for steak. It's also good with pork, chicken, and burgers—or any time you want a barbecue sauce that's spicy and not too sweet.

WORCESTERSHIRE SAUCE

What's the ingredient most frequently used in barbecue sauces? If you answer ketchup, you're close. But I'd put my money on a condiment that comes in a paper-wrapped bottle: Worcestershire sauce.

This thin, brown, sweet-sour condiment turns up in barbecue sauces of all stripes and types—from the tomato-based sauces of Kansas City to the butter sauces of New Orleans to the black dips of Kentucky. The reason is simple: Worcestershire sauce contains something for everyone—sweetness in the form of corn syrup and molasses, acidity from tamarind (page 158) and vinegar, saltiness provided by soy sauce and anchovies, with garlic and cloves for spice.

Like mushroom ketchup and A.1. Sauce, Worcestershire was born in the heyday of the great English table sauces. According to David Burton, author of *The Raj at Table: A Culinary History of the British in India*, the recipe originated in India and was brought back to England by a former governor of Bengal, Lord Marcus Sandys.

In 1835, Lord Sandys took his recipe to the chemist shop of John Lea and William Perrins on Broad Street in Worcester and asked them to brew up a batch. The resulting mixture was so fiery, it "almost blew the heads off Mssrs. Lea and Perrins," according to Burton. They deposited the barrel in a back corner of the cellar and promptly tried to forget it. The chemists stumbled upon it a few years later, and, morbidly curious, they tried it again. With age, the Worcestershire had mellowed into an extraordinary sauce. The recipe was hastily purchased from Lord Sandys and in 1838, commercial Worcestershire sauce was born.

According to Adrian Bailey and Philip Dowell, authors of *Cooks' Ingredients*, the original Lea & Perrins recipe contained walnut and mushroom ketchups, sherry, brandy, and even pork liver, which has been eliminated from the American formula. Today the sauce is enjoyed all over the world. Many companies manufacture Worcestershire sauce today, but no one makes a better one than Lea & Perrins. This is the sauce you should use for the recipes in this book.

Many American rub makers add a freeze-dried Worcestershire sauce to their spice mixes. This flavorful powder is available online at Barbecuebible.com.

PEACH BARBECUE SAUCE

YIELD: Makes about 6 cups

Jason Dady belongs to a growing roster of fine dining chefs who left the rarified realm of French cuisine to get down and dirty with barbecue. If you haven't been to his Two Bros BBQ Market and B&D Ice House in San Antonio, you haven't experienced some of the best barbecue in Texas. Cooking on massive hand-welded steel pits, the Dady brothers turn out briskets of remarkable smoky succulence and ribs with polyphonic layers of flavor. Their Peach Barbecue Sauce is equally polyphonic, pitting lemon, mustard, and Cholula hot sauce against the musky sweetness of peach.

INGREDIENTS

- 2 tablespoons unsalted butter or vegetable oil
- 1 medium-size onion, peeled and finely chopped
- 2 cloves garlic, peeled and finely chopped
- 8 drained canned peach halves, finely diced, plus ¼ cup drained peach syrup
- 2 tablespoons peach schnapps
- 1 cup ketchup
- 1 cup tomato sauce
- ¼ cup red wine vinegar
- ½ teaspoon finely grated lemon zest
- ¼ cup freshly squeezed lemon juice
- ¼ cup molasses
- ¼ cup honey
- ¼ cup packed dark brown sugar
- 3 tablespoons Dijon mustard
- 2 tablespoons Worcestershire sauce
- 1 tablespoon Cholula hot sauce (or sauce of choice)
- 2 teaspoons freshly ground black pepper
- Coarse salt (sea or kosher) to taste

1. Melt the butter in a large saucepan over medium-high heat. Add the onion and garlic and cook until lightly browned, stirring often, 3 minutes. Add the peaches and syrup and the schnapps. Increase the heat to high. Cook until the peaches are really soft, 5 to 8 minutes.

2. Stir in the ketchup, tomato sauce, preserves, vinegar, lemon zest and juice, molasses, honey, brown sugar, mustard, Worcestershire sauce, hot sauce, pepper, and salt and gradually bring to a boil. Reduce the heat and gently simmer the sauce, uncovered, until thick and richly flavored, 20 to 30 minutes. Stir often and add water as needed to keep it from sticking.

3. Transfer the sauce to clean jars and let cool to room temperature for serving. It will keep, covered, in the refrigerator for several weeks.

TEXA-LINA BARBECUE SAUCE

YIELD: Makes 2 cups

TRY THIS!

The considerable vinegar in this sauce makes it a natural for pork, but it also goes well on mammoth beef ribs and barbecued chicken.

To hear Hugh Mangum tell it, he never set out to become a New York barbecue mogul. No, the professional drummer had a career that most guys would kill for: touring with Jakob Dylan and the Wallflowers. But Mangum caught the barbecue bug early, so he started hauling a 16-foot Peoria custom cooker on a trailer to a Brooklyn foodie street fair called Smorgasburg. Today he presides over a barbecue empire that includes Mighty Quinn's Barbeque restaurants in Manhattan and New Jersey. This isn't your old-school barbecue joint, not with its white subway wall tiles, gray slate counters, and triple-thick butcher block communal tables. The restaurant breaks with tradition, too, using beef from hormone-free, pasture-raised cattle and pork from crossbred Duroc-Berkshire heritage hogs. Mangum has Texas roots (his dad grew up in Houston), while his wife comes from North Carolina—hence "Texa-lina." His barbecue sauce combines the fire and spice of the Lone Star State with the mouth-puckering astringency of a Carolina vinegar sauce. Here's how I imagine he makes it.

INGREDIENTS

1 cup ketchup

1 cup cider vinegar

3 tablespoons dark brown sugar

3 tablespoons molasses

3 to 4 tablespoons Dijon mustard

1 teaspoon ground cumin

½ teaspoon ground cayenne pepper

½ teaspoon celery seed

1. Place the ketchup, vinegar, sugar, molasses, mustard, cumin, cayenne, and celery seed in a heavy nonreactive saucepan. Stir and gradually bring the mixture to a boil over medium-high heat.

2. Reduce the heat and gently simmer the sauce, uncovered, until thick, concentrated, and richly flavored, stirring often so it doesn't scorch, 15 to 20 minutes. Transfer to clean jars for serving. Covered and refrigerated, the sauce will keep for several weeks.

MEMPHIS-STYLE BARBECUE SAUCE

YIELD: Makes about 6 cups

John Willingham is a legend on the American barbecue circuit: A winner of dozens of grand championships, like the Memphis in May, Kansas City Royal, and Jack Daniel's Invitational barbecue competitions, he has been an inventor (one of his cookers is on display at the Smithsonian Institution), a restaurateur, author, teacher, and an irrepressible raconteur. His disciples have opened restaurants from Louisville to Dallas.

Willingham calls Memphis home and his sauce contains something for everyone: tomato sauce, steak sauce, mustard, even Coca-Cola. ("I figure with this many ingredients, everybody's bound to like something," Willingham says.) Note the addition of a dry rub to the "wet fixin's." This recipe is an approximation of what Willingham does, as no smoke master would share all his secrets with another barbecue man.

TRY THIS!

In Memphis, pork shoulder and ribs are king, and thus logical destinations for this sauce. But don't stop there. Brush the sauce on grilled chicken, turkey, and vegetables during the last 10 minutes of cooking. Serve plenty of sauce on the side for slathering and dipping.

INGREDIENTS

WET FIXIN'S

4 cups tomato sauce

1 cup cider vinegar

1 cup Coca-Cola, or other cola

¼ cup steak sauce, such as A.1.

¼ cup yellow mustard

¼ cup fresh lemon juice

3 tablespoons molasses

3 tablespoons soy sauce

3 tablespoons Worcestershire sauce

1 teaspoon Tabasco sauce

½ teaspoon liquid smoke

DRY FIXIN'S

½ cup packed dark brown sugar

1 to 2 tablespoons Basic Barbecue Rub (page 19; Willingham uses a rub he manufactures called W'ham)

1 tablespoon chile powder

1 tablespoon freshly ground black pepper

1 tablespoon mustard powder

2 teaspoons garlic salt

1. Combine all the wet fixin's in a large, heavy, nonreactive saucepan and slowly bring to a boil, uncovered, over medium heat.

2. Meanwhile, combine the dry fixin's in a bowl and mix with your fingers.

3. Reduce the heat and stir the dry fixin's into the sauce mixture. Gently simmer the sauce, uncovered, until thick, concentrated, and richly flavored, 15 to 20 minutes. Use right away or transfer to jars, cover, cool to room temperature, and refrigerate. The sauce will keep for several weeks in the refrigerator.

CORROSION PROTECTION

In order to extend the shelf life of your barbecue sauce or relish, place a sheet of plastic wrap between the jar and the metal lid (cover the mouth of the jar with plastic before screwing on the lid). The reason is simple: Eventually, the fumes from the vinegar or salt will corrode the inside of the lid, even a lid coated with rubber or plastic.

SMOKE WRANGLER'S BACON BOURBON BARBECUE SAUCE

YIELD: Makes 1 quart

Bacon and bourbon—two flavorings with deep roots in American barbecue. They come together in this smoky, tangy barbecue sauce created by *Project Smoke* smoke wrangler and frequent Barbecue Board contributor, Rob Baas. Rob is the guy who assembles and fires up all the grills and smokers on our TV show, and his Kentucky roots come through in this sweet-tart red sauce made fiery by sufficient red pepper flakes to let you know it means business.

TRY THIS!

Rob likes to serve this sauce with pulled pork, but don't miss slathering it on your favorite rack of baby backs or spareribs. Yes, that goes for barbecued lamb or mutton, too.

INGREDIENTS

2 strips bacon, finely diced

1½ cups cider vinegar

2½ cups ketchup

¾ cup packed light brown sugar

¼ cup granulated sugar

2 tablespoons red pepper flakes

2 tablespoons freshly ground black pepper

½ cup bourbon

Coarse salt (sea or kosher), to taste

1. Place the bacon in a heavy nonreactive saucepan. Cook over medium heat until the bacon is browned, 3 minutes, stirring with a wooden spoon.

2. Stir in the vinegar and bring to a boil. Then stir in the ketchup, sugars, red pepper flakes, black pepper, and bourbon and gradually bring to a boil.

3. Reduce the heat and simmer the sauce, uncovered, until thick and richly flavored, 15 to 20 minutes. Stir in the salt— you'll need quite a lot to offset the acidity of the vinegar. Use right away or transfer to clean jars, cover, cool to room temperature, and refrigerate. The sauce will keep for several weeks.

THE BARBECUE BURGER

YIELD: Makes 4 huge burgers

YOU ALSO NEED

1½ cups hardwood chips, soaked in water for 30 minutes, then drained

Like most tender quick-cooking meats, hamburgers taste better grilled over a high heat than barbecued (smoked low and slow). Here's a way to infuse the evocative spice and smoke flavors of true barbecue into a conventional fast-cooking burger. It uses a smoke-scented rub and barbecue sauce. I call it The Barbecue Burger; you might call it smoky nirvana. There's a lot to love, literally—each burger tips the scale at 8 ounces.

INGREDIENTS

2 pounds ground beef (preferably a mixture of ground chuck and sirloin, about 18 percent fat)

2 to 3 tablespoons Kansas City Sweet and Smoky Rub (page 24), or your favorite barbecue rub

4 romaine lettuce leaves (taken from near the center)

3 tablespoons extra-virgin olive oil

4 onion rolls or 4 hamburger buns, sliced almost in half through the side

4 thick strips artisanal bacon

4 thick slices red ripe tomato

6 to 8 tablespoons Smoke Wrangler's Bacon Bourbon Barbecue Sauce (page 173), or your favorite barbecue sauce

1. Form the ground beef into 4 patties, each about 3½ inches across and ¾ inch thick. Make a slight depression in the center. (Burgers rise more in the center than on the periphery, so the slight indentation helps give you an even thickness.) Generously season the burgers on both sides with the Kansas City Sweet and Smoky Rub and let marinate in the refrigerator while you light your grill.

2. Set up the grill for direct grilling and preheat to high. Brush and oil the grill grate.

3. Lightly brush the romaine lettuce leaves on both sides with olive oil (you'll need about 1 tablespoon). Brush the insides of the onion rolls with the remaining oil.

4. Arrange the bacon strips on the grill grate and grill until browned on both sides, 3 to 4 minutes per side. (Move them as needed to dodge any flare-ups.)

5. Grill the hamburgers until cooked to taste, about 4 minutes per side for medium (160°F on an instant-read thermometer).

6. Grill the lettuce leaves over the hot fire until lightly browned, 30 seconds per side. Toast the onion rolls, cut side down, over the hot fire, 1 to 2 minutes.

7. To assemble, place a grilled romaine leaf on the bottom half of each onion roll. Top with a burger, then barbecue sauce, then a tomato slice, bacon, and more barbecue sauce. Top with the other onion roll half.

TEXAS BAR-B-QUE SAUCE, KANSAS CITY STYLE

YIELD: Makes about 5 cups

TRY THIS!

If you're feeling *really* ambitious, do as Doug does—start with a rich beef stock made from scratch with oxtails and roasted leg bones. Otherwise, use a really good commercial stock (Doug likes Custom Culinary Gold Label, Orrington Farms, or Better Than Bouillon).

Every once in a while you read a novel with such memorable characters and compelling story line, it stays with you long after you've turned the last page. Such is *Thin Blue Smoke* by former Kansas City reporter Doug Worgul, set in a fictitious Kansas City barbecue joint called Smoke Meat. (If Worgul's name sounds familiar, you may have read his excellent history of Kansas City barbecue, *The Grand Barbecue: A Celebration of the History, Places, Personalities and Techniques of Kansas City Barbecue.*) *Thin Blue Smoke* describes the life of a curmudgeonly pit master named LaVerne Williams. Raised in rural east Texas, Williams moves to Kansas City to play ball for the Athletics. But barbecue is only one theme of this page-turner, which muses on love, loss, religion, blues music, and building families—no blood ties required. Reading it will make you hungry even as it sates your soul.

Texans don't use much sauce on their barbecue, Worgul observes, preferring to let the meat do the talking. In east Texas, barbecue sauce is generally thinner, less tomatoey, less sweet, and more peppery than, say, a Kansas City-style sauce. It is frequently served warm and used more as a dip. Imagine a rich beef stock made with oxtails and spiced up with a little ketchup, vinegar, mustard, Worcestershire sauce, and a dash (or six) of Louisiana Hot Sauce. But first, read Worgul's book.

INGREDIENTS

4 cups beef stock, preferably homemade, or Smoked Stock (page 146)

½ cup skimmed fat from stock, brisket drippings, or ½ cup unsalted butter, if using commercial stock

½ cup ketchup

¼ cup apple cider vinegar

¼ cup packed dark brown sugar

3 tablespoons Louisiana Hot Sauce, or your favorite brand of hot sauce

2 tablespoons Worcestershire sauce

2 tablespoons molasses

1 tablespoons Dijon mustard

½ tablespoon freshly ground black pepper, or to taste

Coarse salt (sea or kosher). to taste

1. Place the beef stock in a heavy saucepan over high heat and bring to a boil. Continue boiling until the stock is reduced by one-quarter (3 cups will remain), 5 to 8 minutes.

2. Reduce the heat to medium and stir in the brisket drippings, ketchup, vinegar, sugar, hot sauce, Worcestershire sauce, molasses, mustard, and pepper. Bring the mixture back to a boil, stirring continuously.

Correct the seasoning, adding salt or more pepper—the sauce should be highly seasoned.

3. Remove the pan from the heat and let the sauce stand for 5 minutes. Stir and serve warm in ramekins or small bowls, one per eater. Spoon it over the meat or use it as a dip for the sandwich. Store any leftover sauce, covered, in the refrigerator, where it will keep for at least 3 days.

DOCTOR SAUCE

YIELD: Makes 2 cups

TRY THIS!

My wife likes to serve this sauce with a grilled rack of lamb. Brush it on during the last 5 minutes of cooking to caramelize the sugar in the marmalade.

Most of the sauces in this book are built and simmered from scratch. This "doctor" sauce lets you customize your favorite commercial barbecue sauce. It contains only three main ingredients and can be made in a matter of minutes. The sauce is sweet, but the bitter oranges in the marmalade keep it from being too sugary. (If using apricot jam, add ½ teaspoon lemon zest and 1 to 2 tablespoons lemon juice to offset the sweetness.)

INGREDIENTS

1 cup commercial tomato-based barbecue sauce, or Sweet-and-Smoky Barbecue Sauce (page 161)

½ cup honey

½ cup orange marmalade or apricot jam

½ to 1 teaspoon freshly ground black pepper

3 tablespoons freshly squeezed lemon juice, or to taste (optional)

Combine all the ingredients in a heavy nonreactive saucepan and stir or whisk to mix. Bring the sauce to a simmer over medium heat and continue simmering and stirring until the marmalade is melted and the sauce is richly flavored, 5 minutes. If desired, add the lemon juice to offset the sweetness. Use right away or transfer to a large jar, cover, cool to room temperature, and refrigerate. The sauce will keep for several weeks.

GUAVA BARBECUE SAUCE

YIELD: Makes 2½ to 3 cups

This satiny, ruby-red sauce sure looks like a traditional American barbecue sauce. It sticks to ribs (and to your fingers) the way a good barbecue sauce should. But one taste lets you know you're not in Kansas anymore. Guava is a perfumed tropical fruit that lends a musky Caribbean sweetness to the sauce, a sultry quality reinforced by ginger and rum. Look for the guava paste sold in flat cans at supermarkets and Latino markets. (The guava paste sold in rectangular cardboard boxes is too soft and sweet.)

INGREDIENTS

1 cup guava paste

6 tablespoons cider vinegar

1 cup cold water

¼ cup dark rum

¼ cup tomato paste

¼ cup fresh lime juice

1 tablespoon soy sauce

2 teaspoons ketchup

2 teaspoons Worcestershire sauce

2 tablespoons minced onion

1 tablespoon minced peeled fresh ginger

2 cloves garlic, peeled and minced

½ Scotch bonnet chile or other hot chile, or to taste, seeded and minced

Coarse salt (sea or kosher) and freshly ground black pepper, to taste

1. Place all the ingredients in a heavy nonreactive saucepan and whisk to mix. Bring the sauce to a simmer over medium heat and continue to simmer, uncovered, until the sauce is slightly thickened and richly flavored, 10 to 15 minutes. Correct the seasoning, adding more salt or pepper if needed. The sauce should be pourable; if too thick, add a little more water.

2. Use right away or transfer to a large jar or squirt bottles, cover, cool to room temperature, and refrigerate. The sauce will keep for several weeks.

TRY THIS!

Guava barbecue sauce is one of the best slathers I know of for ribs and ham (or pork in general), and its exotic fruitiness goes well with chicken, turkey, duck, and even game. Make a double batch and keep some in a squirt bottle in the refrigerator, so you always have it on hand.

JAKE'S THREE C'S BARBECUE SAUCE

YIELD: Makes 2 cups

TRY THIS!

Serve this sauce warm or at room temperature with grilled or smoked poultry, pork, and game.

This may be the strangest sauce you'll find in a barbecue book. Cherries? Chocolate? Are we talking barbecue or dessert? Once you get beyond the initial shock, however, the sauce actually makes sense. The great wild game sauces of Europe play the tartness of vinegar or lemon against the sweetness of cherries and port. The granddaddy of Mexican sauces, *mole poblano*, contains chipotle chiles and a trace of chocolate, prized for its chalky bitterness. This recipe comes from my stepson, Jake Klein, owner-chef of Jake's Handcrafted in Brooklyn.

INGREDIENTS

3 tablespoons unsalted butter

½ medium-size onion, peeled and finely chopped

2 cloves garlic, peeled and thinly sliced

2 cups pitted Bing cherries, fresh, canned (drained), or frozen (thawed and drained)

2 tablespoons unsweetened cocoa powder

1 teaspoon pure chile powder (not a blend)

1½ cups port wine

½ cup sherry vinegar

½ cup honey, or more to taste

1 tablespoon ketchup

1 teaspoon grated lemon zest

2 teaspoons fresh lemon juice, or more to taste

2 canned chipotle chiles, minced, or 2 teaspoons chipotle chile powder

½ teaspoon caraway seeds

½ teaspoon coarse salt (sea or kosher), or more to taste

½ teaspoon freshly ground black pepper

1. Melt the butter in a nonreactive saucepan over medium heat. Add the onion, garlic, and cherries and cook until lightly browned, 3 minutes.

2. Add the remaining ingredients and bring to a boil over medium-high heat. Reduce the heat to gently simmer the sauce, uncovered, until reduced to about 2 cups, 15 to 20 minutes, stirring occasionally.

3. Correct the seasoning, adding salt, lemon juice, or honey; the sauce should be a little sweet, a little sour, and very flavorful. Use right away or transfer to a large jar, cover, cool to room temperature, and refrigerate. The sauce will keep for several weeks.

TAMARIND-BANANA BARBECUE SAUCE

YIELD: Makes 3 cups

The notion of tamarind-banana barbecue sauce sounds exotic, even downright strange, but it makes sense historically and geographically. Barbecue originated in the Caribbean; *barbacoa* was the Arawak Indian word for a grill. And tamarind and bananas are traditional flavorings of the West Indies. (Tamarind is a key ingredient in many commercial steak and barbecue sauces.) In the following recipe, tamarind supplies a fruity acidity, while the sweetness comes from bananas and molasses.

TRY THIS!

The tropical ingredients in this sauce suggest serving it with Caribbean-style barbecue. Come to think of it, it tastes pretty good on American-style barbecue, too.

INGREDIENTS

1½ cups tamarind purée, or more to taste (recipe follows)

1 small onion, peeled and minced

1 tablespoon minced fresh ginger

½ Scotch bonnet chile or other hot chile, seeded and minced

½ green bell pepper, stemmed, seeded, and finely chopped

2 ripe bananas, peeled and chopped

¼ cup dark rum

¼ cup packed dark brown sugar, or more to taste

¼ cup molasses

¼ cup raisins

½ teaspoon ground cumin

¼ teaspoon ground allspice

¼ teaspoon ground cayenne pepper

Coarse salt (sea or kosher), to taste

Freshly ground black pepper, to taste

1. Thaw or prepare the tamarind purée. Combine all the ingredients in a heavy nonreactive saucepan. Bring to a simmer over medium heat and continue simmering, uncovered, until the vegetables and bananas are soft and the sauce is well flavored, 15 to 20 minutes.

2. Transfer the sauce to a blender or food processor and purée. Correct the seasoning, adding salt, brown sugar, or more tamarind purée. The sauce should be sweet, sour, and spicy. If too thick, add a little water. Use right away or transfer to jars, cover, cool to room temperature, and refrigerate. The sauce will keep for several weeks.

TAMARIND PURÉE

YIELD: Makes a generous 1 cup

TRY THIS!

Add 1 or 2 tablespoons tamarind purée to glazes and barbecue sauces for a refreshing fruity tartness.

I think of tamarind as sweet-and-sour sauce in a pod, boasting an acidity reminiscent of fresh lime juice and a sweetness akin to prunes. (The fruit takes its name from the Arabic words *tamr hindi*, literally "Indian date.") The tricky part about using tamarind is reducing the stringy, seed-studded pulp to a smooth purée. Ethnic markets and specialty greengrocers sometimes carry fresh tamarind pods. Look for pods with cracked dusty-brown skins, which indicate ripeness. Alternatively, buy peeled tamarind pulp, which is sold in blocks at Hispanic markets and at many supermarkets. It is easier to use and there's no appreciable difference in flavor. Better still, you may be able to buy frozen tamarind purée (look for it in Indian markets), in which case you can handily skip this recipe. Tamarind purée is sometimes called tamarind water.

INGREDIENTS

8 ounces tamarind pods (8 to 10 pods) or 8 ounces peeled tamarind pulp

1½ cups boiling water

1. If using tamarind pods, peel and pry off the skin with a paring knife. If using a block of pulp, break it into 1-inch pieces. Place the tamarind in a blender with 1 cup of the boiling water. Let the tamarind soften for 10 minutes.

2. Run the blender in short bursts at low speed for 15 to 20 seconds to obtain a thick brown liquid. Do not overblend, or the seeds will break up. Strain the liquid into a bowl, pressing hard with a wooden spoon to extract the juices and scraping the bottom of the strainer with a spatula.

3. Return the pulp in the strainer to the blender and add the remaining ½ cup boiling water. Blend, then strain the mixture into a bowl, pressing well to extract the juices. Tamarind purée will keep for up to 5 days, covered, in the refrigerator and can be frozen for several months. I like to freeze it in plastic ice cube trays, so I have convenient premeasured portions on hand.

SQUIRT BOTTLES:
BARBECUE SAUCE MEETS JACKSON POLLOCK

Once reserved for ketchup and mustard, plastic squeeze bottles have become the paintbrushes of artistic grill masters. Fill them with your favorite sauce or sauces—the more colorful the better—and use them to decorate your food with Jackson Pollock-esque squiggles of flavor. The only thing tricky about squirt bottles is getting the sauce out. When squirting smooth sauces, cut off just the very tip of the nozzle. For a sauce that contains tiny bits of onion, chiles, or spices, you'll need to cut off more of the nozzle to make a wider hole. For a cool presentation at a party, make six different sauces and serve them in a cardboard beer or soda six-pack.

COFFEE BARBECUE SAUCE

YIELD: Makes 1¼ cups

TRY THIS!

Marcus Samuelsson developed this sauce with a sort of Nordic surf and turf (crispy salmon with barbecued boneless veal ribs), which says a lot about its versatility.

"I come from a poor man's culture—it's my job to make it luxurious," says New York uber chef Marcus Samuelsson. (Born in Ethiopia and raised in Sweden, Samuelsson presides over an empire with restaurants in New York, Bermuda, and Scandinavia.) Come to think of it: Isn't that true of all American barbecue, which routinely transforms inexpensive cuts of meat into meals of epicurean wonder?

Like many coffee-based barbecue sauces, it tastes somewhat strange by itself but great with food.

INGREDIENTS

1 tablespoon extra-virgin olive oil

1 tablespoon honey

1 tablespoon dark brown sugar

1 medium-size red onion, peeled and finely chopped

4 ripe tomatoes, peeled, seeded, and diced

1 piece fresh ginger, (3 inches), peeled and finely chopped

1 cup brewed coffee

2 tablespoons ketchup

1 tablespoon prepared chile sauce

1 tablespoon tomato paste

½ teaspoon fresh lemon juice

½ teaspoon Worcestershire sauce

1 canned chipotle chile, minced

2 sprigs fresh rosemary

2 sprigs fresh thyme

1⅓ cups cold water

Coarse salt (sea or kosher), to taste

1. Combine the oil, honey, brown sugar, and onion in a heavy nonreactive saucepan and cook over medium heat until the onion is caramelized (golden brown), 5 to 8 minutes, stirring with a wooden spoon.

2. Stir in the remaining ingredients, except for the salt, and bring to a simmer. Reduce the heat to medium-low and gently simmer the sauce, uncovered, until thick and flavorful, 15 to 20 minutes, stirring from time to time with a wooden spoon.

3. Remove the herb sprigs and transfer the sauce to a

blender. Purée and correct the seasoning, adding salt or any other ingredient if needed. Use right away or transfer the sauce to a jar, cover, cool to room temperature, and refrigerate. The sauce will keep for several weeks.

COCA-COLA BARBECUE SAUCE

YIELD: Makes 2 cups

A lot of people dream of quitting their day job to open a barbecue restaurant. One man who actually did it is Jim Budros. The financial-planner-turned-pit-master and his partners parlayed a championship at the American Royal Barbecue Festival into a chain of City Barbeque and Catering restaurants in the Midwest. What's different about his barbecue sauce is an ingredient people are more likely to drink than cook with: Coke. This isn't quite as strange as it sounds, because Coke is sweet, tart, and spicy—the flavor dynamic in most great barbecue sauces. Still skeptical? Venezuelans braise pot roast in Coke.

TRY THIS!

Use pretty much as you would any sauce, keeping in mind it has a strong affinity for chicken, ribs, and pork.

INGREDIENTS

1 cup Coca-Cola

1 cup ketchup

¼ cup Worcestershire sauce

1 teaspoon liquid smoke

3 tablespoons A.1. Steak Sauce

1 teaspoon dried onion flakes

1 teaspoon dried garlic flakes

½ teaspoon freshly ground black pepper

Combine all the ingredients in a heavy nonreactive saucepan and gradually bring to a boil over medium heat. Reduce the heat slightly to obtain a gentle simmer. Simmer the sauce, uncovered, until reduced by a quarter, 6 to 10 minutes. Use right away or transfer to a large jar, cover, cool to room temperature, and refrigerate. The sauce will keep for several weeks.

PIG PICKER PUCKER SAUCE

YIELD: Makes 2½ cups

TRY THIS!

Serve this sauce with North Carolina-style pulled pork. Mix it in with the pork (this recipe makes enough for 4 to 5 pounds of meat) or spoon it on top. Save some of the sauce to make vinegar slaw (mix it with shredded or chopped cabbage) to pile atop the pork on a hamburger bun. Then imagine you're at a North Carolina pig picking, or a world-class barbecue joint like Wilbur's or Lexington Barbecue.

North Carolina occupies a unique position in American barbecue. Unlike the rest of the country, which enjoys ketchup-based sauces, the condiment of choice here is a piquant mixture of vinegar and red pepper flakes, sometimes with just a touch of sugar to cut the acidity. Because you're eating whole hog or pork shoulder, you're dealing with fatty meat. The vinegar in the sauce offsets the pork's richness. There's another reason vinegar sauce is so well suited to a pig picking. Carolina-style pork is usually served chopped or shredded, so you need a thin sauce that can soak into the tiny pieces of meat. You could prepare this sauce ahead, but why bother? It's so quick and easy to prepare, you should make it from scratch as you need it.

INGREDIENTS

1 small onion, peeled and thinly sliced

1½ cups cider vinegar

¾ cup cold water

2 tablespoons sugar, or to taste

1½ tablespoons coarse salt (sea or kosher), or to taste

1 tablespoon red pepper flakes

½ teaspoon freshly ground black pepper

Combine all the ingredients in a bowl and stir until the sugar and salt are dissolved. Correct the seasoning, adding salt if needed. Serve this sauce on shredded barbecued pork. Store any leftover sauce, covered, in the refrigerator. It will keep for at least 3 days.

CHARLIE TROTTER'S TRUFFLED PORCINI BBQ SAUCE

YIELD: Makes 2 cups

The late Charlie Trotter was one of the pioneer chefs of America's food revolution. For two decades, foodies and chefs the world over made pilgrimages to his eponymous restaurant in a Chicago townhouse—today the headquarters of the Charlie Trotter Project and Culinary Education Foundation. Many years ago, I asked him to create a barbecue sauce; I half expected to be told "We don't serve barbecue sauce at Charlie Trotter's." (Actually, Charlie was way too classy a guy to be supercilious.) Instead, he obliged with a typical Trotteresque recipe—a barbecue sauce flavored with meaty porcini mushrooms and fragrant black or white truffles.

TRY THIS!

This extravagant sauce goes best with simply grilled meats: beef, veal, pork, lamb, or venison. To make it the star attraction, serve it over grilled polenta. Black truffles take you in a French direction; white truffles transport you to northern Italy.

INGREDIENTS

2 cups Smoked Stock (page 146) or beef or veal stock, homemade and/or low-sodium

2 tablespoons grapeseed or vegetable oil

2 shallots, peeled and finely chopped

4 ounces fresh porcini mushrooms, or other exotic mushrooms, trimmed, cleaned, and thinly sliced

1½ cups dry red wine

¼ cup sherry vinegar

2 tablespoons Truffle Oil (page 145)

1 black or white truffle (½ to 1 ounce), scrubbed and finely chopped

2 tablespoons unsalted butter

Coarse salt (sea or kosher) and freshly ground black pepper, to taste

1. Place the stock in a heavy saucepan and bring to a boil over high heat. Continue boiling, uncovered, until reduced by half, about 10 minutes.

2. Heat the oil in a nonreactive saucepan over medium heat. Add the shallots and cook, stirring with a wooden spoon, until lightly browned, about 5 minutes. Add the porcini and sauté for 2 minutes. Add the red wine and simmer briskly (you may need to raise the heat) until reduced by two thirds, 6 to 10 minutes. Add the reduced stock, vinegar, and truffle oil. Simmer the sauce until richly flavored, 3 minutes.

3. Stir in the truffle and remove the pan from the heat. Stir in the butter and season the sauce with salt and plenty of pepper before serving. The sauce tastes best served within a few hours of making. Transfer any extra to a jar, cover, and refrigerate. The sauce will keep for at least 3 days.

JALAPEÑO-MUSTARD BARBECUE SAUCE

YIELD: Makes about 2 cups

TRY THIS!

Originally created for pork, this sauce goes great with just about any smoked or grilled meat.

In South Carolina and parts of Georgia, barbecue just isn't complete without mustard sauce. The basic ingredients are mustard (typically the yellow ballpark variety) with vinegar and some sort of sweetener. The latter could be honey, molasses, brown sugar, or cane syrup—or a combination of two or more. This version owes its kick to jalapeño peppers and its silken sweetness to a fillip of corn syrup. Tip o' the hat to Jack McDavid of Jack's Firehouse in Philadelphia for the idea.

INGREDIENTS

¾ cup distilled white vinegar

½ cup beef or chicken broth

½ cup finely chopped onion

¼ cup minced seeded jalapeño peppers

½ cup Dijon mustard

¼ cup honey mustard or brown deli-style mustard

¼ cup corn syrup, or to taste

2 tablespoons molasses

½ teaspoon freshly ground black pepper

½ teaspoon coarse salt (sea or kosher), or more to taste

¼ teaspoon ground cayenne pepper

Combine all the ingredients in a heavy nonreactive saucepan over high heat and bring to a boil. Reduce the heat and simmer, uncovered, until thick and richly flavored, about 10 minutes, stirring occasionally. Taste the sauce for seasoning, adding salt or corn syrup as desired. Use right away or transfer to jars, cover, cool to room temperature, and refrigerate. The sauce will keep for several weeks.

BUBBA-LINA VINEGAR SAUCE

YIELD: Makes 3 cups

First, the bad news about Joe's Kansas City Barbecue: There's always a waiting line. The good news is that the queue moves quickly. Proprietor and multi American Royal barbecue champ Jeff Stehey wanted to serve a pulled pork sandwich in this city of ribs and brisket, and he wanted to serve it with a North Carolina-style vinegar sauce. To make it more palatable for the locals—visually palatable at least (don't forget, KC was the birthplace of thick sweet red barbecue sauce)—he added tomato paste so that the sauce would look red. The result: a Carolina-style vinegar sauce for Kansas City. Here's my take on a Joe's classic.

TRY THIS!

This sauce—originally designed for North Carolina-style pulled pork—works better mixed in with the chopped meat than spooned over it. You may screw your mouth in a pucker when you first taste it, but the sauce grows on you. A lot.

INGREDIENTS

2 cups cider vinegar

½ cup tomato paste

¼ cup dark corn syrup

¼ cup cold water

2 teaspoons coarse salt (sea or kosher), or more to taste

1 teaspoon freshly ground black pepper

1 to 2 cloves garlic, peeled and minced

½ teaspoon ground cayenne pepper, or red pepper flakes

Combine all ingredients in a nonreactive saucepan and bring to a boil over medium heat. Simmer, uncovered, for 3 minutes. Let cool and correct the seasoning, adding corn syrup, salt, or cayenne to taste. Serve it right away or transfer it to jars, cool to room temperature, and refrigerate. The sauce will keep for at least a week. Stir well before using.

WORLD BARBECUE SAUCES

Americans aren't the only people obsessed with barbecue sauce. Argentineans could no more imagine grilled beef without Chimichurri (page 192) than Thais could enjoy saté without Peanut Sauce (pages 229 and 232). In Spain, grilled fare comes with a roasted vegetable and nut sauce called Romesco (page 212), while in the Republic of Georgia, no barbecue would be complete without a condiment made with sour plums called Tkemali (page 215).

This chapter explores the lip-smacking world of barbecue sauces: from South African Monkey Gland Sauce (page 218—fear not: No primates perished in its preparation) to Moroccan Charmoula (page 216) to Japanese Yakitori Sauce (page 226). Along the way, savor barbecue sauces made with miso, rhubarb, and even chocolate.

CARIBBEAN AND LATIN BARBECUE SAUCES

CHIMICHURRI
ARGENTINE PARSLEY-GARLIC SAUCE

YIELD: Makes 2 cups, enough to serve 6 to 8

TRY THIS!

Serve *chimichurri* with any type of grilled beef, especially T-bones, rib eyes, New York strips, and other steaks. It also goes great with grilled chicken, pork, and sweetbreads.

Chimichurri is a pesto-like sauce comprised of flat-leaf parsley and garlic. (Talk about ingenious: Parsley is nature's mouthwash, so it helps counteract the breath-wilting fumes of the garlic.) There are as many versions as there are Argentinean grill jockeys. Some use dried herbs instead of fresh; others add grated carrot or red bell pepper; others kick up the heat with red pepper flakes or fresh chiles. *Pebre* (page 207) is a sort of Chilean *chimichurri* made with cilantro.

INGREDIENTS

1 bunch fresh flat-leaf parsley, rinsed, stemmed, and dried

8 cloves garlic, peeled

3 tablespoons chopped onion

5 tablespoons distilled white vinegar, or more to taste

5 tablespoons cold water

1 teaspoon coarse salt (sea or kosher)

½ teaspoon dried oregano

1 teaspoon red pepper flakes, or to taste

½ teaspoon freshly ground black pepper

1 cup extra-virgin olive oil or vegetable oil

Finely chop the parsley and garlic in a food processor. Add the onion, vinegar, water, salt, oregano, pepper flakes, and black pepper and process in brief bursts until the salt crystals are dissolved. Add the oil in a thin stream. Don't overprocess; the *chimichurri* should be fairly coarse. Correct the seasoning, adding salt or vinegar if needed. *Chimichurri* is quick to make, so I usually prepare it as I need it. If you do choose to store it, transfer it to a jar, cover, and refrigerate. It will keep for several days, but quickly loses its bright green color. Be sure to taste and re-season before serving.

MOJO
CUBAN CITRUS-GARLIC SAUCE

YIELD: Makes 1½ cups, enough to serve 6 to 8

Here in my hometown, Miami, barbecue calls for a ketchup-free sauce called *mojo* (pronounced MO-ho, not mo-JOE). This edgy citrus sauce starts with the Holy Trinity of Cuban seasonings: oregano, cumin, and garlic. You lightly fry the garlic to boost its flavor. The traditional souring agent is *naranja agria*, sour orange, which in Miami is available at any supermarket. If unavailable, you can approximate its flavor by combining fresh lime and orange juices.

TRY THIS!

Mojo is the traditional sauce for Cuban pit-roasted pork and *palomilla* (a thin steak cut from the round and grilled). You can also serve it with poultry and seafood.

INGREDIENTS

½ cup extra-virgin olive oil

8 large cloves garlic, peeled and thinly sliced crosswise

⅔ cup fresh sour orange juice (see box, page 194), or ½ cup fresh lime juice and 3 tablesoons fresh orange juice

⅓ cup cold water

1 teaspoon ground cumin

½ teaspoon dried oregano

1 teaspoon coarse salt (sea or kosher), or more to taste

½ teaspoon freshly ground black pepper, or more to taste

3 tablespoons chopped fresh cilantro or flat-leaf parsley

Heat the olive oil in a deep saucepan over medium heat. Add the garlic and cook until fragrant and pale golden brown, 2 to 3 minutes. Do not let the garlic burn. Stir in the sour orange juice, water, cumin, oregano, salt, and pepper. Stand back: The sauce may sputter. Bring the sauce to a rolling boil, then remove it from the heat and cool to room temperature.

Stir in the cilantro. Correct the seasoning, adding salt and pepper to taste. To enjoy this *mojo* at its best, serve it within a few hours of making.

Variation

Grapefruit-Mint *Mojo*: Substitute fresh grapefruit juice for the sour orange juice and chopped fresh mint for the cilantro.

SOUR ORANGE

Throughout much of the Caribbean, Central America, and the Yucatán, the preferred souring agent for marinades isn't lime juice or vinegar but the acidic juice of the sour orange. Known as *naranja agria* in Spanish, sour orange looks somewhat like a regular orange, but has a greenish tinge and bumpy rind. The size can range in diameter from 2 to 4 inches.

Sour orange juice has a highly distinctive flavor—imagine fresh lime juice with a hint of regular orange juice and grapefruit. If you're in a hurry, you can use fresh lime juice in place of sour orange juice, but a closer substitute is probably 3 parts lime juice and 1 part fresh orange juice. Sour orange is available in Latino and West Indian markets and a growing number of supermarkets, especially in cities like Miami.

AJILIMOJILI
PUERTO RICAN PEPPER SAUCE

YIELD: Makes 3 cups, enough to serve 8 to 10

Mention *ajilimojili* to a Puerto Rican and his eyes will light with pleasure. *Your* eyes will light with pleasure simply saying this musical word, which is pronounced "a-HEE-lee-mo-HEE-lee" and means something like "little pepper sauce." The peppers in question are green bell and a distinctive Puerto Rican chile called rocotillo. Shaped like a Scotch bonnet, the rocotillo has something of that chile's floral aroma with none of its fierce heat. Put these chiles together with onion, celery, garlic, olive oil, vinegar, cilantro, and *recao* (culantro, a thumb-shape leaf that tastes like a cross between cilantro and celery) and you've got an intensely aromatic sauce that rivals the Argentinean Chimichurri (page 192). Use rocotillos and *recao* if you can find them, but red bell pepper and flat-leaf parsley will work just fine if not.

TRY THIS!

Puerto Ricans traditionally serve *ajilimojili* as a dip for fried vegetables, not as a steak sauce. But I think you'll find its flavors perfectly suited to grilled seafood and meats, and as a sauce or dip for grilled vegetables.

INGREDIENTS

1 medium-size onion, peeled and cut into 1-inch pieces

6 cloves garlic, peeled

1 rib celery, thinly sliced

1 green bell pepper, stemmed, seeded, and cut into 1-inch pieces

8 rocotillo chiles, stemmed and seeded, or ¼ cup diced red bell pepper

1 bunch fresh cilantro, rinsed and stemmed

6 recao (culantro) leaves or 6 sprigs fresh flat-leaf parsley

½ teaspoon dried oregano

½ teaspoon ground cumin

½ teaspoon red pepper flakes

1 cup extra-virgin olive oil

⅓ cup red wine vinegar, or more to taste

1½ teaspoons coarse salt (sea or kosher), or more to taste

½ teaspoon freshly ground black pepper

Combine the onion, garlic, celery, bell pepper, chiles, cilantro, *recao*, oregano, cumin, and pepper flakes in a food processor and process to a coarse purée. Add the oil, vinegar, salt, and pepper and process to mix. Correct the seasoning, adding vinegar or salt; the *ajilimojili* should be highly seasoned. *Ajilimojili* tastes best served within a few hours of making.

MOLE POBLANO
MEXICAN CHOCOLATE-CHILE SAUCE

YIELD: Makes 4 cups, enough to serve 8 to 10

TRY THIS!

Mole poblano is traditionally served with turkey in Mexico. I like it with any type of grilled poultry, from chicken to quail, not to mention with grilled or smoked pork. Because the sauce is thick and brown, you may wish to spread it on the plate, then arrange the grilled bird or vegetables on top.

Mole poblano is one of central Mexico's most famous sauces—a dark rich rib-sticking gravy confected from nuts, raisins, chiles, spices, and chocolate. A good *mole poblano* hits every note on the gustatory scale: sweet, sour, salty, bitter, spicy, earthy, fruity, and pungent. The recipe may look complicated because it contains a lot of ingredients, but actually it's a series of simple steps. To be strictly authentic, you'd use at least five types of dried chiles: anchos, mulatos, pasillas, guajillos, and chipotles. (For a full discussion of the chiles, see page 204.) I call for all five here, but you could replace some of the more esoteric varieties with more ancho chiles. Lard is the traditional fat for frying the sauce ingredients, and it has a smoky meaty flavor that's unique. The real surprise is that lard is actually healthier for you than butter, containing half the cholesterol and a third of the saturated fat. If lard is unavailable, substitute bacon drippings or extra-virgin olive oil.

INGREDIENTS

2 ancho chiles

2 mulato chiles

2 pasilla chiles

2 guajillo chiles

1 to 2 dried chipotle chiles

4 ripe plum tomatoes

1 medium-size onion, peeled and quartered

3 cloves garlic, peeled

1 corn tortilla (5 to 6 inches in diameter)

3 tablespoons slivered almonds

3 tablespoons sesame seeds

½ teaspoon black peppercorns

½ teaspoon coriander seeds

½ cinnamon stick (1 inch)

2 whole cloves

¼ teaspoon anise seeds

Hot water, for soaking the chiles

¼ cup chopped fresh cilantro leaves

3 tablespoons golden raisins

2 cups chicken broth, or more if needed, warm

¼ cup lard, bacon fat, or extra-virgin olive oil

1 ounce unsweetened chocolate

2 teaspoons honey, or more to taste

1 tablespoon red wine vinegar, or more to taste

Coarse salt (sea or kosher), to taste

1. Heat a *comal* or dry cast-iron skillet over medium heat. Roast all the chiles until fragrant, 1 to 2 minutes per side. Transfer to a platter to cool. Roast the tomatoes, onion, and garlic until browned on all sides. The garlic will take 4 to 6 minutes, the tomatoes and onion, 10 to 12 minutes. Set aside to cool. Toast the tortilla until crisp and brown, 2 minutes per side. Set aside to cool, then tear into 2-inch pieces. Toast the almonds, shaking the pan to ensure even browning, until toasted and fragrant but not too brown, 2 to 3 minutes. Set aside to cool. Toast and cool the sesame seeds the same way. Add the peppercorns, coriander, cinnamon, and cloves to the pan and toast until fragrant and toasted, 1 to 2 minutes. Do not let the spices burn. Let cool.

2. Transfer the toasted peppercorns, coriander, cinnamon, and cloves and the anise seeds to a spice mill and grind to a fine powder. Breathe a sigh of relief: The hard part is over.

3. Tear the roasted chiles in half and remove the stems, veins, and seeds. Place the chiles in a bowl with hot water to cover. Soak until pliable, about 30 minutes, and drain well.

4. Place the tomatoes in a food processor or blender. Add the onion, garlic, chiles, tortilla, almonds, sesame seeds, ground spices, cilantro, and raisins. Work in several batches if needed. Purée to a smooth paste, stopping the processor and scraping down the sides of the bowl several times with a rubber spatula. If the mixture is too dry to purée, add a little chicken broth.

5. Heat the lard in a large, deep skillet or saucepan over medium heat. Add the chile mixture and cook, stirring constantly, until thick and fragrant, 5 minutes. Reduce the heat and stir in 2 cups broth, the chocolate, honey, vinegar, and salt. Simmer the sauce, uncovered, stirring occasionally with a wooden spoon, until thick and richly flavored, 10 minutes. The mole should be thick but pourable; add more broth, as needed. It should be very flavorful, with just the faintest hint of sweetness; add salt, vinegar, or just the least bit of honey, as needed. Use right away or transfer to jars, cover, cool to room temperature, and refrigerate. The mole will keep for several days.

CHIRMOL
CENTRAL AMERICAN TOMATO SAUCE

Order a steak in a Honduran or Salvadoran restaurant and you'll be offered a small bowl of a spicy tomato sauce called *chirmol*. At first glance, it looks like Mexican salsa, but the flavor profile is quite different—the result of adding oil and vinegar in addition to the lime juice. There are many types of *chirmol*, including a salsa-like uncooked version and a cooked one made rich with roasted vegetables.

FRESH CHIRMOL

YIELD: Makes about 2 cups, enough to serve 6 to 8

This *chirmol* starts out like a Mexican salsa, but the radishes, vinegar, and olive oil give it a more complex flavor. I like to serve it over *carnitas* (crusty shreds of grilled beef or pork on tortillas).

INGREDIENTS

2 ripe tomatoes, seeded and finely diced (see box, page 285)

½ medium-size sweet onion, such as Vidalia or Walla Walla, peeled and finely chopped

2 radishes, finely chopped

2 scallions (white and green parts), trimmed and finely chopped

2 jalapeño peppers, seeded and finely chopped (for a spicier chirmol, leave the seeds in)

1 clove garlic, peeled and minced

¼ cup chopped fresh cilantro leaves

¼ cup extra-virgin olive oil

2 tablespoons distilled white vinegar

2 tablespoons cold water

1 to 2 tablespoons fresh lime juice, or more to taste

1 teaspoon coarse salt (sea or kosher), or more to taste

½ teaspoon freshly ground black pepper

Combine all the ingredients in an attractive serving bowl and stir to mix. Correct the seasoning, adding lime juice or salt; the *chirmol* should be highly seasoned. Serve within a few hours of making.

TRY THIS!

Use *chirmol* as you would any Mexican salsa. Spoon it over grilled seafood, poultry, and meats (especially steak).

ROASTED CHIRMOL

YIELD: Makes 1½ cups, enough to serve 6

TRY THIS!

This variation has a more robust flavor than the preceding recipe, the result of roasting the vegetables. Serve over grilled meats or seafood.

YOU ALSO NEED (OPTIONAL)

Vegetable grate or 12-inch-long wooden skewers

The traditional way to make this sauce is to roast the vegetables in an ungreased cast-iron skillet for a concentrated, smoky flavor. That set me thinking about my favorite way to achieve a smoke flavor: grilling. Either method will produce a superlative *chirmol*.

INGREDIENTS

4 plum tomatoes

1 small onion, peeled and quartered

2 cloves garlic, peeled

1 to 2 jalapeño peppers, seeded (for a spicier chirmol, leave in the seeds)

3 tablespoons extra-virgin olive oil

3 tablespoons chopped fresh flat-leaf parsley

½ teaspoon dried oregano

2 tablespoons fresh lime juice

1 tablespoon distilled white vinegar, or more to taste

Coarse salt (sea or kosher) and freshly ground black pepper, to taste

1. GRILL METHOD: Set up a grill for direct grilling and preheat to high, placing a vegetable grate in the center. If you don't have a vegetable grate, thread the onion quarters, garlic, and chiles on skewers. Place the tomatoes, onion, garlic, and chiles on the grate and grill until well browned on all sides, 4 to 6 minutes for the garlic and chiles, 10 to 12 minutes for the tomatoes and onions. (If using skewers, place a folded piece of aluminum foil under the exposed ends to keep them from burning.)

SKILLET METHOD: Heat a large cast-iron skillet over medium heat. Add the tomatoes, onion, garlic, and chiles and cook until browned on all sides; the timing is as above.

2. Transfer the vegetables to a food processor or blender and purée. (Don't worry about a few charred pieces of skin; they'll add flavor.)

3. Heat the oil in a nonstick skillet. Add the vegetable purée, parsley, oregano, lime juice, and vinegar and cook, stirring often, until thick and flavorful, 5 minutes. Correct the seasoning, adding salt, pepper, and vinegar as needed. Use right away or transfer to a large jar, cover, cool to room temperature, and refrigerate. The *chirmol* will keep for several days.

SALSA CRIOLLA
COLOMBIAN CREOLE SAUCE

YIELD: Makes 1½ cups, enough to serve 4

Like creole sauces everywhere, this *salsa criolla* is built on tomatoes, ideally the sort that are so ripe and juicy, they go splat if they fall off the table. Don't buy refrigerated tomatoes, and don't refrigerate your tomatoes once you get them home. (Refrigeration destroys a tomato's succulence and flavor.) The cumin, oregano, and red pepper flakes let you know you're in South America.

TRY THIS!

Steak is the destination for this full-flavored Colombian creole sauce, but it goes equally well with grilled chicken, pork, and seafood.

INGREDIENTS

¼ cup extra-virgin olive oil or vegetable oil

1 medium-size onion, peeled and finely chopped

4 scallions (white and green parts), trimmed and finely chopped

1 piece green bell pepper (2 by 3 inches), finely chopped

2 cloves garlic, peeled and finely chopped

½ teaspoon dried oregano

½ teaspoon ground cumin

½ teaspoon red pepper flakes, or to taste

3 medium-size ripe tomatoes, seeded and chopped (see box, page 285)

2 tablespoons red wine vinegar, or to taste

3 tablespoons chopped fresh flat-leaf parsley

Coarse salt (sea or kosher) and freshly ground black pepper, to taste

Heat the oil in a nonstick skillet over medium heat. Add the onion, scallions, bell pepper, garlic, oregano, cumin, and pepper flakes and cook until soft and translucent but not brown, 4 minutes. Increase the heat to high. Add the tomatoes and vinegar and cook until the tomato pieces are soft and most of the tomato liquid has evaporated, 5 minutes. Reduce the heat to medium and stir in the parsley. Cook for 1 minute and add salt and pepper. Serve warm, ideally within a few hours of making.

Variation

Salsa Criolla Fresca (Fresh Colombian Creole Sauce): Place the ingredients above in a mixing bowl and stir to mix. The virtue of this sauce is its spontaneity. Serve it right away.

AJI AMARILLO
PERUVIAN YELLOW PEPPER SAUCE

YIELD: Makes about 1½ cups

TRY THIS!

Serve with Peruvian-style kebabs, grilled beef, and chicken. Also great with grilled seafood.

This piquant yellow sauce accompanies *anticuchos* (beef heart kebabs), Peruvian roast chicken, and other grilled meats for which Peru is so rightly famous. Aji amarillo (yellow chile) gives it heat; *queso fresco* (fresh cheese) makes it tart; and the aromatics come from *huacatay* (also known as black mint—a pungent herb in the marigold family). Look for these ingredients at a Peruvian market or online at Barbecuebible.com. Or, use the work-arounds I suggest in the Notes that follow.

INGREDIENTS

6 to 8 fresh, frozen, bottled, or dried ajis amarillos, or ¾ cup aji amarillo paste (you need ¾ cup chile purée in all; see Notes)

3 tablespoons smooth peanut butter

2 ounces queso fresco or feta cheese, crumbled

⅓ cup cold water

2 tablespoons chopped huacatay, or 1 tablespoon each finely chopped flat-leaf parsley and spearmint or peppermint (see Notes)

2 tablespoons extra-virgin olive oil

1 tablespoon fresh lime juice, or to taste

Coarse salt (sea or kosher) and freshly ground black pepper

1. If using frozen chiles, let thaw at room temperature. If using dried chiles, soak in water to cover for 2 hours, then drain.

2. Stem the chiles and if a milder sauce is desired, remove the seeds. Place the chiles, peanut butter, cheese, and water in a blender and purée until smooth. Blend in the *huacatay*, running the blender in short bursts.

3. Heat the olive oil in a small saucepan over medium-low heat. Add the chile-peanut butter purée and cook, stirring often, until thick, creamy, and richly flavored, 5 to 8 minutes. Reduce the heat as needed—the sauce should gently simmer, not boil.

4. Add 1 tablespoon lime juice, or to taste, and salt: The mixture should be highly seasoned and spicy hot. Serve warm or at room temperature.

NOTES: If you can't find aji amarillo, substitute 1 grilled, peeled, cored, seeded, and diced yellow bell pepper, plus ½ to 1 teaspoon ground cayenne pepper.

Huacatay (sometimes called black mint) is an herb with a minty flavor in the marigold family. Look for it in Peruvian markets or use equal parts mint and parsley.

HOT STUFF:
A GRILLER'S GUIDE TO CHILES

As you travel the world's barbecue trail, heat is a constant. And not just the heat of the fire. Wherever people grill seafood or meat over fire, the chances are you'll find some sort of chile, from the jalapeño-laced salsas of Mexico to the fiery sambals of Penang.

Most of the heat in a chile resides in the seeds and veins. For a milder sauce, rub, or marinade, remove the seeds and veins before using by scraping them out with a paring knife. It's a good idea to wear rubber gloves when handling chiles, especially if you have sensitive skin.

To prepare dried chiles, remove the stems, tear open the chile, and discard the seeds. Soak the chiles in warm water to cover until soft and pliable, 30 to 60 minutes. Sometimes dried chiles are roasted on the grill or on a *comal* or griddle, or under the broiler before soaking to give them a smoky flavor.

FRESH CHILES

AJI DULCE: Sometimes called *aji cachucha*, this tiny pattypan squash-shaped chile has the floral aroma of a Scotch bonnet, but no heat. Used in the Spanish-speaking Caribbean. Substitute red bell pepper.

GHOST PEPPER/BHUT JOLOKIA/RED NAGA/ SCORPION PEPPER: These short, squat, smooth-skinned, botanically related chiles are the world's hottest, routinely tipping the scales at more than 1 million Scovilles. (To put that in perspective, a jalapeño rates 5,000 on the Scoville scale; a Scotch bonnet around 200,000.) Wear gloves to protect your fingers when handling and use with extreme caution.

HABANERO: One of the hottest chiles in Mexico— a country that's no slouch when it comes to gustatory hellfire. Native to Cuba (a *habanero* is a resident of Havana) and the Caribbean, the habanero is the preferred chile of the Yucatán, where it's used in marinades and the fiery salsas for which the region is so famous. The flavor is floral and fruity, with a quality that hints at apricot. Similar to Jamaica's Scotch bonnet.

HORN PEPPER: An elongated bright green chile, tapered and twisted like a steer's horn. The heat ranges from warm to lip-searing. Horn peppers are often grilled whole, especially in Turkey and Japan.

JALAPEÑO: The bullet-shaped jalapeño is our most readily available chile, with a grassy flavor similar to green bell pepper and a gentle heat.

POBLANO: Could be described as a green bell pepper on steroids. Native to Mexico, this large (4 to 6 inches long, 2 to 3 inches wide), tapered, dark green chile is often grilled or roasted to make pepper strips (*rajas*). It's also used for stuffing. The flavor is similar to that of green bell pepper, but hotter and more aromatic.

ROCOTILLO: Similar to the aji dulce (see above) in its floral aroma, delicate bell pepper/Scotch bonnet flavor, and relative lack of heat (some rocotillos can be quite fiery, however). Orange, yellow, or pale green, the rocotillo can look like a miniature pattypan squash or smoother and more elongated, like a small habanero. This is a popular chile in Puerto Rico. Substitute aji dulce or red bell pepper.

SCOTCH BONNET: Red, orange, yellow, or green, the Scotch bonnet is 1 to 2 inches long and puffy and crinkled, like a Highlander's bonnet. Scotch bonnets and their Mexican cousins, habaneros, are 50 times hotter than jalapeños. But behind the heat, there's a floral flavor that hints at apricots and wood smoke. Scotch bonnets are one of the defining flavors of Jamaican Jerk Seasoning (page 85) and French West Indian Scotch Bonnet-Lime Marinade (page 61). Cousins of the Scotch bonnet include the goat pepper of the Bahamas and Haiti's *dame jeanne*. Scotch bonnets and habaneros can be used interchangeably; they are available at West Indian and Latino markets and many supermarkets.

SERRANO: A bright green or red bullet-shaped chile similar in flavor and heat to a jalapeño. The two are interchangeable. Serranos are available at most supermarkets, especially on the West Coast.

THAI CHILES: There are two: the short (1 inch long) slender bumpy *prik kee nu* (literally "mouse droppings") and the longer (2 to 3 inches) slightly milder horn-shaped *prik chee far*. Both are members of the cayenne family and both are extremely hot. In other parts of the world, the *prik kee nu* is called bird pepper. Both types are available at Asian and Indian markets. In a pinch you can substitute jalapeños or serranos.

DRIED, CANNED, AND PRESERVED CHILES

AJI AMARILLO: This long (3 to 4 inches), slender (½ to ¾ inch), fleshy gold-yellow firebrand is Peru's preferred chile. It is used in marinades for *anticuchos* (Peruvian kebabs) as well as in a golden pepper sauce served with all manner of grilled fare (see page 202). Fiery and fruity, the aji amarillo comes in many forms—fresh, dried, frozen, canned, pickled, powdered, and in paste. Look for them at Peruvian markets or online.

ANCHO: A dried poblano chile. Large (3 to 4 inches long and 2 to 3 inches wide), reddish-black in color, and wrinkled like a prune, the ancho has a complex earthy-fruity flavor with hints of dried fruits, tobacco, and coffee. Relatively mild in terms of heat but very flavorful. Essential for Mexican *moles*, like Mole Poblano (page 196).

CASCABEL: A small, brown, cherry-shape chile with loose seeds that rattle when shaken. (The name literally means "sleigh bell.") Hot, with a sweet and woodsy flavor. Used in salsas and marinades.

CAYENNE: An elongated small (1 inch long) red chile enjoyed from Louisiana and Central America to India. Hot but with a fairly monodimensional flavor.

CHINESE DRIED CHILES: Small dried red chiles in the cayenne family. Sold at Asian markets, they're used extensively in Sichuan cooking and for making Chinese Fire Oil (page 142).

CHIPOTLE: This smoked jalapeño—all smoke and fire—is the perfect symbol for barbecue. There are two varieties of chipotles: *grandes* and *moritas*. Grandes are tan-brown, striped, 3 to 5 inches in length, very smoky and fiery, but quite expensive. Moritas are smaller (about 2 inches long), sweeter, milder, and more economical. Both are sold dried and canned. This is one of the few foods I prefer canned on account of the can juices—a spicy sauce called adobo.

DE ÁRBOL: This slender bright red chile in the cayenne family is the preferred chile of northern Mexico and the main ingredient in a fiery salsa served with grilled beef and other meats in Sonora and Chihuahua.

GUAJILLO: A long (4 to 6 inches), slender, smooth-skinned, reddish-brown chile with a sweet mild flavor. The guajillo is one of the most common chiles in Mexico, a veritable workhorse used in numerous marinades, salsas, and *moles*. Fairly mild by Mexican heat standards and earthy and sweet tasting, like paprika.

MALAGUETA: Brazil's chile of choice—a tiny ridged red or green chile usually sold dried but sometimes pickled. The defining ingredient in Brazilian Hot Sauce (page 286).

MULATO: Related to the ancho chile (both are dried poblanos), the elongated, triangle-shaped "half breed" has a wrinkled, shiny, dark-brown to jet-black skin. The flavor is earthy, rich, and smoky, with hints of brandy, tobacco, and chocolate. The heat is gentle, especially if the seeds are removed. The mulato is an important ingredient in Mexican Mole Poblano (page 196).

PASILLA: This long slender chile takes its name from its wrinkled black skin (*pasa* means "raisin" in Spanish). The taste is both sweet and pleasantly bitter, with hints of licorice and raisins. The heat is moderate to quite fiery. If unavailable, substitute ancho or mulato chiles.

PEQUIN: A tiny, reddish-orange Mexican chile with a fiery bite. Substitute ground cayenne.

PEBRE
CHILEAN PEPPER SAUCE

YIELD: Makes 2 cups, enough to serve 8 to 10

This spicy herb-scented salsa is Chile's national table sauce. It may remind you of Argentinean Chimichurri (page 192), but it differs in several key ways. One is the use of cilantro in place of parsley. Another is the use of a fiery green Chilean chile that tastes a little like a Scotch bonnet—the chile called for here. (Some Chileans use hot pepper flakes instead.) Make the *pebre* sauce as spicy or mild as you wish.

TRY THIS!

Like most South American condiments, *pebre* is designed to be spooned over grilled meats, especially steak. Also great with poultry and seafood.

INGREDIENTS

2 medium-size tomatoes, seeded and diced

1 poblano chile, stemmed, seeded, and diced

3 scallions, trimmed, white and green parts sliced crosswise

1 bunch of fresh cilantro, rinsed, stemmed, and dried

3 cloves garlic, peeled and chopped

½ to 1 Scotch bonnet chile or jalapeño pepper, stemmed, seeded, and chopped (for a hotter sauce leave the seeds in)

1 teaspoon coarse salt (sea or kosher), or more to taste

½ teaspoon freshly ground black pepper

½ cup extra-virgin olive oil

¼ cup distilled white vinegar or white wine vinegar, or more to taste

¼ cup cold water

Place the tomatoes, poblano, scallions, cilantro, garlic, Scotch bonnet, salt, and pepper in a food processor and finely chop. Add the remaining ingredients and process to mix. Or the ingredients can be chopped and mixed by hand. Correct the seasoning, adding salt or vinegar; the sauce should be highly seasoned. Like most sauces that contain fresh herbs, *pebre* tastes best served within a few hours of making.

ST. BARTH BARBECUE SAUCE

YIELD: Makes 2 cups, enough to serve 6 to 8

TRY THIS!

Originally created for spiny lobster, this sauce goes great with any grilled fish or shellfish. It's pretty awesome slathered on burgers and grilled chicken, too.

NOTE

Colombo powder is French West Indian curry powder; Indian-style curry powder works well, too.

This sauce dates from the days of Cooking in Paradise, a cooking school I ran in St. Barthélemy in the French West Indies. We would hold our welcome dinner at a beachfront restaurant called the Marigot Bay Club, run by local fisherman Michel Ledée. Michel is gone and so is the restaurant, but we still serve his herb- and Scotch bonnet chile-scented barbecue sauce with grilled seafood.

INGREDIENTS

2 tablespoons unsalted butter

1 small onion, peeled and finely chopped

4 scallions (white and green parts), trimmed and chopped

2 cloves garlic, peeled and minced

½ to 1 Scotch bonnet chile, stemmed, seeded, and minced (for a spicier sauce, leave the seeds in)

3 tablespoons chopped fresh flat-leaf parsley or cilantro

½ teaspoon fresh thyme leaves or dried thyme

1 cup ketchup

¾ cup cold water

2 tablespoons fresh lime juice, or more to taste

1 tablespoon red wine vinegar

2 teaspoons colombo powder or curry powder, or to taste (see Note)

½ teaspoon coarse salt (sea or kosher), or more to taste

½ teaspoon freshly ground black pepper

Melt the butter in a heavy saucepan over medium heat. Add the onion, scallions, garlic, chile, parsley, and thyme and cook until soft but not brown, 3 minutes. Stir in the remaining ingredients and bring the sauce to a boil. Reduce the heat to medium-low and gently simmer the sauce, stirring often, until thick and flavorful, 5 to 10 minutes. Correct the seasoning, adding salt or lime juice; the sauce should be highly seasoned. Use right away or transfer to a large jar, cover, cool to room temperature, and refrigerate. The sauce will keep for at least a week.

EUROPEAN AND AFRICAN BARBECUE SAUCES

SALSA VERDE
ITALIAN GREEN SAUCE

YIELD: Makes 1½ cups, enough to serve 4 to 6

Italians serve this fragrant green sauce with some of their most cherished dishes: *bollito misto* (boiled dinner), for example, or grilled fish fresh from the sea, or seafood roasted in a salt crust. Some people prize the salty tang of diced anchovy; others, the fiery bite of red pepper flakes. I've made both optional, so feel free to customize the recipe to suit your taste.

INGREDIENTS

2 cloves garlic, peeled and minced

½ teaspoon coarse salt (sea or kosher), or more to taste

½ teaspoon freshly ground black pepper

½ teaspoon freshly grated lemon zest

¼ cup fresh lemon juice, or more to taste

¾ cup finely chopped fresh flat-leaf parsley

1 tablespoon drained capers, chopped

2 anchovies, drained and finely chopped (optional)

½ teaspoon red pepper flakes (optional)

¾ cup extra-virgin olive oil

TRY THIS!

Like most vinaigrette-style sauces, *salsa verde* can be used as a marinade, baste, and sauce. It pairs well with light meats, such as grilled seafood, chicken, and veal, but it's rich enough to stand up to lamb or beef.

Place the garlic, salt, pepper, and lemon zest in a bowl and mash to a paste with the back of a spoon. Stir or whisk in the lemon juice, followed by the remaining ingredients. Correct the seasoning, adding salt or lemon juice. The ingredients also can be combined in a jar and shaken or they can be blended in a food processor or blender. If you use the blender, you'll wind up with a smooth, bright green *salsa verde*, which isn't strictly traditional but which is very, very good. Like most fresh herb sauces, *salsa verde* tastes best served within a few hours of making.

ROUILLE
SAFFRON-ROASTED PEPPER SAUCE

YIELD: Makes about 2 cups, enough to serve 6 to 8

TRY THIS!

This sauce goes especially well with grilled fish and shellfish, but I also like it with grilled chicken and veal and pork chops. Spread it on grilled bread slices to make a singular bruschetta (traditionally floated in a bowl of fish soup) or use it as a dip for grilled vegetables.

Sauce rouille (from the French word for "rust") is a garlicky roasted red pepper and saffron sauce traditionally served with bouillabaisse and other fish soups. It's not a huge leap from fish soup to grilled fish and you'll be glad you made it, for this sauce explodes with the Provençal flavors of garlic, saffron, cayenne, and roasted peppers. Tradition calls for the peppers to be roasted in the oven, but I like the smoky sweetness they acquire when cooked on a hot grill grate or in the embers.

INGREDIENTS

2 large red bell peppers

2 slices white bread, crusts removed

½ teaspoon saffron threads

1 cup hot water

3 cloves garlic, peeled and coarsely chopped

1 cup extra-virgin olive oil

1 tablespoon fresh lemon juice, or more to taste

¼ to ½ teaspoon ground cayenne pepper

Coarse salt (sea or kosher) and freshly ground black pepper, to taste

1. Set up a grill for direct grilling and preheat to high. If using a charcoal grill, remove the grate and rake out a bed of hot coals, if desired.

2. Grill or ember-roast the peppers until the skins are charred on all sides, 4 to 6 minutes per side (16 to 24 minutes total). Transfer the peppers to a plate to cool.

3. If you removed the grate from the grill, return it and grill the bread slices until nicely toasted, 2 minutes per side.

4. Scrape off the burnt pepper skins (don't worry about removing every last bit—a few black specks will add character). Stem and seed the peppers and cut into 1-inch pieces.

5. Crumble the saffron threads between your thumb and forefinger and place in a small bowl with 1 tablespoon of the hot water. Let the saffron infuse for 10 minutes. Place the toasted bread in a bowl with the remaining hot water. Let soak for 5 minutes.

6. Wring the water out of the bread slices by squeezing them between your fingers. Place the bread in a food processor with the grilled peppers, saffron, and garlic. Purée to a thick paste. Add the olive oil in a thin stream with the machine running to obtain a thick creamy sauce. Add the lemon juice, cayenne, salt, and pepper. Correct the seasoning, adding salt, cayenne, or lemon juice; the sauce should be spicy and piquant. Use right away or transfer to a large jar, cover, and refrigerate. The sauce will keep for at least 3 days.

ROMESCO SAUCE

YIELD: Makes 2 cups, enough to serve 4 to 6

TRY THIS!

Born in Catalonia, this roasted nut and vegetable sauce traditionally accompanies *calçots*, a leek-like vegetable grilled with its roots, dirt, and all, and served wrapped in newspapers. But don't overlook it as a condiment for grilled meats, seafood, poultry, and vegetables. Make Catalan-style bruschetta by slathering romesco on grilled bread slices.

Romesco is one of the most distinctive grill sauces in Europe—a thick purée of charred vegetables, chiles, and nuts spiced up with a Spanish dried chile called *nyora*—or ñora (If unavailable, substitute an ancho chile.) It isn't particularly pretty to look at (like most Catalan dishes, it's brown). But it's hard to imagine a grilled food—be it from sea, land, or air—that wouldn't shine in its presence. Try it with grilled green Vidalia onions or scallions.

INGREDIENTS

3 dried nyora chiles, or 1 ancho chile, stemmed

Hot water, to soak the chiles

3 tablespoons slivered almonds

3 tablespoons hazelnuts

3 medium-size ripe tomatoes, cut in half

1 small onion, peeled and quartered

½ red bell pepper, stemmed and seeded

1 jalapeño pepper, halved and seeded

5 cloves garlic, peeled

1 slice white bread

¼ cup finely chopped fresh flat-leaf parsley

½ cup extra-virgin olive oil, preferably Spanish

2 tablespoons red wine vinegar, or more to taste

½ teaspoon sugar, or more to taste

Coarse salt (sea or kosher) and freshly ground black pepper, to taste

1. Soak the dried chile in the hot water until soft and pliable, 30 minutes. Drain, reserving the soaking liquid, and blot dry.

2. Meanwhile, set up a grill for direct grilling and preheat to medium-high.

3. Place the almonds and hazelnuts in a dry cast-iron skillet and toast on the grill until fragrant, 4 to 6 minutes, shaking the pan 2 or 3 times to ensure even browning. Transfer the nuts to a plate to cool. Rub the hazelnuts between the palms of your hands to remove the skins (don't worry about removing every last bit).

4. Brush and oil the grill grate. Arrange the tomatoes, onion, bell pepper, jalapeño, and garlic on the grill and cook until darkly browned, turning to ensure even browning, 4 to 8 minutes per side, depending on the vegetable. Transfer the vegetables to a plate and let cool.

5. Grill or toast the bread slice until darkly toasted, 1 to 2 minutes per side. Break the toast into several pieces, transfer to a food processor, add the nuts, and process to a fine powder. Add the vegetables and parsley and process to a coarse paste. Add the oil, vinegar, sugar, salt, and pepper and process to mix. The romesco should be thick but pourable; if too thick, add a little chile soaking liquid. Correct the seasoning, adding salt, sugar, or vinegar; the romesco should be highly seasoned. It tastes best served within a few hours of making.

RED CURRANT PORT SAUCE

YIELD: Makes 2 cups, enough to serve 4 to 6

If you like the robust flavor of game, this spice-scented, sweet-sour Central European sauce is your the ticket. Lemon makes it sour; currant jelly and port wine make it sweet; and orange marmalade adds the right note of bitterness to keep it from being cloying. Delicious with game, but also welcomed with pork and poultry.

TRY THIS!

If ever there were a sauce to go with spit-roasted partridge or pheasant or grilled venison or elk, this is it. Also excellent with turkey, duck, chicken, and quail.

INGREDIENTS

1 orange, scrubbed

1 lemon, scrubbed

4 whole cloves

1 cinnamon stick (3 inches)

⅓ cup red currant jelly

1 cup chicken broth

½ cup plus 1 tablespoon
port wine

⅓ cup orange marmalade

2 teaspoons cornstarch

⅛ teaspoon ground cayenne
pepper, or to taste

Coarse salt (sea or kosher) and
freshly ground black pepper,
to taste

1. Using a vegetable peeler, remove 2 strips of zest from the orange and 2 strips from the lemon. Stick 1 clove in each piece of zest.

2. Squeeze the orange and lemon and strain the juice into a medium-size nonreactive saucepan. Add the zests, cinnamon stick, red currant jelly, and stock and gradually bring to a boil over high heat. Reduce the heat to medium and simmer the mixture, uncovered, until the jelly is melted and the mixture is reduced by one quarter, about 10 minutes. Remove and discard the orange and lemon zest and cinnamon stick.

3. Add the ½ cup port and the orange marmalade and simmer, uncovered, until the marmalade is melted and the sauce is richly flavored, 5 minutes.

4. Dissolve the cornstarch in the remaining 1 tablespoon port. Stir or whisk this mixture into the sauce and simmer for 15 seconds; the sauce will thicken. Correct the seasoning, adding cayenne, salt, and pepper. Serve the sauce warm or at room temperature, or transfer to a large jar, cover, and refrigerate. The sauce will keep for at least 3 days. Warm to room temperature before serving.

TKEMALI
GEORGIAN RHUBARB SAUCE

YIELD: Makes 2 cups, enough to serve 8

The Republic of Georgia is a hotbed not only of politics but of grilling. According to Greek mythology, it was here, in the Caucasus Mountains, that Prometheus gave man the gift of fire. Barbecue sauce in this region means *tkemali*, a mouth-puckering purée of sour plums or other sour fruit, garlic, and dill. This isn't quite as strange as it sounds: After all, many Americans add lemon or pineapple to their barbecue sauce. Here's a *tkemali* made with fresh rhubarb, which comes in season just in time for the start of barbecue season. The sauce is very intense: A little dab spread on meat or used as a dipping sauce will do.

TRY THIS!

Serve *tkemali* at room temperature in tiny bowls or ramekins, providing one for each guest. It goes great with grilled chicken, pork, lamb, salmon, and vegetables.

INGREDIENTS

1 pound rhubarb, trimmed and cut into ½-inch slices

1 cup cold water

2 tablespoons fresh lemon juice, or to taste

2 tablespoons extra-virgin olive oil

3 cloves garlic, peeled and minced

1 teaspoon ground coriander

½ teaspoon coarse salt (sea or kosher), or more to taste

½ teaspoon red pepper flakes, or to taste

2 tablespoons finely chopped fresh cilantro leaves

2 tablespoons finely chopped fresh dill

½ teaspoon sugar, or more to taste

1. Combine the rhubarb and water in a heavy nonreactive saucepan and cook, uncovered, over medium heat until the rhubarb is soft and mushy, 5 to 8 minutes.

2. Stir in the lemon juice, oil, garlic, coriander, salt, and pepper flakes and simmer for 3 minutes. Transfer the mixture to a food processor and process to a smooth purée. Return the purée to the saucepan and stir in the cilantro and dill.

3. Continue simmering the sauce until thick and flavorful, 3 minutes. Correct the seasoning, adding salt or sugar to taste; *tkemali* should be highly seasoned and tart (but not unpalatably sour). Use right away or transfer to a large jar, cover, and refrigerate. The sauce will keep for up to 2 weeks.

CHARMOULA
MOROCCAN HERB AND PAPRIKA SAUCE

YIELD: Makes 1 cup, enough to serve 4

TRY THIS!

Use as a marinade, baste, and/or sauce with just about everything—from grilled chicken to lamb to seafood.

Imagine the spices of North Africa, the pungency of Italian pesto, and the tang of French vinaigrette. Put them together and you get *charmoula*. There are probably as many versions as there are Moroccan grill masters. Use the following recipe as a road map, following the spicing that suits your taste.

INGREDIENTS

½ cup chopped fresh flat-leaf parsley

½ cup chopped fresh cilantro leaves

2 cloves garlic, peeled and chopped

1 teaspoon coarse salt (sea or kosher), or more to taste

1 teaspoon sweet or smoked paprika

½ teaspoon freshly ground black pepper

½ teaspoon ground cumin

½ teaspoon red pepper flakes, or to taste

¼ cup fresh lemon juice, or more to taste

¾ cup extra-virgin olive oil

3 tablespoons water

Combine the parsley, cilantro, and garlic in a food processor and finely chop. Add the salt, paprika, pepper, cumin, pepper flakes, lemon juice, oil, and water and process to a coarse purée, running the machine in short bursts. Correct the seasoning, adding salt and/or lemon juice; the *charmoula* should be highly seasoned. Like most sauces made with fresh herbs, *charmoula* tastes best served within a few hours of making.

MOROCCAN LAMB KEBABS

YIELD: Serves 4

T our (make that lose yourself in) the souk in Fez and you'll find these tiny kebabs at grill stalls strategically located in the labyrinthine warren of alleyways. The *charmoula* does double duty as a marinade and a sauce.

YOU ALSO NEED

6- to 8-inch bamboo skewers, soaked in water to cover, then drained

INGREDIENTS

1½ pounds boneless lamb shoulder

1 medium-size onion, peeled

Coarse salt (sea or kosher) and freshly ground black pepper

Charmoula (facing page)

2 ripe red tomatoes

Pita or Moroccan bread, for serving

1. Cut the lamb into ½-inch cubes. Cut the onion in half widthwise. Cut each half in quarters and break each quarter into individual layers.

2. Thread the lamb cubes onto bamboo skewers alternating with pieces of onion. Arrange the kebabs in a baking dish or aluminum foil pan just large enough to hold them. Season on all sides with salt and pepper.

3. Spoon half of the *charmoula* over the lamb kebabs, turning the kebabs so they marinate evenly. Cover and let marinate in the refrigerator while you light the grill.

4. Make the sauce: Cut the tomatoes in half widthwise and wring out the seeds. Grate each tomato on the coarse side of a box grater into a mixing bowl. The idea is to grate the tomato flesh. Discard the skin. Stir the remaining *charmoula* into the grated tomatoes. Taste for seasoning, adding salt and pepper to taste.

5. Set up your grill for direct grilling and preheat to high. Brush and oil the grill grate.

6. Drain the kebabs and arrange them on the grate. Discard the marinade. Grill the kebabs until browned on the outside and cooked through, about 3 minutes per side. Serve with the *charmoula*-tomato sauce for spooning over them, and pita or Moroccan bread on the side.

MONKEY GLAND SAUCE

YIELD: Makes 1¼ cups, enough to serve 4 to 6

TRY THIS!

This sauce is customarily served warm or at room temperature, with grilled meats, such as steak and lamb chops. It can also be used for basting.

Spend time at a South African *braai* (barbecue) and you'll experience one of the most curiously named condiments in the world of live-fire cooking: Monkey Gland Sauce. The very notion might alarm a North American, but for a South African, nothing tastes better at a barbecue than this sweet-spicy blend of chutney, wine, and hot sauce. This version comes from the Mount Nelson Hotel in Capetown. For chutney, you could also use one of the recipes in this book (see pages 321 to 328) or a good commercial brand, like Major Grey's. The butter and liquid smoke aren't strictly traditional, but I like the way they round out the flavor of the sauce.

INGREDIENTS

1 cup fruit chutney

3 tablespoons dry red wine

3 tablespoons port wine

2 tablespoons salted butter

1 teaspoon Piri-Piri Sauce (page 289), or your favorite hot sauce

½ teaspoon freshly ground black pepper

½ teaspoon liquid smoke

Coarse salt (sea or kosher)

Combine all the ingredients in a heavy nonreactive saucepan over medium-high heat and bring to a boil. Reduce the heat to medium and simmer the sauce, uncovered, stirring often until the chutney melts and the sauce is richly flavored, 5 to 10 minutes. For a chunky sauce, serve as is. For a smooth sauce, purée in a food processor or blender. Use right away or transfer to a jar, cover, and refrigerate. The sauce will keep for several weeks; bring to room temperature before serving.

Variation

Tomato Monkey Gland Sauce: Replace half the chutney with ketchup.

ASIAN BARBECUE SAUCES

BEIJING BARBECUE SAUCE

YIELD: Makes 1 cup, enough to serve 4

Sweet-salty barbecue sauce is a constant on the world's barbecue trail. In North America we play ketchup and brown sugar against the saline flavors of salt, mustard, and Worcestershire sauce. The Chinese achieve a similar effect with hoisin sauce, a thick purplish-brown condiment made from soybean paste, sugar, and spices. Hoisin sauce varies widely in quality: Recommended brands include Pearl River Bridge, Ma Ling, Amoy, and Koon Chun.

TRY THIS!

Serve with barbecued pork and poultry. To heighten the Asian effect, rub the chicken or ribs with Sweet and Licoricey Duck Rub (page 46) before grilling or smoking.

INGREDIENTS

½ cup hoisin sauce

3 tablespoons Chinese rice wine, sake, or dry sherry

2 tablespoons soy sauce

2 tablespoons sugar or honey

2 tablespoons ketchup

1 to 2 tablespoons rice vinegar or distilled white vinegar, or to taste

1 tablespoon Asian (dark) sesame oil

1 teaspoon minced fresh ginger

1 clove garlic, peeled and minced

Combine all the ingredients in a nonreactive saucepan and slowly bring to a boil over medium heat. Reduce the heat slightly and simmer the sauce, uncovered, until richly flavored, 5 minutes. The sauce should be thick but pourable—if too thick, add a few tablespoons water. Use right away or transfer to a jar; cool to room temperature, cover, and refrigerate until using. The sauce will keep for at least 1 week.

CHINATOWN DUCK

YIELD: Serves 2 to 4

YOU ALSO NEED

A needle stuck in a cork
(the cork prevents you
from losing the needle!)

Here's the barbecue version of the crisp aromatic duck that hangs in Chinatown shop windows. Note that the Chinese like their duck well done and very tender.

INGREDIENTS

1 duck (5 to 6 pounds), cut in half, excess neck skin and any lumps of fat removed and discarded

2 tablespoons Asian (dark) sesame oil, plus more for basting

2 tablespoons Sweet and Licoricey Duck Rub (page 46), or to taste

¼ cup chopped fresh cilantro leaves

2 scallions (white and green parts), trimmed and thinly sliced on the diagonal

Beijing Barbecue Sauce (page 219)

1. Place the duck halves in a baking dish. Prick the skin (but not the meat below it) on all sides with a needle stuck in a cork. (This helps release the fat.) Brush the duck on all sides with sesame oil. Sprinkle all over with the rub. Marinate in the refrigerator for at least 4 hours or as long as overnight, uncovered.

2. Set up a grill for indirect grilling and preheat to medium-high (375°F). Brush and oil the grill grate.

3. Arrange the duck halves, cut sides down, on the grate over the drip pan away from the heat. Indirect grill the duck until the skin is sizzling and browned and the meat is cooked through, 1 to 1½ hours. Baste the duck a couple times with the sesame oil. The internal temperature in the thigh will be about 180°F when read on an instant-read thermometer.

4. Transfer the duck to a platter or plates and sprinkle with cilantro and scallions. Serve the barbecue sauce on the side.

RAITA

YIELD: Makes 3½ cups, enough to serve 6 to 8

TRY THIS!

Serve this sauce with tandoori and other Indian-style dishes, or with any type of assertively seasoned grilled meat or seafood.

VARIATIONS

Banana Raita: Substitute ground cardamom for the cumin (there's no need to toast it) and replace the tomato with a diced ripe banana. Add 1 to 2 teaspoons brown sugar for sweetness.

Pineapple Raita: Substitute 1 cup diced fresh pineapple for the tomato. Add 1 teaspoon minced fresh ginger, ½ teaspoon ground coriander, and ¼ teaspoon crumbled saffron threads.

Carrot Raita from Goa: Substitute 1 cup finely diced cooked carrots for the cucumber and tomato. Add 1 teaspoon black mustard seeds and toast them with the cumin. Add 1 seeded and minced jalapeño pepper. Carrot raita goes especially well with lamb.

The hops heads have it wrong. Beer isn't what you drink for a gullet scorched by chiles. The best way to put out the fires is with a dairy product like yogurt. Which brings us to a classic accompaniment to Indian barbecue: raita. This cooling yogurt-cucumber dip soothes taste buds inflamed by chiles and spices. The sour cream isn't strictly traditional, but I love how it enriches the sauce. Some Indian kebab wallahs add chopped fresh chiles. This partially defeats the cooling effect, but it tastes great. It's up to you.

INGREDIENTS

½ teaspoon cumin seeds

2 cups plain whole milk Greek-style yogurt

½ cup sour cream

1 cucumber, peeled, seeded, and cut into ¼-inch dice

1 ripe tomato, seeded and cut into ¼-inch dice (see page 285)

3 tablespoons chopped fresh mint

1 jalapeño pepper, seeded and minced (optional)

1 clove garlic, peeled and minced

½ teaspoon coarse salt (sea or kosher), or to taste

¼ teaspoon freshly ground black pepper

1. Heat a dry skillet over medium heat. Add the cumin seeds and toast until fragrant, 2 minutes. Let cool.

2. Grind the cumin in a spice mill, then transfer it to a bowl. Add the yogurt and sour cream and stir to mix. Stir in the cucumber, tomato, mint, jalapeño, if using, garlic, salt, and pepper. You can serve the raita right away, but it will taste better if you let the flavors meld in the refrigerator for 10 to 15 minutes. Serve it the same day you make it.

KB SAUCE
KOREAN BARBECUE SAUCE

YIELD: Makes about 6 cups, enough to serve 8 to 10

When I wrote the original *Barbecue! Bible*, few Americans had ever tasted Korean barbecue. Today, we can't seem to grill without it. Defined by the umami flavors of *gochujang* (a pungent spicy condiment made from fermented soybeans and sticky rice) and the slow burn of hot pepper powder, Korean barbecue satisfies our inexhaustible hunger for barbecue, fire, and spice. And few people do it better than Cody Taylor and Jiyeon "Jiji" Lee of Heirloom Market BBQ in Atlanta. Taylor comes from Houston, Jiji from Seoul, and their popular barbecue joint (located in a former convenience store), with its fusion of East-West flavors, typifies new school American barbecue. The poultry and pork shoulders here marinate for 48 hours in Korean *gochujang* prior to being slow-smoked over hickory and oak. The spicy pork sandwich gets a triple blast of flavor from Korean barbecue sauce, sriracha, and Thai sweet chili sauce.

TRY THIS!

You'll need to know about one special ingredient here—*gochujang*—a dark, thick, salty, spicy paste made from fermented soy beans, rice, salt, garlic, and chiles. Look for it at Korean and Asian markets, or order it from Amazon.

INGREDIENTS

1½ cups cold water

1 cup Sprite, or other lemon-lime soda

¾ cup granulated sugar

½ cup packed dark brown sugar

¼ cup soy sauce

1 tablespoon Asian (dark) sesame oil

2 cups (about 1 pound) gochujang

1 tablespoon rice vinegar, or to taste (optional)

Place the water, Sprite, sugars, and soy sauce in a heavy saucepan and bring to a boil over high heat. Boil until the sugars are dissolved, 3 minutes, whisking well. Remove the pan from the heat and let cool slightly, then whisk in the sesame oil, *gochujang*, and rice vinegar, if using. Transfer the sauce to clean jars. Covered and refrigerated, the sauce will keep for at least 1 month.

KOREAN PULLED PORK

YIELD: Serves 8 to 10

YOU ALSO NEED

Insulated rubber gloves or meat claws for pulling and shredding the pork; wood for the smoker

Gochujang and KB Sauce give this pork shoulder a slow burn and soulful umami flavors you don't normally associate with Southern-style pulled pork. For the full flavor, start 48 hours before you plan to serve the pork.

INGREDIENTS

PORK

1 Boston butt (bone-in pork shoulder roast, preferably skin-on; 5 to 6 pounds)

1 cup gochujang

2 cups KB Sauce (page 223)

4 tablespoons (½ stick) melted butter

12 sesame seed buns, split

OPTIONAL FLAVORINGS

Kimchi (page 314)

Sriracha

Thai sweet chili sauce (one good brand is Mae Ploy)

1. Place the pork in a deep baking dish. Spread the *gochujang* over it on all sides. Loosely cover with plastic wrap and marinate in the refrigerator for 24 to 48 hours; the longer, the richer the flavor.

2. Set up a smoker following the manufacturer's instructions and preheat to 250°F. Add wood as specified by the manufacturer.

3. Smoke the pork shoulder until darkly browned and crusty on the outside and the meat reaches an internal temperature of 195°F, 5 to 6 hours. Another test for doneness is to pull on the ends of any protruding bones— they should come out easily. Replenish the charcoal and wood as needed. There's no point in rushing the process: If you don't achieve the desired internal temperature, the pork won't shred properly.

4. When the pork is cooked, transfer it to a large cutting board or chopping block. *Loosely* tent with aluminum foil and let rest for 15 minutes.

5. Pull off any skin and scrape any excess fat off of the cooked pork. Crisp the skin over a hot fire on your grill, starting meat side down, or in a hot oven.

6. Pull out and discard any bones. Pull the meat into fist-size pieces, discarding any large lumps of fat. (Remember, you need some fat to keep the pork moist.) Using a cleaver or a heavy chef's knife, coarsely chop the pork—the pieces should be between ¼ and ½ inch in size. Alternatively, pull the pork into shreds using meat claws or two large forks.

7. Transfer the pork to a large mixing bowl and stir enough KB Barbecue Sauce to give the meat a terrific flavor and make it moist (but not soupy). You'll need about 1 cup.

8. Now's a good time to butter and grill or toast the buns.

9. To serve, pile the meat on the buns—about ¼ pound (¾ cup) per sandwich. Top with kimchi and drizzle with sriracha and Thai sweet chili sauce, if using. Serve the remaining KB Sauce on the side. Wow!

YAKITORI SAUCE

YIELD: Makes 2 cups, enough for 2 pounds of chicken

TRY THIS!

Brush some of this sauce on grilled chicken as a glaze (or dip the chicken in it—see facing page). Use the rest as a spooning or dipping sauce. The sauce was created for grilled chicken (in Japanese, *yaki* = grilled or roasted; *tori* = chicken), but it's also excellent with grilled beef and pork.

These tiny skewers of chicken and various chicken parts, such as skin, liver, and embryonic eggs, are enjoyed at innumerable *yakitori* parlors throughout Japan, for lunch or as a snack when workers gather for drinks and camaraderie after work. Many *yakitori* masters simmer this shiny sweet-salty sauce with a roasted chicken leg bone for extra flavor. Tradition holds for the partially cooked *yakitori* to be dipped in the sauce, then returned to the grill for glazing and final cooking. If you wish to try this, please follow the food safety notes on page 8. Mirin is sweetened Japanese rice wine. If unavailable, use sake or sherry with a little more sugar.

INGREDIENTS

1 cup soy sauce

¾ cup sugar

½ cup chicken stock or Smoked Stock (page 146)

½ cup mirin

1 scallion (white part only), flattened with a cleaver

1 strip lemon zest

1 roasted or grilled chicken leg bone (optional)

Combine all the ingredients in a nonreactive saucepan and gradually bring to a boil over medium-high heat. Reduce the heat and gently simmer the sauce, uncovered, until glossy and slightly thickened, 15 minutes, stirring with a wooden spoon as needed to prevent scorching. Discard the scallion, lemon zest, and chicken bone (if using). Use right away or transfer to a large jar, cover, cool to room temperature, and refrigerate. The sauce will keep for at least 5 days.

YAKITORI

YIELD: Serves 6 to 8

Like most denizens of Planet Barbecue, the Japanese prefer chicken thighs to breasts because they're fattier, moister, and more flavorful. Substitute 1½ pounds boneless skinless chicken breasts if you desire. While not strictly traditional, the scallions add color and flavor.

YOU ALSO NEED

6- to 8-inch bamboo skewers, soaked in water to cover for 30 minutes, then drained

INGREDIENTS

1½ pounds boneless chicken thighs

2 bunches scallions (white and green parts), trimmed

Yakitori Sauce (facing page)

1. Cut the chicken into ½-inch cubes (I like to leave the skin on). Cut the scallions into ½-inch pieces. Skewer the pieces onto small bamboo skewers, alternating chicken and scallion. Place half the *yakitori* sauce into a deep bowl. It will be used for dipping the skewers.

2. Preheat the hibachi or set up a grill for direct grilling and preheat to high. Brush and oil the grill grate.

3. Place the *yakitori* on the grate and grill until almost cooked, about 3 minutes per side.

4. Dip the skewers in one of the sauce bowls to coat the chicken and scallions, then return them to the grill. Grill for 1 minute per side, dip again, and continue grilling until the *yakitori* are browned and cooked through, 1 to 2 minutes more. If you'd rather not dip, brush the sauce on the chicken as it grills using a basting brush.

5. Serve the *yakitori* with small bowls of the remaining yakitori sauce for dipping or spooning.

NOTE: If you use the dip method and want to store any remaining sauce to use again, boil it for at least 3 minutes before storing, covered, in the refrigerator.

MISO BARBECUE SAUCE

YIELD: Makes 2 cups, enough to serve 6 to 8

TRY THIS!

Miso sauce is the traditional topping for Japanese grilled tofu and eggplant. It's fantastic on grilled salmon and other fish. I even serve it with steak.

This creamy beige condiment is one of Japan's national barbecue sauces. And like barbecue sauces in the West, it's sweet, salty, and tangy. The sweetness comes from sugar and mirin (sweet rice wine), while saltiness is one of the defining characteristics of the main ingredient, miso. Think thick sweet-salty paste of fermented soybeans and grains, and know that it tastes a lot better than it sounds. The tang comes from sake and grated lemon zest.

INGREDIENTS

1 cup white miso, at room temperature

½ cup boiling water, vegetable stock, or chicken stock

3 tablespoons sugar

3 large egg yolks, or 2 tablespoons mayonnaise

3 tablespoons sake

3 tablespoons mirin

½ teaspoon grated lemon zest

1. Pour water to a depth of 2 inches into the bottom of a double boiler or saucepan and bring it to a simmer over medium-high heat. Place the miso and boiling water in the top of the double boiler or in a smaller saucepan and whisk to mix.

2. Meanwhile, whisk the sugar, egg yolks (or mayonnaise, if using), sake, mirin, and lemon zest into the miso mixture.

3. Set the pan with the miso mixture over the simmering water. Cook the miso sauce over the simmering water until thick and creamy, 6 to 10 minutes, whisking steadily. Adjust the heat to keep the water at a simmer.

4. Remove the pan from the heat and let cool to room temperature. Transfer the miso sauce to serving bowls if serving immediately. Or transfer to a large jar, cover, and refrigerate. The miso sauce will keep for at least 3 days.

RICH PEANUT DIPPING SAUCE

YIELD: Makes 2½ cups, enough to serve 8 to 10

Peanut sauce accompanies saté in most of Southeast Asia. Here's how they make it in Penang in northern Malaysia. Penang enjoys the sort of mythical food status in Southeast Asia that New Orleans does in America. For a caramelized flavor, fry the aromatics—garlic, shallots, lemongrass—in a wok. If you're in a hurry, try the Quick Peanut Dipping Sauce on page 232.

TRY THIS!

Spoon the sauce into small bowls and serve with satés and other Asian-style barbecue.

INGREDIENTS

2 tablespoons peanut oil

2 to 3 shallots, peeled and minced (about ½ cup)

3 cloves garlic, peeled and minced

3 Thai chiles or jalapeño peppers, seeded and minced (for a spicier sauce leave the seeds in)

1 tablespoon minced fresh ginger

1 stalk lemongrass, trimmed and minced

½ cup peanut butter

1½ cups unsweetened coconut milk

3 tablespoons finely chopped fresh cilantro leaves

3 tablespoons fish sauce or soy sauce, or more to taste

2 tablespoons fresh lime juice, or more to taste

1½ tablespoons dark brown sugar

1 teaspoon ground coriander

½ teaspoon freshly ground black pepper

1. Heat the oil in a wok or nonreactive saucepan over medium heat. Add the shallots, garlic, chiles, ginger, and lemongrass and stir-fry to a rich golden brown. Reduce the heat to obtain maximum caramelization without burning. When ready, the oil will start to separate out, 8 to 10 minutes.

2. Add the peanut butter and stir-fry for 1 minute. Add the remaining ingredients and simmer the sauce until thick and richly flavored, stirring or whisking to blend, 6 to 10 minutes. Correct the seasoning, adding fish sauce or lime juice. Cool to room temperature and serve within a few hours of making.

SINGAPORE PORK SATÉ

YIELD: Serves 4 as an appetizer, 2 or 3 as a light main course

Saté is enjoyed throughout Southeast Asia. Singapore's version features a fragrant cumin-turmeric rub and soulful garlicky peanut sauce. Leave the point of the skewer exposed and use it for spearing and eating the cucumber relish.

INGREDIENTS

1 pound boneless pork shoulder, loin, or tenderloin (make sure there's some fat on it), cut into ½-inch cubes

1½ tablespoons Singapore Saté Rub (page 46), or to taste

4½ tablespoons vegetable oil

1 small sweet onion, peeled

Rich Peanut Dipping Sauce (page 229) or Quick Peanut Dipping Sauce (page 232)

Thai Cucumber Relish (page 298)

YOU ALSO NEED

6- to 8-inch bamboo skewers soaked in water to cover for 30 minutes, then drained; sheet of aluminum foil folded in thirds to make a grill shield

1. Place the pork in a medium-size bowl and stir in the saté rub, coating the meat cubes on all sides with the spices. Stir in 2 tablespoons of the oil to coat. Let marinate, covered in the refrigerator, for at least 1 hour or as long as 6.

2. Cut the onion in half widthwise. Cut each half in quarters and break each quarter into individual layers.

3. Set up a grill for direct grilling and preheat it to high. Use ½ tablespoon of the oil to brush and oil the grill grate.

4. Skewer the pork cubes on bamboo skewers, placing a piece of onion between each. Leave half the skewer without meat so you have a handle for holding the saté.

5. Arrange the satés on the grate, sliding the aluminum foil shield under the exposed part of the skewers to keep them from burning. Grill, basting with the remaining 2 tablespoons oil, until the pork is sizzling, browned, and cooked through, 1 to 2 minutes per side, 4 to 8 minutes in all. Serve with peanut sauce of choice and Thai Cucumber Relish on the side.

QUICK PEANUT DIPPING SAUCE

YIELD: Makes about 2 cups, enough to serve 6 to 8

TRY THIS!

Place the sauce in bowls or ramekins and serve as a dip for satés.

The sweet nutty flavor of Asian peanut sauce goes great with smoky charred chicken, pork, beef, and lamb. There are probably as many different recipes as there are individual saté vendors, which is to say a lot. Here's a quick peanut sauce that can be made in a food processor in a couple of minutes. For a richer, more complex sauce, see facing page.

INGREDIENTS

- 1 tomato, peeled, seeded, and diced
- 2 cloves garlic, peeled and chopped
- 2 scallions (white and green parts), trimmed and minced
- 1 to 3 Thai chiles or jalapeño peppers, seeded and chopped (for a spicier sauce leave the seeds in)
- 3 tablespoons chopped fresh cilantro leaves
- ½ cup chunky peanut butter

- ½ cup coconut milk, or chicken or vegetable broth, or more as needed
- 3 tablespoons fish sauce or soy sauce, or more to taste
- 3 tablespoons fresh lime juice, or more to taste
- 1 tablespoon light brown sugar, or more to taste
- ½ teaspoon freshly ground black pepper
- Sprigs of fresh cilantro, for garnish

Place the tomato, garlic, scallions, chiles, and chopped cilantro in a food processor and process to a fine paste. Add the peanut butter, coconut milk, fish sauce, lime juice, brown sugar, and black pepper and process to obtain a smooth sauce. Correct the seasoning, adding fish sauce, lime juice, or brown sugar. The sauce should be salty, tart, and sweet. It should also be thick but pourable; if too thick, add a little more coconut milk. Transfer the sauce to a bowl or ramekins and use right away garnished with sprigs of cilantro. It tastes best served within a few hours of making.

CAMBODIAN DIPPING SAUCE

YIELD: Makes about 2 cups, enough to serve 6 to 8

Like most Southeast Asian barbecue sauces, this dip offers an electrifying spectrum of flavors: the umami tang of fish sauce and soy sauce, the sharp bite of vinegar, the pungency of garlic, and the explosive freshness of mint. I often make a double batch of the sauce, using half as a marinade and half for dipping.

INGREDIENTS

- 3 cloves garlic, peeled and minced
- ⅓ cup sugar, or to taste
- ½ cup fish sauce
- ½ cup distilled white vinegar
- ¼ cup soy sauce
- 1 to 3 teaspoons Vietnamese chile paste, sambal oelek (Indonesian chile paste), or your favorite hot sauce
- 3 tablespoons chopped scallion greens
- 3 tablespoons chopped fresh cilantro leaves
- 3 tablespoons chopped fresh mint leaves
- ¼ cup finely chopped dry-roasted peanuts
- ¾ cup water, or to taste

Combine the garlic and 2 tablespoons of the sugar in a bowl and mash to a paste with the back of a spoon. Add the remaining sugar, fish sauce, vinegar, soy sauce, and chile paste and stir or whisk until the sugar is completely dissolved. Stir in the scallion greens, cilantro, mint, peanuts, and enough water to make a mellow sauce. Serve this sauce within a few hours of making.

TRY THIS!

Cambodians serve this big-flavored dipping sauce with thin slices of grilled beef and pork. Also great with satés, grilled tofu and vegetables, and as a dressing for grilled beef salad.

VIETNAMESE DIPPING SAUCE
NUOC MAM

YIELD: Makes 1 cup, enough to serve 4

TRY THIS!

Use this sauce as a dip for grilled thin slices of beef, pork, poultry, seafood, or tofu.

This clear delicate dipping sauce turns up wherever Vietnamese people fire up the grill. Sugar makes it sweet; lime juice and rice vinegar make it sour; fish sauce gives it that salty umami flavor so characteristic of Southeast Asian cuisines.

INGREDIENTS

1 medium-size carrot, peeled

2 tablespoons sugar

1 clove garlic, peeled and minced

3 tablespoons fresh lime juice

3 tablespoons rice vinegar

3 tablespoons fish sauce

3 tablespoons cold water, or to taste

1 small hot red or green chile, stemmed, seeded, and cut crosswise into paper-thin slices

2 tablespoons chopped fresh cilantro leaves

1. Using a vegetable peeler, cut 4 paper-thin strips of carrot. Pile these one on top of the other and, using a sharp chef's knife, cut lengthwise into paper-thin threads. Place these in a small bowl. Stir in 1 tablespoon sugar and let stand for 10 minutes. The carrot threads will soften.

2. Place the garlic and remaining sugar in a nonreactive bowl. Mash to a paste with the back of a spoon. Add the lime juice, rice vinegar, and fish sauce and stir until the sugar is dissolved. Stir in the carrot threads and sugar and enough water to make a mellow, well-balanced sauce. Taste the sauce for seasoning: It should be sweet, sour, salty, and aromatic.

3. Divide the sauce among 4 small serving bowls. Sprinkle each with thinly sliced chiles and chopped cilantro. The dipping sauce tastes best served within a few hours of making.

FISH SAUCE

A malodorous condiment made from fermented anchovies may not be your idea of a winning barbecue sauce ingredient. But for legions of grill jockeys in Thailand, Cambodia, Laos, and Vietnam, satés and other grilled foods just wouldn't taste right without it. Made from pickled anchovies, this salty brown condiment is used throughout Southeast Asia the way soy sauce is in China and Japan.

Known as *nam pla* in Thai and *nuoc mam* in Vietnamese, fish sauce serves as a marinade ingredient, as in the Basic Thai Saté Marinade (page 80), and as a table sauce (see the Cambodian Dipping Sauce on page 233). The strong, cheesy aroma can be off-putting, but the flavor quickly becomes addictive.

Fish sauce is available at Asian markets and in the Asian food section in most supermarkets. The best grades come in glass bottles. My favorite is Red Boat. (Other good brands include Flying Lion, Three Crabs, and Squid.) Avoid the cheap fish sauce sold in plastic bottles or Filipino fish sauce, which most Americans will find unpalatably fishy.

MAM NEM
VIETNAMESE PINEAPPLE-SHRIMP DIPPING SAUCE

YIELD: Makes 2 cups, enough to serve 6 to 8

The global barbecue trail abounds with fruit-based barbecue sauces. Few are as distinctive as *mam nem*, Vietnamese pineapple-shrimp sauce. Pineapple, shrimp, and fish sauce (sometimes anchovies are used) may sound like odd bedfellows—until you stop to think that American steak sauces often contain tamarind and anchovies. The sweet and salty flavors go great with grilled foods of all sorts, be they Asian or Western.

TRY THIS!

This shrimp and pineapple dipping sauce is a no-brainer for grilled seafood, but don't overlook it for grilled chicken, pork, or beef.

INGREDIENTS

2 tablespoons peanut oil

3 cloves garlic, peeled and minced

1 shallot, peeled and minced

3 Thai chiles or 1 to 2 jalapeño peppers, seeded and minced

8 ounces fresh shrimp, peeled, deveined, and minced

1 cup finely chopped fresh pineapple with juice

3 tablespoons fish sauce, or more to taste

1 tablespoon Vietnamese chile paste, or more to taste

½ teaspoon freshly ground black pepper

1. Heat the oil in a nonreactive wok or deep skillet over medium heat. Add the garlic, shallot, and chiles and stir-fry until just beginning to brown, about 1 minute. Add the shrimp and stir-fry until opaque, 1 to 2 minutes. Stir in the pineapple with the juice and bring to a boil. Stir in the fish sauce, chile paste, and pepper and bring back to a boil.

2. Reduce the heat and simmer the sauce, uncovered, until thick and richly flavored, 3 minutes. Correct the seasoning, adding fish sauce or chile paste. Let the sauce cool to room temperature before serving. The dipping sauce tastes best served within a few hours of making.

FINADENE

VINEGAR-SOY BARBECUE SAUCE FROM GUAM

YIELD: Makes 1 cup, enough to serve 4

This salty-tart condiment constitutes barbecue sauce in Guam (motto: "Where the sun first rises over American barbecue"). When it comes to counterpointing the fatty richness of barbecued pork or adding tart umami flavors to grilled seafood, few sauces can beat it. Finadene (pronounced "fee-na-DEE-nee") echoes the Filipino flavor triad of soy sauce, vinegar, and onion, but with tiny fiery chiles for heat. Some versions are quite mild; others downright incendiary—your dose of chiles should suit your heat tolerance.

TRY THIS!

Finadene is the traditional sauce served with *Chamorro* (Guamanian) barbecued chicken and pork. It also goes well with grilled lobster, prawns, and fish.

INGREDIENTS

½ cup soy sauce

3 tablespoons freshly squeezed lemon juice

3 tablespoons distilled white vinegar

¼ cup finely chopped onion

1 scallion (white and green parts), trimmed and very thinly sliced crosswise

1 to 3 Thai or other small Asian fresh chiles, thinly sliced crosswise, or ½ teaspoon red pepper flakes

Combine the soy sauce, lemon juice, vinegar, onion, scallion, and chiles in an attractive serving bowl and stir to mix with a fork. The sauce tastes best served within a few hours of making.

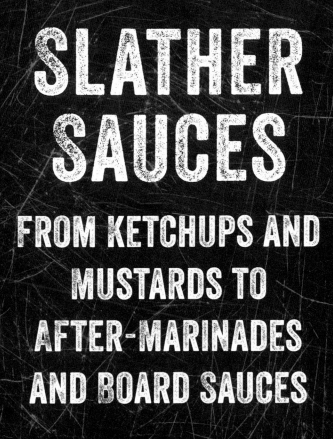

SLATHER SAUCES

FROM KETCHUPS AND MUSTARDS TO AFTER-MARINADES AND BOARD SAUCES

Slather sauces is a catchall term for the ketchups, mustards, steak sauces, egg sauces, and vinaigrettes we love to slather on burgers, chops, and steaks. You may learn some surprising things about these seemingly commonplace condiments.

That ketchup, for example, derives from a Chinese pickled fish sauce called *ket-tsiap*. That mustard was so important in the Middle Ages, Pope John XXII had his own private mustard maker. That Worcestershire sauce came from India and was a big flop before it became a commercial success. That A.1. Steak Sauce got its name from King George IV. That aïoli (garlic mayonnaise) is the focal point of a community feast in Provence.

In this chapter you'll find recipes for making ketchup and mustard from scratch, and not just the likely suspects, but exotic Banana Ketchup (page 244), Mango-Mint Ketchup (page 242), and even a Purple Mustard (page 248). Blast your guests' tongues with Hell's Fury hot sauce (page 284) and soothe them with a silky French Béarnaise Sauce (page 257). Make a simple but satisfying steak sauce from one of the most celebrated chefs in New York. And don't forget main-course vinaigrettes, which provide a health-conscious way to sauce grilled meats.

KETCHUPS, MUSTARDS, MAYONNAISE, STEAK SAUCES, AND SO ON

MADE-FROM-SCRATCH KETCHUP

YIELD: Makes 4 cups

This citrusy ketchup blurs the boundary between traditional ketchup and chutney. Orange and lemon add an unexpected tropical touch that's reinforced by the ginger and allspice. Tip o' the hat to Todd English of the popular Olives and Figs restaurants, who inspired this recipe.

TRY THIS!

Finally, a ketchup you won't be embarrassed to ask for to put on steak. Use pretty much as you would any commercial ketchup—only it's better.

INGREDIENTS

2 tablespoons extra-virgin olive oil

1 small onion, finely chopped

2 cloves garlic, peeled and minced

½ cup red wine vinegar

½ cup packed dark brown sugar

½ cup honey

½ cup fresh orange juice

1 lemon, peeled (remove both zest and rind), seeded, and diced

2 teaspoons coarse salt (sea or kosher)

2 teaspoons ground allspice

1 teaspoon ground ginger

½ teaspoon mustard powder

½ teaspoon freshly cracked black peppercorns

½ teaspoon ground cloves

1 can (28 ounces) whole plum tomatoes, juices strained and reserved, tomatoes coarsely chopped by hand or in a food processor

1. Heat the olive oil in a medium-size nonreactive saucepan over medium heat. Add the onion and garlic and cook until lightly browned, stirring with a wooden spoon, 4 minutes. Increase the heat to high, stir in the vinegar and brown sugar, and boil until the mixture is reduced by half, 3 to 5 minutes. Add the honey, orange juice, lemon, salt, spices, and reserved tomato juices. Reduce the heat to medium and gently simmer, uncovered, until syrupy, 5 minutes. Stir in the chopped tomatoes and simmer the ketchup, uncovered, until thick and flavorful, 20 to 30 minutes. The mixture should be concentrated but not too thick (think the consistency of ketchup). Add water as needed (½ to 1 cup).

2. Transfer the mixture to a food processor and process to a coarse purée. Correct the seasoning, adding salt, vinegar, or any other ingredient; the ketchup should be highly seasoned. Transfer the purée to jars, cover, cool to room temperature. Refrigerate until serving. The ketchup will keep for several weeks in the refrigerator.

MANGO-MINT KETCHUP

YIELD: Makes 4 cups

TRY THIS!

This tropical ketchup pairs well with grilled seafood and poultry, not to mention grilled or fried sweet potatoes.

Mango has been described as a peach that grew up in the tropics. We grow a lot of them in my hometown, Miami, and after we've all gorged ourselves on fresh mango and mango salsa for a few weeks, we find ways to preserve this fragrant fruit for the months when it's not in season. Enter this mango ketchup—a perfect fit for the grilled seafood so popular here in South Florida.

When a mango is ripe, it smells very fragrant and feels soft, or at least yielding, to the touch. You can't go by the color, as some mangos remain green even when ripe. Note: If you have sensitive skin, wear gloves when peeling the mangos. The oils in the mango skin can cause a poison ivy-like rash.

INGREDIENTS

3 or 4 ripe mangos
(about 2 pounds)

2 tablespoons unsalted butter

¼ cup minced shallots

½ to 1 Scotch bonnet or
habanero chile, seeded and
minced (for a hotter ketchup
leave the seeds in)

1 tablespoon minced fresh
ginger

½ teaspoon ground cinnamon

¼ teaspoon ground allspice

⅛ teaspoon ground cloves

3 tablespoons dark brown sugar,
or more to taste

3 tablespoons cider vinegar

2 tablespoons fresh lime juice,
or more to taste

1 to 2 teaspoons Caribbean-style
hot sauce, such as Matouk's
or Busha Browne's

½ teaspoon coarse salt
(sea or kosher), or more
to taste

½ teaspoon freshly ground
black pepper, or more to
taste

¼ cup chopped fresh mint
leaves

Cold water, as needed

1. Peel the mangos, cut the flesh off the seeds, and dice.

2. Melt the butter in a heavy nonreactive saucepan over medium heat. Add the shallots and cook until lightly browned, 4 minutes. Stir in the remaining ingredients, except for the mint leaves and water, and cover the pan. Cook the ketchup over medium heat, stirring often, until the mango is soft and the flavors are well blended, 10 to 15 minutes.

3. Transfer the ketchup to a blender or food processor and purée until smooth. Return the ketchup to the saucepan and stir in the mint. Simmer until the mint has lost its rawness, 2 minutes. Correct the seasoning, adding brown sugar, lime juice, salt, or pepper; the ketchup should be sweet and sour, and highly seasoned. If too thick, add a little water. Transfer the ketchup to jars, cover, cool to room temperature, and refrigerate until serving. Mango ketchup will keep for several weeks in the refrigerator.

BANANA KETCHUP

YIELD: Makes 4 cups

TRY THIS!

The musky sweetness of the bananas makes this a perfect ketchup for grilled chicken, pork, and seafood. Serve it with snapper and tuna burgers. Or use it as a dip for grilled vegetables.

Fruit ketchups belong to a centuries-old tradition. Thumb through an eighteenth-century English cookbook and you'll find recipes for ketchups made with gooseberries, walnuts, and even mushrooms. This banana ketchup explodes with the Caribbean flavors of allspice, lime, and rum.

INGREDIENTS

3 ripe bananas, peeled and diced

1 small onion, peeled and finely chopped

2 cloves garlic, peeled and chopped

½ to 1 Scotch bonnet or habanero chile, minced (for a spicier ketchup leave the seeds in)

Cold water

¼ cup fresh lime juice

¼ cup cider vinegar, or more to taste

¼ cup molasses

¼ cup golden raisins

¼ cup honey, or more to taste

¼ cup tomato paste

¼ cup dark rum, or more to taste

½ teaspoon ground cinnamon

¼ teaspoon ground allspice

¼ teaspoon ground nutmeg

¼ teaspoon ground cloves

¼ teaspoon freshly ground black pepper

¼ teaspoon ground cayenne pepper

1. Place all the ingredients, including 1 cup of the cold water, in a heavy nonreactive saucepan and bring to a boil over high heat. Reduce the heat to medium and simmer, partly covered, until the mixture is thick and richly flavored, 15 minutes.

2. Transfer the ketchup to a blender or food processor and blend until smooth. Return it to the saucepan and simmer for 3 minutes. Correct the seasoning, adding honey, rum, or vinegar; the ketchup should be highly seasoned. If too thick, add a little cold water. Transfer to jars, cover, cool to room temperature, and refrigerate. The ketchup will keep for several weeks.

KETCHUP

Ketchup could be called the lifeblood of American grilling. Not only would hamburgers look positively anemic without it, ketchup is the main ingredient in innumerable barbecue sauces, not to mention cocktail sauce and its variations, which go so well with grilled seafood. It's hard to imagine a cookout without at least one squeeze bottle of a condiment that feels as American as apple pie.

So you may be surprised to learn that ketchup originated in China and was introduced to the West more than three centuries ago. Our term ketchup (also spelled catsup and catchup) comes from a Chinese pickled fish sauce known as *ket-tsiap*. British seafarers acquired a taste for it in Malaysia in the eighteenth century. They described the condiment to cooks back home, who set out to recreate *ket-tsiap*, using more familiar English ingredients, like mushrooms and walnuts. By 1748, ketchup was so popular that the author of a book called *The Housekeeper's Pocketbook* cautioned the homemaker "never to be without [it]."

The ketchups of the eighteenth and nineteenth centuries differed dramatically from what we use today. A recipe in a 1778 cookbook, *The Experienced English House-Keeper*, called for red wine, anchovies, shallots, ginger, and "two quarts of old strong beer." The resulting ketchup could be kept for seven years, the author boasted. *The Cook's Oracle*, published in 1823, proposed a mushroom ketchup, which, when boiled down to double strength, became a "dog-sup."

Tomatoes didn't enter ketchup until 1792. Most Americans considered the tomato to be poisonous well into the nineteenth century. Only prolonged cooking, it was believed, could rid the tomato of its toxins. And ketchup was an excellent use for lengthily cooked tomatoes.

Thus reasoned an enterprising young man from Sharpsburg, Pennsylvania, who at the age of 25 began bottling and selling homemade condiments. He designed a special wide-based, slender-necked bottle for ketchup. His name was Henry Heinz. In 1876, armed with $3,000, he founded the H. J. Heinz Company, and the modern age of ketchup was born.

Today, we've come full circle. Cutting-edge grill restaurants now serve ketchups made from banana, pineapple, and even guava. Fruit ketchups capture the flavor dynamics of traditional tomato ketchups—the yin-yang of sweet and sour (sugar and vinegar) combined with the spicy sweetness of allspice and ground cloves.

SWEET AND SPICY MUSTARD

YIELD: Makes 2 cups

TRY THIS!

Use as you would any mustard, especially on grilled hot dogs, sausages, ham, and pork.

Cinnamon, allspice, and cloves lend this mustard a spicy sweetness. The mustard seeds are only partially ground, producing a speckled appearance and pleasing semisoft crunch. The actual preparation time is brief, but because of the various infusions and soakings, you'll need to budget a couple of hours from start to finish.

INGREDIENTS

2 tablespoons yellow mustard seeds

2 tablespoons brown mustard seeds

5 tablespoons mustard powder

1 cup cider vinegar

¼ cup hot water

3 tablespoons dark corn syrup

1 small onion, peeled and minced

1 clove garlic, peeled and chopped

3 tablespoons dark brown sugar

2 teaspoons coarse salt (sea or kosher)

½ teaspoon ground cinnamon

¼ teaspoon ground allspice

⅛ teaspoon ground cloves

1. Combine the yellow and brown mustard seeds, mustard powder, ½ cup of the vinegar, and the water in a small bowl and stir to mix. Let stand for 1 hour at room temperature.

2. Combine the remaining ½ cup vinegar, the corn syrup, onion, garlic, brown sugar, salt, cinnamon, allspice, and cloves in a saucepan. Bring to a boil over high heat and boil, uncovered, for 1 minute.

Remove the pan from the heat, cover, and let stand for 1 hour.

3. Combine the soaked mustard mixture and the spice mixture in a food processor and purée to a coarse paste. Transfer the purée to the top of a nonreactive double boiler placed over simmering water or to a nonreactive saucepan sitting in a sauté pan of simmering water and cook, stirring often, until thick and creamy, 15 to

20 minutes. Don't worry if the mixture isn't quite as thick as commercial mustard; it will thicken on cooling. Transfer the mustard to a large jar, cover, cool to room temperature, and refrigerate. The mustard will keep for several weeks.

CUTTING THE MUSTARD

Wherever there's a grill, there are hot dogs. (Not to mention bratwurst, chorizo, linguiça, kielbasa, and merguez.) And wherever you find grilled sausages, you'll also find a condiment that's practically as old as live-fire cooking itself: mustard.

Mustard seeds have been found at Stone Age archaeological sites across Europe. According to food historian Waverley Root, the ancient Egyptians chewed mustard grains when they ate meat and the Greeks used mustard to cure scorpion bites. Others have suggested it was the Romans who made the first spreadable mustard by mashing mustard seeds with must (unfermented grape juice). They called the preparation *mustum ardens*, literally "burning must"— the origin of our word mustard.

Mustard has other linguistic associations. "To cut the mustard" means to succeed. In France, a person with a particularly overinflated sense of self-importance thinks himself *le premier moutardier du pape*, or the Pope's mustard maker, a colorful expression dating to the papacy of Pope John XXII, who created the office of Papal Mustard Maker in the fourteenth century to keep a foolish nephew out of trouble.

Prepared mustard begins with mustard seeds, which are ground and mixed with some sort of liquid (water, wine, and/or vinegar) and seasonings (which may include salt, pepper, sugar, honey, or turmeric). White (yellow) mustard seeds produce the mildest mustard, followed by brown mustard seeds, a key ingredient in deli-style mustards. Black mustard seeds—a staple in Indian cooking—are the hottest of all. Mustard seeds can be ground to make a smooth mustard (Dijon style), or left whole to make a grainy mustard (Meaux style).

French mustards are tart and salty; German mustards, hot and sweet. American mustards owe their sharp tang to vinegar and their bright yellow color to turmeric. The Chinese mix mustard powder with water to create a sinus-blasting paste. New Englanders have a long-standing tradition of sweet mustards, flavored with maple syrup or honey.

PURPLE MUSTARD

YIELD: Makes ¾ cup

TRY THIS!

Serve as you would conventional mustard. Scandinavians like it with fish.

A reduction of red wine and port gives this mustard a vivid purple color and interesting vinous tartness. Look for purple and black mustard seeds at Indian markets or online.

INGREDIENTS

3 cups dry red wine

1 cup port wine

2 shallots, peeled and finely chopped

¼ teaspoon ground white pepper

2 sprigs fresh tarragon, finely chopped

1 tablespoon purple or black mustard seeds

1 teaspoon mustard powder

3 tablespoons Dijon mustard

Coarse salt (sea or kosher) and freshly ground black pepper, to taste

Combine all the ingredients in a heavy nonreactive saucepan and bring to a boil over high heat. Reduce the heat slightly and briskly simmer the mixture, uncovered, until only ¾ cup remains, 20 to 30 minutes.

Let cool to room temperature. Correct the seasoning, adding more salt and pepper as needed. Transfer to a jar, cover, and refrigerate. The mustard will keep for several weeks.

GREEN PEPPERCORN MUSTARD

YIELD: Makes ⅔ cup

Green peppercorns are the fresh fruit of a tropical vine native to India. (When dried, they become black peppercorns; when peeled and dried, they become white peppercorns.) They possess not just heat, but a fruity herbal quality that endears them to chefs from Penang to Paris. Sometimes you can find them fresh or frozen in Southeast Asian markets. Otherwise, look for them freeze-dried or packed in water or brine in jars.

TRY THIS!

Use as you would any mustard, keeping in mind the special affinity green peppercorns have for grilled chicken, tuna, and beef.

INGREDIENTS

3 tablespoons yellow mustard seeds

⅓ cup mustard powder

½ cup white wine vinegar

½ cup dry white wine

3 tablespoons green peppercorns, drained if water-packed

2 teaspoons honey

1 teaspoon coarse salt (sea or kosher), or to taste

1. Combine all the ingredients in a small nonreactive saucepan and stir until the mustard powder is dissolved. Let stand for 1 hour at room temperature.

2. Bring to a boil over high heat, then reduce the heat to low and gently simmer, covered, until the mustard seeds and peppercorns are semi-soft, 30 to 45 minutes. Stir often and add water as needed to keep the mustard seeds and peppercorns from drying out.

3. Transfer the mixture to a spice mill or food processor with a small work bowl and purée to a coarse paste. Don't worry if the mixture isn't as thick as commercial mustard; it will thicken on cooling. Transfer the mustard to a glass jar, cool to room temperature, cover, and refrigerate. The mustard will keep for several weeks.

HORSERADISH MUSTARD

YIELD: Makes 1½ cups

TRY THIS!

Spicier than conventional mustard and especially well suited to sausages, burgers, steak, and roast beef.

First, the good news about this fiery mustard: If you have a cold, it will blast you back to health, and if you have stuffed-up sinuses, it will clear them. The bad news is that if you've got a delicate palate, you're toast. The actual preparation takes only 15 minutes, but you'll need to allow a couple of hours from start to finish for soaking the mustard seeds and cooling the mustard. For the full effect use freshly grated horseradish root.

INGREDIENTS

¼ cup yellow mustard seeds

¼ cup brown mustard seeds, or more yellow

½ cup white wine vinegar

½ cup dry white wine

3 tablespoons hot water

2 teaspoons light brown sugar

1 teaspoon coarse salt (sea or kosher), or to taste

1 teaspoon freshly ground black pepper, or to taste

2 ounces (about 2 inches) fresh horseradish root, peeled and cut into ½-inch pieces, or 4 tablespoons prepared white horseradish

1. Combine the yellow and brown mustard seeds, vinegar, wine, and hot water in a nonreactive saucepan and bring to a boil over high heat. Remove the pan from the heat and cool to room temperature. Soak the mustard seeds at room temperature until soft, 1 hour.

2. Transfer the mustard seed mixture to a blender or food processor and process to a coarse purée. Transfer the purée to the top of a nonreactive double boiler over simmering water or to a nonreactive saucepan sitting in a sauté pan of simmering water. Add the brown sugar, salt, and pepper, and cook, stirring often, until thick and creamy, 15 to 20 minutes. Don't worry if the mixture isn't quite as thick as commercial mustard; it will thicken on cooling. Remove the pan from the heat and let the mustard cool to room temperature.

Correct the seasoning, adding salt and pepper to taste.

3. Place the horseradish in a food processor fitted with a chopping blade and finely chop. (Take care not to inhale the volatile fumes.) Add the mustard and process to mix. Transfer the mustard to a large jar, cover, and refrigerate. The mustard will keep for several weeks.

Variation

Sun-Dried Tomato Mustard: Prepare as for Horseradish Mustard, substituting 4 sun-dried tomatoes for the horseradish. Soak the tomatoes in hot water until soft, 1 hour. Chop and add them to the mustard mixture when you puréed it in Step 2.

MAYONNAISE AND COMPANY

YIELD: Makes 2 cups

Mayonnaise enters barbecue in strange but compelling ways. As the base for Alabama white barbecue sauce (made by mixing mayonnaise with vinegar and pepper). Mixed with sriracha and slathered on short rib tacos from Korean food trucks in Los Angeles. Ninety-nine percent of us (most of the time including me) will reach for a good commercial mayonnaise, like Hellmann's (aka Best Foods west of the Rocky Mountains). But as a guy who started his culinary career in Paris, I'd be remiss if I didn't point out that, if you own a food processor, you can make mayonnaise from scratch in a couple of minutes. Why would you bother? Organic eggs, Meyer lemon juice, and a premium oil, like grapeseed. That's why. Below find the original recipe, plus six flavored mayonnaises that will whisk you around the world's barbecue trail. All the variations will keep up to 3 days when stored, covered, in the refrigerator. Note: this mayonnaise contains raw eggs, so be sure to use only fresh eggs that have been kept refrigerated.

TRY THIS!

Homemade mayonnaise belongs on the usual suspects—BLTs, grilled fish, roast (or should I say smoked) beef. Call me an oddball, but I also like it on hamburgers. Simple twists will give you amazing variations: Meyer lemon juice or lime, yuzu, or calamansi juice instead of lemon. (Or replace some of the lemon juice with rice vinegar.) Olive oil or sesame oil to cut the vegetable oil. You get the idea.

INGREDIENTS

3 large eggs

1 teaspoon coarse salt
   (sea or kosher)

½ teaspoon freshly ground
   white pepper

2 cups vegetable oil or a mixture
   of half vegetable oil and half
   extra-virgin olive oil

¼ cup fresh lemon juice, or
   to taste

Crack the eggs into the bowl of a food processor, add the salt and pepper, and process to blend. With the machine running, add the oil in a very thin stream through the feed tube: The mixture will thicken. Drizzle in the lemon juice. The mixture will be thick—the consistency of, well, mayonnaise. Correct the seasoning, adding lemon juice or salt to taste. Store in a clean jar in the refrigerator; it will keep for at least 3 days.

MUSTARD MAYONNAISE

YIELD: Makes 1 cup

Great on grilled fish or chicken and fish sandwiches.

INGREDIENTS

⅔ cup mayonnaise

⅓ cup Dijon mustard, or grainy
   Meaux-style mustard

½ teaspoon grated fresh lemon
   zest (the oil-rich outer peel)

Combine the ingredients in a mixing bowl and whisk to mix.

Transfer to a clean jar, cover, and refrigerate.

HORSERADISH MAYONNAISE

YIELD: Makes 1 cup

Excellent with prime rib, roast beef, and tri-tip.

INGREDIENTS

⅔ cup mayonnaise

⅓ cup prepared or freshly grated horseradish (or as much as you can bear)

½ teaspoon grated fresh lemon zest (the oil-rich outer peel)

1 tablespoon fresh lemon juice

Coarse salt (sea or kosher) and freshly ground black pepper to taste

Combine the ingredients in a mixing bowl and whisk to mix.

Transfer to a clean jar, cover, and refrigerate.

CHIPOTLE MAYONNAISE

YIELD: Makes 1 cup

Slather on burgers and tacos, not to mention grilled chicken and shrimp.

INGREDIENTS

1 cup mayonnaise

1 to 2 canned chipotle chiles (depending on your capsaicin tolerance), minced, plus 2 teaspoons can juices

1 tablespoon fresh lime juice

Combine the ingredients in a mixing bowl and whisk to mix.

Transfer to a clean jar, cover, and refrigerate.

WASABI MAYONNAISE

YIELD: Makes 1 cup

Great on grilled tuna. Squirt flavorful zigzags from a squeeze bottle onto your favorite grilled chicken or fish.

INGREDIENTS

1 tablespoon wasabi powder

1 tablespoon warm water

1 tablespoon Asian fish sauce or soy sauce

1 cup mayonnaise

Place the wasabi and water in a bowl and whisk into a smooth paste. Let stand for 5 minutes. Add the fish sauce and mayonnaise and whisk to mix. Transfer to a clean jar, cover, and refrigerate.

SRIRACHA MAYONNAISE

YIELD: Makes 1 cup

Flavored with Thai garlic chile sauce. Terrific on just about everything.

INGREDIENTS

¾ cup mayonnaise

3 tablespoons sriracha

1 tablespoon fresh lime juice

Combine the ingredients in a bowl and whisk to mix. Transfer to a clean jar, cover, and refrigerate.

AÏOLI
GARLIC MAYONNAISE

YIELD: Makes 1 cup

The traditional condiment for grilled fish in the south of France.

INGREDIENTS

3 to 5 cloves garlic, peeled and minced

½ teaspoon coarse salt (sea or kosher)

1 cup mayonnaise

Place the garlic and salt in a bowl and mash to a paste with the back of a spoon. Whisk in the mayonnaise. Transfer to a clean jar, cover, and refrigerate.

A.1. STEAK SAUCE

The original A.1. Steak Sauce was invented by one Henderson William Brand, chef to King George IV of England from 1824 to 1831. The king relished the sauce so much, he proclaimed it "A.1." Armed with this endorsement, Brand went into the condiment business, but he turned out to be a better sauce maker than businessman. His sauce venture ended in bankruptcy. (Happily, he also found the time to write several cookbooks, including *The Complete Modern Cook.*)

In 1906, the liquor distributors G. F. Heublein & Brother acquired the exclusive right to manufacture and distribute A.1. Steak Sauce in the United States. It proved to be a lifesaver for the company, for the sauce kept Heublein afloat during Prohibition. Now, with the current enthusiasm for steak, martinis, and cigars, A.1. is enjoying a heyday.

A.1. Steak Sauce is a popular ingredient among barbecue sauce makers, who prize it for its thick consistency and complex sweet-sour flavor. A.1. owes its sweetness to corn syrup, its pucker to distilled vinegar, and its richness to puréed raisins, oranges, and tomato paste. As befits any good meat sauce, it also contains onions and garlic.

BURGER SAUCE FOR GROWN-UPS

YIELD: Makes about 1 cup

TRY THIS!

Slather on burgers, of course, and it also makes a pretty interesting sauce for tacos.

Every burger joint has its "special sauce"—which, generally, tastes like it was made by mixing the packets of ketchup, mustard, mayonnaise, and the sweet pickle relish you find by the carryout window. Add sugar or corn syrup and you've got your basic industrial burger sauce. Here's a version for grown-ups, with pickled jalapeños and Cognac—and a *lot* less sugar.

INGREDIENTS

½ cup mayonnaise

2 tablespoons Dijon mustard

2 tablespoons prepared horseradish

2 tablespoons steak sauce, such as A.1.

2 tablespoons smoky barbecue sauce (see pages 161, 166, 167, 171), or use your favorite commercial brand

2 tablespoons Cognac

2 tablespoons minced pickled jalapeños

2 tablespoons minced pimento olives

Place the ingredients in a bowl and whisk to mix. Refrigerate, covered, until using. The sauce will keep for at least 3 days.

BÉARNAISE SAUCE

YIELD: Makes about 1¼ cups

T his wantonly rich condiment is the closest the French get to steak sauce. Yes, it's rich. How could it not be? The main ingredients are egg yolks and butter. But offsetting the richness are an acidic reduction of white wine and vinegar, a blast of black pepper, and a licoricey hit of fresh tarragon. I learned to make béarnaise at La Varenne cooking school in Paris, but until writing this book, I hadn't prepared it for twenty years. It's amazing how thoroughly satisfying this classic French sauce tastes on an American grilled steak.

I won't say that béarnaise is easy to make. There are three tricks that will help ensure success. First, use a heavy non-aluminum saucepan. This keeps the eggs from scorching or discoloring. Second, have handy a bowl of ice water to shock-cool the pan if the yolks start to scramble. Finally, add the melted butter when hot but not scalding and add it in a very thin stream. Traditionally, the sauce would be strained for extra suaveness, but I like the crunchy texture of the shallots.

TRY THIS!

In France, this tarragon- and shallot-scented sauce is the classic accompaniment to filet mignon and grilled salmon. Delectable on lamb and grilled asparagus. Which just goes to show that the classics never go out of fashion.

INGREDIENTS

⅔ cup dry white wine

⅓ cup tarragon vinegar or white wine vinegar, or more to taste

½ cup minced shallots

3 tablespoons chopped fresh tarragon leaves

Freshly ground black pepper

1 tablespoon cold water

4 large egg yolks

12 tablespoons (1½ sticks) unsalted butter, melted and cooled slightly

⅛ teaspoon ground cayenne pepper

Coarse salt (sea or kosher), to taste

1. Combine the wine, vinegar, shallots, 1½ tablespoons of the chopped tarragon, and 10 grinds of pepper in a nonreactive saucepan. Bring to a boil over high heat and boil, uncovered, until only 3 tablespoons liquid remain, 5 to 8 minutes. Add the cold water and let the mixture cool to room temperature in the pan. Have ready a large bowl of ice water.

2. Add the egg yolks to the vinegar mixture and cook over medium-low heat, whisking for all you're worth, until the mixture thickens to the consistency of mayonnaise and you can see traces of the whisk on the bottom of the pan, 1 to 2 minutes. Do not overcook, or the yolks will scramble. If the yolks start to scramble, set the pan in the bowl of ice water. (A little scrambling won't harm the final sauce.)

3. Remove the pan from the heat and add the melted butter in a thin stream, whisking steadily; the sauce will thicken. Whisk in the cayenne, the remaining tarragon, and salt; the sauce should be highly seasoned. If additional tartness is desired, add a few more drops of tarragon vinegar. Keep the sauce warm on a shelf over the stove or in a pan of hot tap water. Do not attempt to warm the sauce over direct heat or in a double boiler or it will curdle. Use within 2 hours of making.

PEPPERY CREAM SAUCE
FOR GRILLED STEAK

YIELD: Makes 1 cup

If there's one dish that epitomizes the French bistro, it's *steak au poivre*—the cream sauce simmered right in the frying pan where the filet mignons were sautéed in butter. I've deconstructed the recipe, so you can serve the sauce on a steak you char on the grill.

TRY THIS!

Spooning it over any grilled steak or chop is a no-brainer, but it's also excellent on grilled tuna and other seafood and rotisserie chicken.

INGREDIENTS

2 tablespoons unsalted butter

2 to 3 shallots, peeled and minced (½ cup)

2 teaspoons coarsely crushed or cracked black peppercorns

½ cup dry white wine

¼ cup Cognac

1 cup heavy (whipping) cream

2 tablespoons Dijon mustard

Coarse salt (sea or kosher), to taste

1. Melt the butter in a heavy saucepan over medium heat. Add the shallots and peppercorns and cook until they just begin to brown, 3 minutes.

2. Add the wine and increase the heat to high. Boil until the wine is level with the shallots, 3 minutes. Add the Cognac and boil for 2 minutes. Add the cream and boil until you have about 1 cup sauce, 3 to 5 minutes. Whisk in the mustard and salt to taste; the sauce should be highly seasoned. Keep the sauce warm until serving and serve within 2 hours of making.

VOLCANIC HORSERADISH SAUCE

YIELD: Makes 2 cups

TRY THIS!

Serve Volcanic
Horseradish Sauce
in a bowl alongside
grilled steaks, chops,
and prime rib.

It's hard to imagine a more perfect English dish than roast beef (ideally spit-roasted) with horseradish sauce. This sauce owes its volcanic heat to freshly grated horseradish and its airy consistency to unsweetened whipped cream. Spoon the cool sauce on the hot meat and watch it melt into an aromatic puddle.

INGREDIENTS

1 piece fresh horseradish root (about 3 inches)

½ cup mayonnaise

¼ cup sour cream

1 tablespoon fresh lemon juice, or more to taste

½ teaspoon grated lemon zest

½ teaspoon coarse salt (sea or kosher), or more to taste

½ teaspoon freshly ground black pepper, or more to taste

¾ cup heavy (whipping) cream, chilled

1. Peel the horseradish and finely grate it by hand or in a food processor. If using the latter, cut the horseradish into ¼-inch-thick slices before processing. Transfer the horseradish to a bowl and stir or whisk in the mayonnaise, sour cream, lemon juice, lemon zest, salt, and pepper.

2. Pour the cream into a chilled mixer bowl and beat to soft peaks. Gently fold the whipped cream into the mayonnaise mixture. Correct the seasoning, adding salt or lemon juice to taste. Cover and refrigerate until using. The horseradish sauce tastes best served within a couple of hours of making.

CAJUN RÉMOULADE

YIELD: Makes 2 cups

If you like the bold flavors of Cajun cooking, you'll love this creamy sauce, which is assertively seasoned with mustard, horseradish, and Tabasco sauce and audibly crunchy with finely chopped celery and shallots. Louisianans aren't particularly famous for barbecue, but this singular sauce will spice up anything from barnyard, bayou, or ocean you may choose to throw on the grill. Try to use Creole mustard, which is sharper than your average American mustard. One good brand is Zatarain's.

TRY THIS!

A variation on classic rémoulade, this Cajun sauce goes well with grilled seafood, especially redfish, snapper, and shrimp.

INGREDIENTS

1 cup mayonnaise

¼ cup Creole mustard

2 tablespoons prepared horseradish

2 tablespoons Worcestershire sauce

2 tablespoons fresh lemon juice

1 tablespoon ketchup

1 to 2 teaspoons Tabasco sauce, or more to taste

1 tablespoon sweet paprika

½ teaspoon freshly ground black pepper

¼ teaspoon sugar

1 large shallot, peeled and minced

1 rib celery, minced

3 tablespoons finely chopped fresh flat-leaf parsley

1 scallion (white and green parts), trimmed and finely chopped

Coarse salt (sea or kosher), to taste

Combine all the ingredients in a mixing bowl and stir or whisk to mix. Correct the seasoning, adding salt or hot sauce to taste. Transfer to a large jar, cover, and refrigerate. The sauce will keep for at least 3 days.

CAJUN TUNA

YIELD: Serves 4

YOU ALSO NEED

Plancha or cast-iron skillet
(optional)

Here's a simple tuna steak that explodes with Louisiana flavors. For a blackened version, cook it on a fire-heated plancha or in a cast-iron skillet set on the grill grate. Serve with Cajun Rémoulade.

INGREDIENTS

4 tuna steaks, about 1 inch thick
(about 8 ounces each)

3 tablespoons Cajun Rub, or
to taste (page 33)

3 tablespoons unsalted butter,
melted

1 cup Cajun Rémoulade
(page 261)

1. Sprinkle the tuna steak on both sides with half of the rub. Cover and marinate in the refrigerator for 30 minutes.

2. Set up a grill for direct grilling and preheat to high. Brush and oil the grill grate. If using a plancha or cast-iron skillet, place it on the grill grate and preheat.

3. Brush each tuna steak on both sides with melted butter, then sprinkle with the remaining rub.

4. Place the tuna on the grate (or on the plancha) and grill until darkly seared on the outside, but still rare (make that raw) in the center, about 2 minutes per side, turning with tongs. Transfer the tuna to a platter and spoon the sauce on top.

JALAPEÑO TARTAR SAUCE

YIELD: Makes 1½ cups

TRY THIS!

Serve with any sort of grilled seafood.

Tartar sauce was once one of the great American condiments, but the sugary versions dispensed at fast food joints have reduced it to a culinary cliché. I say it's time to rehabilitate this classic sauce with jalapeños for heat, and without a single grain of sugar.

INGREDIENTS

- 1 cup mayonnaise
- 1 hard-cooked egg, finely chopped
- 1 tablespoon finely chopped pickled or fresh jalapeño pepper
- 1 tablespoon minced shallots
- 1 tablespoon finely chopped cornichons or dill pickles

- 1 tablespoon chopped drained capers
- 2 tablespoons mixed chopped fresh herbs, such as parsley, tarragon, basil, and/or cilantro
- Freshly ground black pepper, to taste
- 1 tablespoon fresh lemon juice, or to taste

Place the mayonnaise in a bowl and stir or whisk in the remaining ingredients, adding pepper and lemon juice as desired. The tartar sauce should be highly seasoned. Transfer to a jar, cover, and refrigerate. The tartar sauce will keep for at least 3 days.

SMOKED TOMATO SAUCE

YIELD: Makes 3 cups

Eighteenth and Vine is a rarity among barbecue restaurants: a smoke joint run by a pit master from Kansas City and a French-trained chef who worked at Le Bernardin in New York City. What results is a menu equally remarkable for its chutzpah (Kansas City-style barbecue in Dallas, really?) and its creativity and finesse. Where else would you find the likes of BBQ-braised osso buco, smoked Texas quail with eggplant cream, and a vegetarian wood-grilled cauliflower "steak"?

"Even our European-inspired dishes contain at least one element that has spent time in our wood-burning pit," says chef Scott Gottlich, who runs the restaurant (named for Kansas City's blues district) with his pit master partner Matt Dallman. True to message, the tomato sauce (sometimes served with house-made pasta) starts with fresh tomatoes, which are roasted not in the oven, but in a The Good-One barbecue pit. The smoke and fire make this one of the most interesting tomato sauces you'll ever taste.

TRY THIS!

Smoked tomatoes (through Step 3) are delectable eaten by themselves, or combine them with smoked mozzarella and fresh basil leaves to make a smokehouse Caprese salad. Serve the sauce with pasta (not grilled), seafood (definitely grilled), or smoked or grilled pork or veal chops.

YOU ALSO NEED

Wood chunks or chips, like oak or cherry

INGREDIENTS

6 plum tomatoes, cut in half lengthwise, seeds squeezed or scooped out

Coarse salt (kosher or sea) and freshly ground black pepper

2 cloves garlic, peeled and minced

2 tablespoons slivered fresh basil leaves

2 teaspoons fresh thyme leaves

3 tablespoons extra-virgin olive oil, or as needed

8 tablespoons (1 stick) unsalted butter, or half butter and half extra-virgin olive oil

1. Set up a smoker following the manufacturer's instructions (or set up a grill for indirect grilling) and preheat to 250°F. Add wood as specified by the manufacturer.

2. Arrange the tomato halves cut side-up on a sheet pan. Season each with salt and pepper. Top with garlic, basil, and thyme and 1 teaspoon olive oil. Place the tomatoes in the smoker and smoke until smoky and tender, 30 to 50 minutes.

3. Transfer the tomatoes to a cutting board and let cool. At this point they'd be incredible served as a snack or on grilled bread.

4. To continue with the sauce, peel and dice the tomatoes. Melt the butter in a heavy saucepan over medium heat. Add the tomatoes and cook until sizzling and soft, 3 minutes. Purée the sauce using an immersion blender, or transfer to a blender or food processor and purée. (For a silky-smooth sauce, strain through a sieve back into the saucepan—a step I rarely do.) Correct the seasoning, adding salt and pepper to taste.

VINAIGRETTES

BASIC HERB VINAIGRETTE

YIELD: Makes 1 cup, enough to serve 6 to 8

Here's the granddaddy of vinaigrettes—a simple emulsification of oil and vinegar, with mustard for stability and fresh herbs for fragrance. You may be surprised by the use of canola oil instead of olive oil, but bland oil is what makes a true French vinaigrette taste French. If you add the oil gradually and whisk like crazy, you should wind up with an emulsified sauce. If it breaks (the oil separates), a few tablespoons of ice water may help the ingredients re-emulsify. The vinaigrette is best served immediately after making.

INGREDIENTS

2 tablespoons Dijon mustard

½ teaspoon coarse salt (sea or kosher), or more to taste

½ teaspoon freshly ground black pepper

2 tablespoons white wine vinegar, tarragon vinegar, or Champagne vinegar, or more to taste

¾ cup canola or grapeseed oil

2 tablespoons fresh lemon juice

3 tablespoons mixed chopped fresh herbs, including chives, chervil, tarragon, and/or flat-leaf parsley

TRY THIS!

Spoon or drizzle this vinaigrette over grilled seafood, chicken, pork, veal, lamb, beef, or vegetables. You can also use part of the vinaigrette as a marinade.

WHISK METHOD: Combine the mustard, salt, pepper, and vinegar in a heavy bowl and whisk to mix. Gradually whisk in the oil in a very thin stream; the sauce should thicken. Whisk in the lemon juice and herbs. Correct the seasoning, adding more salt or vinegar.

JAR METHOD: Combine all the ingredients in a jar with a tight-fitting lid. Shake vigorously until blended.

BLENDER METHOD: Combine the mustard, salt, pepper, vinegar, and lemon juice in a blender and blend to mix. Add the oil through the hole in the blender lid, running the blender on low, then medium speed. Stop the blender and stir in the herbs by hand.

Whichever method you use, the vinaigrette tastes best within a few hours of making. Shake or whisk well before using.

BARBECUE VINIAGRETTE

YIELD: Makes 1 cup

TRY THIS!

Spoon this smoky vinaigrette over grilled or smoked seafood, poultry, meats, and yes, hamburgers.

When a conventional barbecue sauce would be too heavy—for example, on grilled seafood—use this smoky vinaigrette. For a sweeter vinaigrette, add a Kansas City–style sauce, like the Sweet-and-Smoky Barbecue Sauce (page 161), Smoke Wrangler's BBQ Sauce (page 173), or B.B.'s Lawnside Spicy Apple Barbecue Sauce (page 166); for a spicier vinaigrette, try a Texas-style sauce, like Lean-and-Mean Texas Barbecue Sauce (page 167) or the Jalapeño-Mustard Sauce (page 188).

INGREDIENTS

⅔ cup vegetable oil

3 tablespoons red wine vinegar

2 tablespoons barbecue sauce (see above)

½ to 1 teaspoon of your favorite hot sauce

½ teaspoon coarse salt (sea or kosher)

½ teaspoon freshly ground black pepper

Combine all the ingredients in a blender and blend to mix. Or combine in a jar with a tight-fitting lid and shake to mix. The vinaigrette tastes best at room temperature and used within a few hours of making. Shake or whisk well before serving.

CATALAN VINAIGRETTE

YIELD: Makes 2 cups, enough to serve 6 to 8

D ine at a grill joint in Barcelona and you'll receive a trio of sauces: Romesco (page 212), Aïoli (garlic mayonnaise, page 255), and this intensely flavorful vinaigrette. What makes it more than mere salad dressing is the addition of capers, shallots, tomato, and tiny tart cornichon pickles. This recipe comes from the lively Barcelona chophouse, La Tomaquera.

INGREDIENTS

1 clove garlic, peeled and minced

½ teaspoon coarse salt (sea or kosher), or more to taste

1 tablespoon Dijon mustard

¼ cup red wine vinegar or sherry vinegar, or to taste

1 cup extra-virgin olive oil

1 large or 2 medium-size shallots, peeled and minced (about ¼ cup)

2 tablespoons capers with juices

6 cornichons, finely chopped

1 ripe tomato, peeled, seeded, and finely chopped (see box, page 285)

Freshly ground black pepper, to taste

Place the garlic and salt in a large bowl and mash to a paste with the back of a spoon. Add the mustard and vinegar and whisk until the salt crystals are completely dissolved. Gradually whisk in the oil in a thin stream; the sauce should emulsify. Whisk in the shallots, capers, cornichons, and tomato. Correct the seasoning, adding salt, pepper, and more vinegar if needed to taste. Cover and refrigerate. Tastes best served at room temperature and used within a few hours of making. Whisk well before serving.

Variation

Some Spanish cooks enrich their vinaigrette with flat-leaf parsley and finely chopped hard-cooked eggs.

TRY THIS!

Try this vinaigrette with Spanish-style kebabs (see the recipe for Pincho Powder on page 41). Serve it with grilled salmon, shrimp, and other seafood, grilled pork chops, and even steak. It's also good on grilled vegetables—especially asparagus and mushrooms.

SESAME-GINGER-SOY VINAIGRETTE

YIELD: Makes 1¼ cups

TRY THIS!

This sesame-soy vinaigrette goes great with just about anything: grilled shellfish, chicken breasts, pork loin, steak, and of course grilled vegetables.

Here's an Asian-inflected vinaigrette based on soy sauce, sesame oil, and rice vinegar, with ginger juice for pungency and black and white sesame seeds for color and crunch. The easiest way to extract ginger juice is to press fresh ginger in a garlic press. Or you can grate the ginger on a Japanese ginger grater or the fine side of a box grater.

INGREDIENTS

1 clove garlic, peeled and minced

1 scallion (white part only), trimmed and minced

1 teaspoon ginger juice

2 teaspoons sugar

¼ cup soy sauce

¼ cup rice vinegar

5 tablespoons canola oil

3 tablespoons Asian (dark) sesame oil

¼ cup boiling water

1 tablespoon toasted sesame seeds (see box, page 112)

Combine the garlic, scallion, ginger juice, sugar, soy sauce, vinegar, and canola and sesame oils in a blender and blend at high speed until mixed. Add the water and blend for 10 seconds. Add the sesame seeds and run the blender in short bursts just to mix. Or place all the ingredients in a jar, tightly cover, and shake to mix. Store in a jar, covered, in the refrigerator for at least 3 days. Bring to room temperature and shake or whisk well before using.

ITALIAN DRESSING FROM SCRATCH

YIELD: Makes 2¼ cups

I talian salad dressing is a popular sauce and marinade base on the barbecue competition circuit. The purist in me rebels at using a bottled salad dressing, but people win big with it. Here's an Italian dressing you can make from scratch. It tastes almost factory made, only better!

INGREDIENTS

2 teaspoons cornstarch

½ cup cold water

¾ cup distilled white vinegar

2 teaspoons sugar

1 teaspoon coarse salt (kosher or sea)

2 teaspoons dried red bell pepper flakes (optional)

2 teaspoons dried garlic flakes

2 teaspoons dried oregano

2 teaspoons dried parsley

2 teaspoons freeze-dried chives

1 teaspoon dried onion flakes

1 teaspoon mustard powder

½ teaspoon red pepper flakes

½ teaspoon freshly ground black pepper

1 cup canola oil

1. Combine the cornstarch and 1 tablespoon of the water in a small bowl and stir to form a thick paste. Place the remaining water, the vinegar, sugar, and salt in a nonreactive saucepan and bring to a boil over medium heat. Stir the cornstarch mixture again and whisk it into the boiling vinegar mixture. Bring to a boil, whisking steadily; the mixture should thicken. Remove the pan from the heat and let cool to room temperature.

2. Transfer the vinegar mixture to a bowl and whisk in the remaining ingredients. Transfer to a jar, cover, and refrigerate. The dressing will keep for at least 1 week. Shake or whisk well before using.

TRY THIS!

Use this Italian dressing to marinate poultry, meat, and seafood both for grilling over a hot fire and slow-smoking in a pit. It also makes a fit dressing for the iceberg lettuce salads that go so well with steak.

SPIEDIES
CHICKEN KEBABS

YIELD: Serves 6 to 8

YOU ALSO NEED

8-inch bamboo skewers; sheet of aluminum foil folded in thirds to make a grill shield; a basting brush

I f you come from upstate New York, you probably grew up on spiedies—chicken shish kebabs—and if you live anywhere else, you probably ignore their very existence. The name spiedie comes from the Italian *spiedo*, "skewer" or "kebab." The dish was brought to America by Italian immigrants and popularized as spiedies (pronounced "SPEE-dees"). These days, they often soak in a prosaic marinade of bottled Italian dressing, but you, comrade in smoke and fire, will make that Italian dressing from scratch. I'm partial to the rich fatty thigh meat, but you can certainly make spiedies with lean chicken breast, too.

INGREDIENTS

KEBABS

1 sweet onion, peeled

2 pounds boneless chicken (if possible with some skin on it)

2 red bell peppers, stemmed, seeded, and cut into 1-inch squares

1 cup Italian Dressing from Scratch (page 271)

¼ cup extra-virgin olive oil, or as needed, for basting

SERVING

6 to 8 pita breads

1 cup plain Greek-style yogurt

2 ripe tomatoes, diced

1 cucumber, peeled and diced

1. Cut the onion in half crosswise and cut each half into 4 quarters. Break each quarter into individual layers. Finely chop the small pieces for sprinkling on the spiedies at the end.

2. Thread the chicken pieces onto bamboo skewers, alternating with pieces of onion and red bell pepper. Arrange the skewers in a glass baking dish just large enough to hold them in a single layer. Pour the Italian dressing over them. Marinate the spiedies in the refrigerator for at least 4 hours or as long as overnight (the longer, the richer the flavor).

3. Set up a grill for direct grilling and preheat to high. Brush and oil the grill grate.

4. Drain the spiedies, discard the marinade, and arrange the skewers on the grill grate, sliding the aluminum foil shield under the exposed part of the bamboo skewers to keep them from burning. Grill until browned on the outside and cooked through, 2 to 3 minutes per side, 8 to 12 minutes in all. Start basting with olive oil after 4 minutes. Transfer the spiedies to a platter or plates.

5. Lightly brush the pita breads with olive oil. Grill until warm and pliable, 1 minute per side.

6. To serve, place a spiedie on a pita bread. Fold the bread around it to hold the meat and pull out the skewer. Top with yogurt and diced tomato, cucumber, and chopped onion, if using. Roll it up and eat like a burrito.

BALSAMIC DRIZZLE

YIELD: Makes 1 cup

TRY THIS!

Drizzle this fruity sweet-sour syrup over grilled veal chops, salmon steaks (or other fish), or grilled vegetables. Or, for a surprising dessert, pour a few drops on grilled fresh fruit or smoked ice cream.

Aceto balsamico tradizionale owes its extraordinary richness (not to mention its lofty price) to a minimum of twelve years' aging in a series of barrels, each made of a different wood. There's a way to simulate the concentrated flavor of a *tradizionale* without having to mortgage your home: Boil affordable commercial balsamic vinegar down to a thick fragrant syrup.

INGREDIENTS

1 cup good commercial balsamic vinegar

⅓ cup honey

⅓ cup sugar

3 tablespoons soy sauce

Place all the ingredients in a large, heavy, nonreactive saucepan over medium heat and bring to a boil. Reduce the heat and simmer the mixture, uncovered, until reduced to 1 cup, about 15 minutes. Skim off and discard any foam that may rise to the surface. Strain the mixture into a bottle and cool to room temperature. Cork or cap the bottle. The drizzle will keep for several weeks at room temperature.

AFTER-MARINADES AND BOARD SAUCES

DECONSTRUCTED PESTO AFTER-MARINADE

YIELD: Makes enough for 4 servings of grilled poultry, meat, or seafood

D o you crave brighter, more direct flavors—and an opportunity for theatrics when you serve? Use an after-marinade—an intensely flavored mixture of condiments, herbs, and spices you apply to meat or seafood *after* it comes off the grill. Look for pointillistic flavor bursts from fresh basil, toasted pine nuts, fried garlic, cheese, lemon zest, and of course extra-virgin olive oil. You're about to get a whole new perspective on pesto.

TRY THIS!

This is a barbecue book, so this after-marinade is destined for grilled meat and seafood (like the Grilled Shrimp on page 280). But I have to tell you it makes a hell of a pasta with pesto.

INGREDIENTS

¼ cup plus 3 tablespoons extra-virgin olive oil

¼ cup pine nuts

3 cloves garlic, peeled and thinly sliced

Finely grated zest and juice of 1 lemon (about 1 teaspoon of the former and 3 tablespoons of the latter)

1 cup (about 4 ounces) freshly grated Parmigiano-Reggiano cheese

1½ cups fresh basil leaves

Coarse salt (sea or kosher) and freshly ground black pepper, to taste

1. Place the ¼ cup olive oil in a small saucepan and heat over medium heat. Add the pine nuts and garlic and sauté until golden, 2 minutes. Do not let the garlic chips burn. Pour the mixture into a large heatproof mixing bowl. Stir in the lemon zest and juice.

2. Place the cheese in a small bowl. Right before serving, slice the basil leaves into ¼-inch-wide ribbons.

3. To serve, slice the hot grilled meat or seafood (if it needs slicing). Add to the bowl with the pine nut mixture and toss to mix. Add the basil leaves and toss. Stir in the remaining 3 tablespoons of olive oil. Stir in the cheese and salt and pepper and serve at once.

AFTER-MARINADES

Conventional wisdom holds that marinades are as indispensable to barbecuing and grilling as charcoal is to fire.

According to Chris Schlesinger, conventional wisdom is wrong. Schlesinger founded the East Coast Grill in Cambridge, Massachusetts, one of the first serious modern grill restaurants in America. And he sparked a grilling revolution with his 1990 book, *The Thrill of the Grill*—one of the best books on grilling ever, and still a must-read today. Chris remains one of my barbecue heroes, so when he speaks, I listen. He definitely has some surprising things to say about marinades.

In a nutshell, Chris believes that we have it all wrong about marinades—that most of their supposed benefits get lost in the fiery heat of the grill. Take a marinade's supposed tenderizing properties. Common wisdom holds that the lemon juice, vinegar, yogurt, or other acids in marinades tenderize meat and seafood. According to Schlesinger, marinades rarely penetrate deeper than ⅛ inch, so the tenderizing effect is minimal.

Ditto for imparting flavor, as no matter how intensely spicy or fiery a marinade may be, it chiefly works at the surface level.

Even when a marinade contains such intense flavorings as fresh herbs, freshly ground spices, chiles, and soy sauce or Worcestershire sauce, the overall effect is to meld these flavors together, diminishing the taste of each, rather than letting them shine by themselves. Which may be fine for sauce making, Schlesinger says, but in grilling, you want these bold flavors to come through as individual tastes.

Which brings us to what Schlesinger calls the "post-marinade era of grilling," and what I like to call the "after-marinade." An after-marinade goes on your food *after* it's grilled, giving you separate but simultaneous blasts of chile, garlic, cilantro, lime juice, and so on. After-marinades give your food a lot more flavor, Schlesinger argues, than when the meat soaks in those ingredients beforehand. The net effect is to light up your taste buds like the fireworks of a July Fourth sky.

Almost any traditional marinade can become an after-marinade simply by applying it to the grilled sliced meat right before serving. You'll find Chris Schlesinger's recipe for Deconstructed Pesto After-Marinade on page 275 and Thai Flavor After-Marinade on the facing page.

THAI FLAVOR AFTER-MARINADE

YIELD: Makes 2 cups, enough for 3 pounds of grilled meat or seafood

After-marinades are spice, herb, and condiment blends applied to grilled foods *after* they come off the fire. Among their benefits: The individual flavors stay fresh and separate and there's no dilution of taste. This one features the bold flavors of *yam nua*—Thai grilled beef salad.

TRY THIS!

This is truly a protean seasoning—equally delectable on grilled meat, poultry, seafood, vegetables, and tofu.

INGREDIENTS

FIRST LAYER

2 cloves garlic, peeled and minced

1 piece ginger (2 inches), peeled and minced

1 piece lemongrass (the pale stalk, 2 inches), peeled and minced

2 tablespoons cilantro roots, washed and minced (optional)

5 tablespoons sugar

1 teaspoon freshly ground black pepper

½ cup fish sauce

½ cup fresh lime juice

FINISHING LAYER

½ cup fresh mint leaves

½ cup fresh Thai or Italian basil leaves

½ cup fresh cilantro leaves

1 to 2 jalapeño peppers or red serrano chiles, stemmed and thinly sliced (for a milder after-marinade, seed the chiles)

½ cup coarsely chopped dry-roasted peanuts

Hot grilled meat or seafood

1. Place the garlic, ginger, lemongrass, and cilantro roots (if using) in a large bowl and stir to mix. Sprinkle the sugar and pepper on top and mash well with the back of a spoon. Add the fish sauce and lime juice and whisk to mix. Set aside.

2. Place the mint, basil, cilantro leaves, and jalapeño in another bowl and toss to mix. Place the peanuts in a separate bowl.

3. To serve, slice the hot grilled meat or seafood. Add to the first bowl with the garlic and fish sauce and toss to mix. Stir in the second bowl with the herbs and toss to mix. Sprinkle on the peanuts and serve at once.

THAI GRILLED BEEF SALAD

YIELD: Serves 4

Yam nua—grilled beef salad—is one of the high holies of Thai cuisine. And one of the healthiest dishes on Planet Barbecue, thanks to the high proportion of plant foods to meat.

INGREDIENTS

BEEF

1 small skirt steak
(about 1 pound)

Coarse salt (sea or kosher)
and freshly ground
black pepper

2 tablespoons vegetable oil

SALAD

1 head Boston or bibb lettuce,
broken into leaves, rinsed,
and spun dry

1 cucumber, peeled (optional)
and thinly sliced crosswise

1 pint cherry tomatoes, cut in half

1 small sweet onion, peeled and
sliced paper-thin (optional)

Thai Flavor After-Marinade,
prepared through Step 2
(page 277)

1. Generously season the steak with salt and pepper on both sides. Drizzle with oil, rubbing it into the meat.

2. Set up a grill for direct grilling and preheat to high. Brush and oil the grill grate.

3. Grill the steak until cooked to taste, 3 to 4 minutes per side for medium-rare, turning with tongs. Transfer the steak to a cutting board and let rest for 1 minute.

4. Meanwhile, arrange the lettuce leaves on a platter. Top with the cucumber, tomatoes, and onion.

5. Thinly slice the steak on the diagonal and add the hot slices to the bowl with the garlic and fresh after-marinade. Toss to mix. Using tongs, arrange the steak slices with two-thirds of the after-marinade over the salad. Sprinkle the finishing layer (the mint, basil, cilantro, and jalapeños) over the steak. Sprinkle on some of the peanuts and serve with a bowl of the remaining after-marinade mixed with the remaining peanuts.

GRILLED SHRIMP
WITH DECONSTRUCTED PESTO AFTER-MARINADE

YIELD: Serves 4

YOU ALSO NEED

12-inch bamboo or metal skewers (optional)

C hef Chris Schlesinger originally created this recipe for grilled chicken thighs, but it also works wonders on shrimp. Use local shrimp with heads on when possible, for example, Key West pinks in Florida or spot prawns in the Pacific Northwest.

INGREDIENTS

2 pounds jumbo shrimp, peeled and deveined

Coarse salt (sea or kosher) and freshly ground black pepper

Red pepper flakes (optional)

2 tablespoons extra-virgin olive oil

Deconstructed Pesto After-Marinade, prepared through Step 2 (page 275)

1. Generously season the shrimp on all sides with salt, pepper, and red pepper flakes, if using. Toss with the olive oil. If grilling large shrimp, you can arrange them directly on the grill. For smaller shrimp, thread them on bamboo or metal skewers for grilling. (It's easier to turn 5 kebabs on the grill than it is 30 small shrimp.) Have the ingredients for the Deconstructed Pesto After-Marinade ready.

2. Set up a grill for direct grilling and preheat to high. Brush and oil the grill grate.

3. Arrange the shrimp on the grate and grill until sizzling and browned on the outside and cooked through, about 2 minutes per side.

4. Have ready the Deconstructed Pesto pine nut mixture and the rest of the pesto ingredients. Stir the hot shrimp into the pine nut mixture and toss to mix. Add the basil leaves and toss. Stir in the remaining 3 tablespoons olive oil. Stir in the cheese and salt and pepper to taste, and serve.

"BOARD SAUCE" FOR STEAK

YIELD: Makes enough sauce for a 1½- to 2-pound steak

Adam Perry Lang helped pioneer New York City's barbecue revolution. Here was a French-trained chef (who worked with the likes of Guy Savoy in Paris and Daniel Boulud in New York), yet when it came time to open his first restaurant, it was a barbecue joint called Daisy May's. In addition to the restaurant's exemplary ribs and brisket, with advance notice you could order a whole hog to share with friends.

Lang brings to barbecue a refined palate and decidedly unconventional thinking. When it comes to steak sauce, for example, he advocates preparing it right on the cutting board when you slice the meat. In a nutshell, you lay the steak on a bed of fresh herbs, chiles, and olive oil, which mix with the meat juices to form the sauce. The hot steak partially cooks these flavorings—yet not so long as to take away their fresh taste. He calls it a "board dressing." I call it one of the best sauce ideas to come along in a long time. Here's my version.

TRY THIS!

Originally created for steak, this board sauce goes great with grilled poultry, pork, and lamb.

INGREDIENTS

- 6 fresh sage leaves
- 1 tablespoon fresh rosemary or thyme leaves
- 2 scallions (white and green parts), trimmed, or a small bunch chives
- 1 red or green serrano chile (for a milder sauce, seed it before chopping)
- ⅓ cup really good extra-virgin olive oil
- Coarse salt (sea or kosher) and freshly ground black pepper, to taste
- 1 grilled steak (1½ to 2 pounds of your favorite, such as New York strip, rib, rib eye, or flank steak)

1. Working on a large cutting board with a well (groove around the periphery), finely chop the sage, rosemary, scallions, and chile. Season with salt and pepper and pour half the olive oil over the top. Mix with the blade of the knife.

2. Remove the hot steak from the grill and lay it directly on top of the herbs on the cutting board. Slice it thickly for tender steaks, like strip steaks, or thinly for tougher steaks, like flank. Pour the remaining olive oil over the steak and toss on the board with a spoon and the blade of the knife: The idea is to coat the steak slices with herbs and oil and mix them with the meat juices. Add salt and pepper to taste. The whole process of slicing, tossing, and serving should take only a few minutes.

HOT SAUCES

XNI PEC

YIELD: Makes about 2 cups

TRY THIS!

Serve this fiery salsa with such Yucatecan dishes as *tikin xix* (achiote-marinated grilled snapper) and *pok chuk* (brined grilled pork). Excellent with all manner of grilled seafood, poultry, or pork. If you're feeling sadistic, serve it in the salsa bowl with chips.

In the Yucatán, this sauce goes by the curious name of *xni pec*, "dog's nose," literally—a reference to its biting heat, or perhaps because it makes your nose run. Habaneros provide the fire power; tomatoes and cabbage offset the heat.

INGREDIENTS

1 small red onion, peeled and cut into small dice (about ¾ cup)

Ice water

3 tablespoons fresh sour orange juice (see box, page 194), or 2 tablespoons fresh lime juice and 1 tablespoon fresh orange juice, or more to taste

2 medium-size ripe tomatoes, peeled, seeded, and cut into small dice (about 2 cups; see box, page 285)

½ to 1 habanero or Scotch bonnet chile, seeded, and minced (for spicier xni pec, leave the seeds in)

¼ cup finely chopped green cabbage or 3 or 4 radishes, cut into small dice

3 tablespoons chopped fresh cilantro leaves

½ teaspoon coarse salt (sea or kosher), or more to taste

1. Place the onion in a bowl with ice water to cover and let soak for 10 minutes. Drain well in a strainer and gently blot dry with paper towels. Transfer the onion to a bowl and stir in the sour orange juice. Let stand for 5 minutes.

2. Gently stir in the remaining ingredients. Correct the seasoning, adding salt or sour orange juice. The salsa tastes best served within a few hours of making.

Variation

Grill masters in the Yucatán also make a grilled version of this salsa. Char the onion, tomato, and chile on the grill or in the embers, then make the salsa.

JALAPEÑO SAUCE

YIELD: Makes 1½ cups

This simple salsa turns up on the tables of grill restaurants throughout Central America. A Honduran or Salvadoran steak just wouldn't taste right without it. The salsa can be made in not much more time than it takes to pull out your food processor. Don't be intimidated by the seemingly large quantity of jalapeños: You can manage the heat by seeding the chiles.

TRY THIS!

Here's a simple fiery salsa to serve with any sort of grilled seafood, poultry, or meat.

INGREDIENTS

1 medium-size sweet onion, such as Vidalia or Walla Walla, peeled and finely chopped

8 jalapeño peppers, seeded and diced (for a hotter salsa leave some of the seeds in)

3 tablespoons chopped fresh cilantro leaves

¾ cup distilled white vinegar

2 teaspoons coarse salt (sea or kosher), or more to taste

½ teaspoon freshly ground black pepper, or more to taste

Place the onion and chiles in a food processor and process to a coarse purée. Add the cilantro, vinegar, salt, and pepper and pulse to blend. Correct the seasoning, adding salt or pepper; the salsa should be highly seasoned. The salsa tastes best served the day it's made. Transfer any leftovers to a jar, cover, and refrigerate. The salsa will keep for several days.

HELL'S FURY

YIELD: Makes about 2 cups

TRY THIS!

Use as you would any hot sauce. I like it slathered with mayonnaise (page 251) on grilled chicken and fish sandwiches.

Hell's Fury derives its heat from Scotch bonnet chiles and mustard, balanced by the musky sweetness of fresh mango. The overall effect is rather like eating a peach, taking a whiff of turpentine (mango has a turpentiney aroma), then biting a high voltage cable. Exercise caution when serving. I've given a range of chiles: Two will give you a very hot sauce; six makes it incendiary.

INGREDIENTS

1 cup diced ripe mango or frozen mango purée

2 to 6 Scotch bonnet chiles, seeded and chopped

½ small onion, peeled and chopped

3 cloves garlic, peeled and chopped

⅔ cup fresh orange juice

¼ cup Dijon mustard

¼ cup distilled white vinegar

3 tablespoons vegetable oil

3 tablespoons chopped fresh cilantro leaves

2 tablespoons light brown sugar, or more to taste

1 tablespoon fresh lime juice

2 teaspoons coarse salt (sea or kosher), or more to taste

½ teaspoon freshly ground black pepper, or more to taste

Combine all the ingredients in a nonreactive saucepan and cook, uncovered, over medium heat until the mango and onion are soft, 10 minutes. Transfer the mixture to a blender or food processor and process to a coarse or smooth purée. Correct the seasoning, adding salt or brown sugar. Transfer the sauce to a jar. You can use it right away, but the flavor will improve if you let it age for a few days. Cover and refrigerate. The sauce will keep for several weeks. Shake well before serving.

HOLY TOMATO

Tomatoes are a major player in the world of barbecue—an indispensable ingredient in the sauces, salsas, sambals, and relishes that accompany grilled meats and seafoods. Most grill jockeys are pretty informal when it comes to using tomatoes, but occasionally a recipe asks you to peel and seed them. Here's how to do it.

To peel a tomato (grill method): Preheat the grill to high. Grill the tomatoes until the skins are blackened on all sides, 6 to 8 minutes total. (Or char them in the embers.) Transfer the tomatoes to a plate to cool, then pull off the burnt skins with your fingers. Don't worry about removing every last bit of black. A little burnt skin adds character. I prefer the grill method because it gives the tomato a smoky flavor.

To peel a tomato (water method): Bring a saucepan of water to a boil. Cut a small shallow "X" on the rounded end of the tomato. Using the tip of a paring knife, cut out the stem. Plunge the tomato into rapidly boiling water for 15 to 60 seconds. (The riper the tomato, the shorter the cooking time you'll need.) Transfer the tomato to a plate and let cool. Pull off the skin with your fingers.

To seed a tomato: Cut the tomato in half crosswise and gently squeeze each half, cut side down, to wring out the seeds and liquid. If necessary, help the seeds out with a small spoon. Work over a bowl and strainer, so you can catch the tomato water for adding to drinks and soups.

One final word of advice: Avoid refrigerating tomatoes. If they're not completely ripe when you buy them, they will continue to ripen at room temperature. Cold deadens the flavor.

BRAZILIAN HOT SAUCE

YIELD: Makes 1¼ cups

TRY THIS!

Brazilians serve this fiery salsa wherever they put meat on a rotisserie over fire. Which is to say everywhere. Serve with simply grilled chicken, pork, beef, and seafood.

No Brazilian barbecue would be complete without some sort of hot sauce. The firepower in this one comes from a tiny chile called *malagueta*. Think slow burn in the front of your mouth that continues down your gullet. Look for malagueta chiles dried or packed in vinegar at Brazilian markets or online. If unavailable, use dried Chinese chiles or red pepper flakes.

INGREDIENTS

1 clove garlic, peeled and minced

1 teaspoon coarse salt (sea or kosher)

1 to 4 tablespoons dried malagueta chiles or other dried chiles, or 1 to 3 teaspoons red pepper flakes

⅓ cup fresh lime juice

½ medium-size onion, peeled and finely chopped

⅔ cup extra-virgin olive oil, preferably Portuguese

½ teaspoon freshly ground black pepper

Combine the garlic and salt in a bowl and mash to a paste with the back of a spoon. If using whole dried chiles, crumble them into the bowl with your fingers. If using red pepper flakes, there's no need to crumble them. Add the lime juice and stir until the salt is dissolved. Stir in the onion, olive oil, and black pepper. You can serve the sauce right away, but it will be even more flavorful if you let it sit for 30 minutes. Stir again with a fork before serving. This sauce tastes best served the day it's made.

Variation

Country-Style Hot Sauce: For a more elaborate country-style hot sauce, stir in 1 finely diced seeded tomato, ¼ cup finely diced green bell pepper, and 3 tablespoons finely chopped flat-leaf parsley.

PIRI-PIRI SAUCE

YIELD: Makes 1 cup

S outh Africa's contribution to the world of hot barbecue sauces is *piri-piri*. Don't let its size fool you, because the tiny piri-piri pepper is a scorcher. Piri-piri chiles may be hard to come by in the United States, unless you live near an African or Iberian market. (This sauce is very popular in Portugal, too.) Substitute fresh cayenne peppers, Thai chiles, Mexican pequins, or even red serranos. To keep the traditional heat level, I use whole chiles, but you could remove the veins and seeds if a milder sauce is desired. The mustard and garlic aren't strictly traditional, but I like the way they round out the flavor. Purists can leave them out.

TRY THIS!

This fiery sauce is popular on three continents, so you could serve it with Portuguese, Brazilian, or African-style barbecue. Spoon it over your favorite grilled seafood, chicken, pork, or beef.

INGREDIENTS

1 clove garlic, peeled and finely chopped

½ teaspoon coarse salt (sea or kosher)

1 to 3 tablespoons finely chopped fresh red chiles

1 tablespoon Dijon mustard

¼ cup white wine vinegar

¾ cup extra-virgin olive oil, preferably Portuguese

1. Place the garlic and salt in a bowl and mash to a paste with the back of a spoon. Add the chiles and continue to mash. Add the mustard. Whisk in the vinegar in a thin stream, then whisk in the oil; the sauce should thicken slightly. Or combine all the ingredients in a jar and shake to mix.

2. If not mixed in a jar, transfer to one, placing a sheet of plastic wrap between the top of the jar and the lid, cover, and refrigerate. Piri-Piri Sauce will keep for several days at room temperature. Stir before serving.

ZEHUG
YEMENITE PEPPER SAUCE

YIELD: Makes 2 cups

TRY THIS!

The obvious destination for *zehug* is Middle Eastern–style shish kebab, grilled fish, or vegetables. It also makes an electrifying dip for grilled pita bread.

Israeli grill masters heat up their food with a fiery pepper sauce called *zehug*. Brought to Israel by Yemenite Jews, *zehug* starts with puréed chiles and garlic and can be embellished with cumin, cilantro, lemon, tomatoes, or a combination of all these ingredients. To make a red *zehug*, use red chile peppers; a green *zehug*, use green.

INGREDIENTS

2 ripe tomatoes, peeled and seeded (see box, page 285)

3 to 6 red or green jalapeño peppers, seeded and coarsely chopped (for a hotter zehug leave the seeds in)

6 cloves garlic, peeled and coarsely chopped

1 teaspoon coarse salt (sea or kosher)

1 teaspoon ground cumin

1 teaspoon ground coriander

½ teaspoon freshly ground black pepper

3 tablespoons fresh lemon juice

¼ cup extra-virgin olive oil

¼ cup chopped fresh cilantro leaves

Combine all the ingredients in a blender and blend until smooth. Correct the seasoning, adding any of the ingredients as desired. Use right away or transfer to a large jar, cover, and refrigerate. The sauce will keep for at least a week.

SCOTCH BONNET SAUCE

YIELD: Makes 1¼ cups

Think of this Scotch bonnet sauce as pepper jelly on steroids. It's easy to make and even easier to customize: You could add yellow or green bell peppers for color, for example, or add an auxiliary chile, like smoky chipotle.

TRY THIS!

Serve this colorful sauce with any grilled food that benefits from heat and sweetness. Grilled shrimp, fish, and lobster come to mind; also poultry, pork, and Asian satés.

INGREDIENTS

1 large red bell pepper, stemmed, seeded, and cut into ½-inch dice

½ to 1 Scotch bonnet chile, seeded and minced (for a really spicy jam leave the seeds in)

1 cup sugar

1 tablespoon fresh lemon juice

1 teaspoon coarse salt (sea or kosher)

1 strip (2 by ½ inch) lemon zest

Combine all the ingredients in a nonreactive saucepan and cook, uncovered, over medium-low heat until the pepper pieces have released their juices and are translucent and the cooking liquid is thick and syrupy, about 15 minutes. (If the syrup gets too thick, add a few drops of water.) Transfer the mixture to a food processor and coarsely purée. (Omit the puréeing if you prefer a chunkier sauce.) Transfer to a large jar, cover, and refrigerate. The sauce will keep for several months.

SALSAS, RELISHES, SAMBALS, AND CHUTNEYS

They may not have the sex appeal of barbecue sauces or spice rubs, but a cookout wouldn't be quite complete without the electrifying condiments known variously as salsas, relishes, sambals, and chutneys.

Well, actually, salsas do have sex appeal and they aren't just limited to Mexico. Salsas add a fresh vibrant flavor to grilled food from anywhere on the planet. And speaking of anywhere on the planet, relishes range from the cucumber salads served with saté in Southeast Asia to the *encurtidos* (chopped pickled vegetables) dished up with Central American steaks to the sweet-spicy pickle relishes served on American hot dogs and brats. Our word relish seems to come from the French *relever*, "to heighten or sharpen" (as in a flavor). Relishes increase the thrill quotient of any grilled meats and seafood.

Malaysia and Indonesia are home to another great family of barbecue condiments: sambals (sometimes called *sambars*). The catchall term is broad enough to include fiery chile pastes, mild sweet peanut sauces, fragrant relishes of lemongrass and coconut milk, and even condiments made from pickled seafood. Sambals are an integral part of the barbecue scene in Southeast Asia. Tiny bowls accompany satés in Indonesia, Malaysia, and Singapore.

Chutneys are jam-like concoctions of fruits, spices, vinegar, and sugar. As the name suggests (*chatni* is a Hindi word), chutneys come from India. Actually, the spicy fruit mixtures that most Westerners think of as chutney are an English invention (or at least an English adaptation of an Indian dish). Like sambals, chutneys are made with everything from coconut to cilantro to onion. In fact, the latter are among the most popular chutneys served with kebabs and tandoori. Thick or thin, mild or spicy, savory or sweet, chutneys belong at your barbecue.

SALSAS AND RELISHES

SALSA FRESCA

YIELD: Makes 2½ to 3 cups, enough to serve 6 to 8

Salsa fresca (aka *salsa Mexicana* or *pico de gallo*) turns up wherever Mexicans fire up the grill. Make it with the sort of produce Mexicans use—shockingly red ripe tomatoes that have never seen the inside of a refrigerator, crisp sweet white onion, fresh cilantro, and fresh lime juice.

TRY THIS!

Spoon this salsa over any type of grilled seafood, poultry, or meat. Serve it on tacos and fajitas. Use it as a dip for chips or as a sauce for grilled fish or mussels or scramble it with your morning eggs.

INGREDIENTS

3 medium-size ripe tomatoes, seeded (see box, page 285)

½ medium-size onion, peeled

2 to 4 serrano or jalapeño chiles, seeded and minced (for a spicier salsa leave the seeds in)

1 clove garlic, peeled and minced (optional)

¼ cup finely chopped fresh cilantro leaves

3 tablespoons fresh lime juice, or more to taste

½ teaspoon coarse salt (sea or kosher), or more to taste

Cut the tomatoes and onion into ¼-inch dice and transfer to a bowl. Stir in the chiles, garlic (if using), cilantro, lime juice, and salt. Correct the seasoning, adding salt or lime juice; the salsa should be highly seasoned. The virtue of this salsa lies in its freshness. Serve it within 1 hour of making.

FLAME-CHARRED SALSA VERDE

YIELD: Makes 3 cups, enough to serve 6 to 8

TRY THIS!

Often served alongside *salsa fresca*, this tart green salsa has a natural affinity for seafood, poultry, and pork.

YOU ALSO NEED (OPTIONAL)

12-inch bamboo or metal skewers

Salsa verde owes its piquancy to a green fruit with a papery husk that tastes and looks like a green tomato: the tomatillo. Botanically speaking, it's a fruit, and there's something fruity about its acidity. *Salsa verde* contains virtually the same ingredients in roughly the same proportions wherever you go in Mexico, but how you cook those ingredients gives you strikingly different salsas. For the mildest *salsa verde*, you would boil the tomatillos and vegetables. For a richer flavor, roast them on a *comal* or griddle. For even more flavor, fry the resulting purée in lard. But the most dynamic flavor of all is obtained by a nontraditional method: charring the tomatillos and vegetables in the embers or on the grill.

INGREDIENTS

1 pound fresh tomatillos, husked

½ medium-size onion, peeled and cut in half

3 cloves garlic, peeled

4 serrano or 2 jalapeño chiles, stemmed

1 cup chopped fresh cilantro leaves

½ teaspoon sugar, or more to taste

½ teaspoon coarse salt (sea or kosher), or more to taste

2 tablespoons lard or olive oil

1 cup chicken broth or Smoked Stock (preferably homemade, page 146) or water, or more as needed

1. Set up a grill for caveman grilling (see Note) or preheat a conventional grill to high and set a vegetable grate on top. If you don't have a vegetable grate, thread the tomatillos, onion, garlic, and chiles on skewers.

2. Place the tomatillos in the embers or on the grate and grill until soft and lightly browned, 4 to 6 minutes, turning with tongs. Remove to a cutting board. Grill the onion, garlic, and chiles in the embers or on the grate. The garlic and chiles will take 2 to 4 minutes, the onion 6 to 8 minutes. Transfer to a cutting board and let cool. For a milder salsa, cut the chiles in half and scrape out the seeds. For a hotter salsa, leave them in.

3. Place the grilled vegetables, cilantro, sugar, and salt in a food processor or blender and process to a coarse paste.

4. Heat the lard in a deep saucepan over medium-high heat. Add the vegetable mixture and fry until thick, aromatic, and slightly darkened, 3 to 5 minutes. Stir the mixture with a long-handled wooden spoon as it fries and watch out for spatters. Stir in the broth and simmer the salsa, uncovered, until thick but pourable and richly flavored, 6 to 8 minutes. If too thick, add more stock. Correct the seasoning, adding salt or sugar. Serve at room temperature. Transfer leftover salsa to a jar, cover, and refrigerate. It will keep for at least 3 days, but may thicken. Let the salsa come to room temperature before serving and thin with water if needed.

NOTE: Caveman grilling means directly on the embers. Build a hot charcoal fire, then rake out the embers into a single layer. (A grill hoe or garden hoe works well for this.) Fan the embers to dislodge any loose ash, then lay the food directly on the embers.

SMOKY TWO-CHILE SALSA

YIELD: Makes 2 cups, enough to serve 6 to 8

Many salsas in Mexico are made not with tomatoes, but puréed dried chiles. It's a very ancient taste, almost as ancient as Mexico itself. The chile varies as you move through Mexico—fiery de árbols, mild guajillos, smoky chipotles. Use canned chipotles, so you can add a spoonful of the flavorful adobo (can juices).

TRY THIS!

Serve the salsa on tacos, fajitas, and *carne asada*, and with Mexican-style grilled meats and poultry.

INGREDIENTS

8 guajillo chiles or dried
  New Mexican red chiles
  (2½ to 3 ounces), stemmed

2 cups hot water

½ medium-size onion, peeled
  and cut in half

3 cloves garlic, peeled

1 to 2 canned chipotle chiles

2 teaspoons chipotle can juices,
  or more as needed

¼ cup chopped fresh cilantro
  leaves

1 teaspoon fresh lime juice, or
  more to taste

½ teaspoon coarse salt
  (sea or kosher), or more
  to taste

1. Place the guajillos in a bowl, add the hot water, and soak until soft and pliable, 30 minutes. Drain the chiles, reserving the soaking liquid, tear them open, and discard all of the seeds.

2. Heat a *comal* or cast-iron skillet over medium heat. Add the onion and garlic and roast, turning with tongs, until the vegetables are darkly browned. The garlic will take 2 to 4 minutes, the onion 6 to 8 minutes. Alternatively, grill the vegetables.

3. Combine the guajillos, 1 cup of the soaking liquid, the onion, garlic, chipotles, chipotle juice, cilantro, lime juice, and salt in a blender and purée until smooth. Add soaking liquid as needed to obtain a thick but pourable salsa; it should be the consistency of heavy cream. Correct the seasoning, adding lime juice or salt to taste. Use right away or transfer to a large jar, cover, and refrigerate. The salsa tastes best served within a few hours of making, but will keep for at least a week in the refrigerator.

SALSA BORRACHA
DRUNKEN SALSA

YIELD: Makes 2 cups, enough to serve 8 to 10

This is one of Mexico's most unusual salsas. Bitter and piquant, it's not the sort you'd serve with chips, but *barbacoa* (pit-roasted lamb or goat) just wouldn't taste right without it. The salsa owes its mahogany color, smoky flavor, and gentle heat to the pasilla, a wrinkled dried chile whose name literally means "raisin." (Look for it in Mexican markets or order online.) Pulque is a sort of hard cider made from agave cactus. If unavailable, substitute beer.

TRY THIS!

This salsa is traditionally served with pit-roasted lamb or goat.

INGREDIENTS

¼ cup vegetable oil

8 pasilla chiles

1 large onion, peeled and finely chopped (2 cups)

⅔ cup pulque or beer

½ cup distilled white vinegar

½ cup cold water

2 tablespoons mezcal or tequila

¼ cup chopped fresh cilantro leaves

1 teaspoon honey

1 teaspoon coarse salt (sea or kosher), or more to taste

½ teaspoon freshly ground black pepper

½ cup grated salty cheese, like Mexican queso fresco, or feta

1. Heat the oil in a skillet over medium heat to 350°F on a deep-fry thermometer. Add the chiles a few at a time and fry until puffed and crisp, 10 to 20 seconds per side. Do not let the chiles burn. Transfer them to a paper towel–lined plate and let cool. Stem the chiles and break into 1-inch pieces.

2. Add the onion to the pan and fry until golden brown, 4 to 6 minutes. Let cool slightly, then transfer the onion to a blender or food processor. Add the chiles, beer, vinegar, water, mezcal, cilantro, honey, salt, and pepper and blend to a coarse purée. Correct the seasoning, adding salt, as needed. Transfer to a jar, cover, and refrigerate. The salsa will keep for several days. Just before serving, transfer the salsa to bowls and sprinkle with grated cheese.

THAI CUCUMBER RELISH

YIELD: Makes 2 cups, enough to serve 4

TRY THIS!

Serve with saté and any
Southeast Asian-style
barbecue.

This colorful dish—part salad, part relish—traditionally accompanies saté. The cool crisp cucumber nicely counterpoints the sizzling meat. For the best results choose smallish cucumbers with a minimum of seeds.

INGREDIENTS

DRESSING

⅓ cup distilled white vinegar

⅓ cup sugar

⅓ cup cold water

Generous ½ teaspoon coarse
salt (kosher or sea)

1 clove garlic, lightly flattened
with the side of a cleaver

RELISH

2 small or 1 large cucumber

1 shallot, peeled and thinly sliced

1 hot red chile, seeded and
minced

2 tablespoons chopped fresh
cilantro leaves

2 tablespoons chopped dry-
roasted peanuts

1. Prepare the dressing: Combine the vinegar, sugar, water, salt, and garlic in a saucepan over high heat and bring to a boil. Reduce the heat and simmer until the sugar and salt are completely dissolved, 3 minutes. Transfer the mixture to a bowl and let cool to room temperature. Discard the garlic.

2. Peel the cucumber with a vegetable peeler, removing the skin in lengthwise strips about ⅛ inch apart. This will give you green stripes when you slice the cucumber. Cut the cucumber lengthwise in quarters, then crosswise into ¼-inch slices. Add the cucumber to the cooled dressing. Add the shallot, chile, and cilantro and toss to mix. Just before serving, sprinkle the relish with peanuts. You can serve the relish right away, but it will taste better if you let the flavors blend for 1 hour. Serve it the same day you make it.

HOW TO PEEL AND SEED CUCUMBERS

Recipes usually call for the cucumbers to be peeled, and from time to time, seeded. Here's how to do it.

Wash the cucumber and remove the skin in lengthwise strips with a vegetable peeler. Leave a little space between each strip—this will give you thin dark green stripes running the length of the cucumber.

When you cut the cucumber crosswise, you'll get decorative stripes on the slices.

To seed a cucumber, cut it in half lengthwise. Use a melon baller or spoon to scrape out the seeds. For half moon-shaped slices, slice each cucumber in half crosswise. For cucumber chunks, slice each half in half again lengthwise and then crosswise.

MELON-MINT RELISH

YIELD: Makes 4 cups, enough to serve 4 to 6

Here's a relish designed to keep you cool under fire. It's made with melon, or, even better, with an assortment of melons, such as watermelon, cantaloupe, and honeydew. You can cut the melon into as large or as small dice as you have patience for—I generally go ½ inch. Or cut miniature spheres with a melon baller.

TRY THIS!

This refreshing relish goes especially well with grilled chicken, smoked turkey, and seafood.

INGREDIENTS

¼ cup fresh lime juice

2 tablespoons light brown sugar, or more to taste

4 cups diced mixed ripe melons

1 cucumber, peeled, seeded, and cut into ½-inch dice (see box)

⅓ cup finely diced red onion

2 to 4 jalapeño peppers, seeded and finely chopped (for a spicier relish leave the seeds in)

2 tablespoons finely chopped candied ginger

¼ cup chopped fresh mint leaves

Combine the lime juice and sugar in a bowl and stir or whisk until the sugar is dissolved. Add the remaining ingredients and gently toss to mix. Taste and add more sugar as needed. Serve within a few hours of making.

GRILLED STRIPED BASS
WITH MELON-MINT RELISH

YIELD: Serves 4

YOU ALSO NEED

A grill basket lightly oiled with vegetable oil

Stripers or blues? These are two of the best eating fish on the planet, and for the six months a year I live on Martha's Vineyard, our local fishermen pursue striped bass and bluefish with relentless enthusiasm. I like to keep the preparation simple: a quick basting of garlic-cilantro butter or sesame oil and soy sauce. The fireworks come from a supremely refreshing Melon-Mint Relish. Note: The easiest way to grill fish that are likely to stick to the grate—like stripers and blues—is in a grill basket. (You turn the basket, not the fish.)

INGREDIENTS

2 pounds striped bass or bluefish fillets

Garlic Butter Baste (page 111) or Sesame Soy Butter Baste (page 113)

Coarse salt (sea or kosher) and freshly ground black pepper

Melon-Mint Relish (page 299)

1. Set up a grill for direct grilling and preheat to high.

2. Brush the fish on both sides with some of the Garlic Butter Baste. Season the fish on both sides with salt and pepper. Place the fish in the oiled grill basket.

3. Grill the fish until browned on the outside and cooked through (the internal temperature will be about 140°F on an instant-read thermometer), 4 to 6 minutes per side. Brush the fish with the remaining butter baste as it cooks.

4. Transfer the fish to a platter or plates. Top with Melon-Mint Relish and dig in!

SPICY CORN RELISH

YIELD: Makes 2¼ cups, enough to serve 6 to 8

TRY THIS!

This tangy relish goes well—hot or cold—with almost any sort of grilled seafood, poultry, or meat.

You can make this corn relish with grilled or ungrilled corn. (Guess which I prefer?) To grill the corn, husk it, brush it with oil or melted butter, season with salt and pepper, and grill until browned over a hot fire. The peanuts, cilantro, and chile sauce recall the sambals of Southeast Asia.

INGREDIENTS

2 ears of fresh corn (1½ cups kernels)

2 tablespoons extra-virgin olive oil

2 shallots, peeled and finely chopped

1 clove garlic, peeled and minced

2 teaspoons minced or grated fresh ginger

1 to 2 jalapeño peppers, seeded and finely chopped (for a spicier relish leave the seeds in)

½ red bell pepper, stemmed, seeded, and cut into ¼-inch dice

½ green bell pepper, stemmed, seeded, and cut into ¼-inch dice

1 ripe tomato, seeded and diced (see box, page 285)

2 tablespoons dark brown sugar, or more to taste

2 tablespoons rice vinegar or cider vinegar, or more to taste

1 to 3 teaspoons Thai chile sauce, or sriracha

Coarse salt (sea or kosher) and freshly ground black pepper to taste

3 tablespoons coarsely chopped dry-roasted peanuts

3 tablespoons chopped fresh cilantro leaves

1. Cut the kernels off the corn cobs. The easiest way to do this is to lay the ears flat on the cutting board and slice off the kernels with broad lengthwise strokes of a chef's knife.

2. Heat the oil in a skillet, preferably nonstick, over medium heat. Add the shallots, garlic, ginger, and chiles and cook over medium heat until just beginning to brown, 3 minutes. Increase the heat to high and add the corn, red and green bell peppers, and tomato. Cook until the vegetables render their juices and most of those juices evaporate, 3 to 5 minutes.

3. Add the brown sugar, vinegar, chile sauce, salt, and pepper and cook until the vegetables are tender and the relish is richly flavored, 5 minutes. Stir in the peanuts and cilantro and cook for 1 minute. Correct the seasoning, adding salt, sugar, or vinegar; the relish should be highly seasoned. The relish can be served hot or at room temperature. Transfer to jars, cover, cool to room temperature, and refrigerate. The relish will keep for at least 3 days.

CHILE PASTE AND CHILE SAUCE

These fiery sauces and pastes are found in every corner of Asia. The basic ingredients—chiles, garlic, and salt—are often placed in giant jars to pickle. The flavor of each chile paste and sauce is quite different, so you should try to use the one called for in a particular recipe. But in the end, it's better to substitute one Asian chile paste or sauce for another than do without it entirely.

Here are some of the regional variations:

- Chinese hot bean paste has the added richness of fermented soybeans.

- Thai chile pastes often contain fresh Thai basil. Sriracha (Thai chile garlic sauce) has become one of the world's bestselling hot sauces. Think of it as turbocharged ketchup.

- Indonesian *sambal ulek* (sometimes spelled *oelek*) is a bright red fiery purée of chiles, garlic, and salt.

- Vietnamese chile paste contains fiery red chiles, vinegar, and salt.

AVOCADO SALSA

YIELD: Makes 2 cups, enough to serve 4 to 6

TRY THIS!

For even more flavor, flash char the avocado halves on the grill before puréeing.

It's a short jump from everyday guacamole to this offbeat avocado salsa, but it's one that's definitely worth taking. I first tasted it atop *tacos al pastor* at the taqueria El Lago de los Cisnos (Swan Lake) in Mexico City. To get the right effect, start with ripe, squeezably soft Hass avocados.

INGREDIENTS

5 medium-size tomatillos, husked

2 to 4 jalapeño peppers, seeded and minced (for a hotter salsa leave the seeds in)

½ cup chopped fresh cilantro leaves

¼ cup minced onion

1 clove garlic, peeled and minced

1 tablespoon fresh lime juice, or more to taste

½ teaspoon sugar

½ teaspoon coarse salt (sea or kosher), or more to taste

½ teaspoon freshly ground black pepper

1 ripe Hass avocado, peeled, seeded, and diced

1. Set up a grill for direct grilling and preheat to high.

2. Place the tomatillos on the grate and grill until lightly browned on all sides and soft, 6 to 8 minutes. Transfer to a plate and let cool. (Or bring 2 cups water to a boil in a saucepan. Add the tomatillos and simmer, covered, until soft, about 4 minutes. Drain the tomatillos, reserving the cooking liquid.)

3. Transfer the tomatillos to a food processor and process to a coarse purée. Add the chiles, cilantro, onion, garlic, lime juice, sugar, salt, and pepper and process just to mix. The mixture should be soupy; if too thick, add a few tablespoons of water or tomatillo cooking liquid. Add the avocado and process just to mix. Don't overprocess; the avocado should remain in small pieces. Correct the seasoning, adding salt or lime juice; the salsa should be highly seasoned. Serve within 1 to 2 hours of making.

HOW TO PEEL, PIT, AND DICE AN AVOCADO

There are at least two ways to peel, seed, and dice an avocado. Use the first when you want large pieces of avocado. Use the second when you need smaller dice. Whichever method you use, squeeze fresh lime juice over the cut avocado to keep it from browning.

To cut large pieces: Using the tip of your knife, make four shallow lengthwise slits evenly spaced around the avocado from end to end. Pinching one corner of one section of the peel between the knife blade and your thumb, gently pull it away from the avocado—almost like peeling a banana. Repeat to remove all four sections of the skin. Cut the flesh off the pit in lengthwise strips.

To cut small pieces: Cut the avocado in half lengthwise with a single cut to the seed, rotating the knife 360 degrees while cutting. Twist the halves in opposite directions: The pit will stick out of one half. Sink the blade into the pit with a flick of the knife. Gently rotate the knife: The pit will pop out completely. Carefully remove the pit from the tip of your knife. Using the tip of the knife, make a series of cuts through the avocado flesh to, but not through, the skin. The cuts should be parallel and spaced ½ inch apart. Make another series of cuts at a 90-degree angle to the first. Use a spoon to scrape the avocado out of the skin: The flesh will come out in neat dice.

MEDITERRANEAN RELISH

YIELD: Makes 2 cups, enough to serve 4 to 6

TRY THIS!

Serve the relish with grilled lamb or seafood. For a Greek-style sandwich, grill lamb shish kebabs and wrap the meat in pita bread with Mediterranean Relish and plain yogurt.

You may have enjoyed this colorful relish on crostini. It also makes a terrific topping for grilled seafood, chicken, and veal chops.

INGREDIENTS

1 ripe red tomato, seeded and diced (see box, page 285)

1 ripe yellow tomato (or use another red tomato), seeded and diced

1 ripe green tomato, such as Green Zebra (or use another red tomato), seeded and diced

8 fresh basil leaves, thinly slivered

3 tablespoons finely chopped fresh flat-leaf parsley

3 tablespoons pitted black olives, preferably Kalamata

3 tablespoons toasted pine nuts (optional, see box, page 146)

2 tablespoons drained capers

3 tablespoons extra-virgin olive oil

1 tablespoon balsamic vinegar, or more to taste

¼ to ½ teaspoon red pepper flakes (optional)

Coarse salt (sea or kosher) and freshly ground black pepper, to taste

Combine all the ingredients in a bowl and gently toss to mix. Correct the seasoning, adding salt or vinegar; the relish should be highly seasoned. You won't need much salt, as the olives and capers are quite salty. Serve within 1 hour of making; the virtue of this relish lies in its freshness. You can have the ingredients prepped ahead of time, but mix at the last minute.

HELLAS RELISH

YIELD: Makes 3 cups, enough to serve 4 to 6

Greeks love barbecue—especially grilled lamb and seafood. They keep the accompaniments simple. Cucumber, red onion, and tomatoes are the primary ingredients in a simple relish that invariably accompanies grilled meats and seafood in Greece, particularly souvlaki (lamb shish kebab) and spit-roasted lamb. There are two ways to serve the relish—plain or dressed with olive oil and vinegar.

INGREDIENTS

1 cucumber, peeled, seeded, and cut into ¼-inch dice (see box, page 299)

1 large or 2 medium-size ripe tomatoes, peeled, seeded, and cut into ¼-inch dice (see box, page 285)

½ medium-size red onion, peeled and cut into ¼-inch dice

½ cup chopped fresh flat-leaf parsley

3 tablespoons extra-virgin olive oil, preferably Greek

2 tablespoons fresh lemon juice, or more to taste

1 tablespoon red wine vinegar

½ teaspoon dried oregano

½ teaspoon coarse salt (sea or kosher)

½ teaspoon finely ground black pepper, or more to taste

Combine the cucumber, tomatoes, onion, and parsley in a serving bowl. Add the oil, lemon juice, vinegar, oregano, salt, and pepper. Toss to mix. Correct the seasoning, adding salt or lemon juice. The virtue of this relish is its freshness. So, don't make it more than 1 or 2 hours before you plan to serve it.

TRY THIS!

Every which way you can. Spread it on grilled bread to make bruschetta. Spoon it over grilled seafood, poultry, or meat.

HELLISH RELISH

YIELD: Makes 2 cups, enough to serve 8 to 10

TRY THIS!

Serve this relish with any grilled fare you want to blast with fire—chicken, pork, lamb, seafood. Spoon it atop grilled bread to make a fire-eater bruschetta.

YOU ALSO NEED

6-inch bamboo skewers (about 10); a sheet of aluminum foil folded in three to make a grill shield (place under the exposed part of the skewers)

The relish features the smoky sweetness of fire-roasted peppers. The fire power comes from fresh habaneros. How fiery? Well, chile heat is measured in units called Scovilles. A jalapeño pepper rings in at 5,000 Scovilles. A habanero at 200,000 to 300,000. For even more heat, use a ghost or scorpion pepper (1 million Scovilles or more).

INGREDIENTS

1 medium-size onion, peeled and quartered

3 cloves garlic, peeled

1 to 3 habanero chiles

1 green bell pepper

1 red bell pepper

1 yellow bell pepper

3 tablespoons finely chopped fresh cilantro leaves

3 tablespoons extra-virgin olive oil

2 tablespoons distilled white vinegar, or more to taste

2 tablespoons fresh orange juice

1 tablespoon fresh lime or lemon juice

2 teaspoons sugar, or more to taste

Coarse salt (sea or kosher) and freshly ground black pepper to taste

1. Set up a grill for direct grilling and preheat to high.

2. Thread the onion quarters, garlic cloves, and habanero chiles onto separate skewers.

3. Brush and oil the grill grate. Grill the vegetables, including the bell peppers (these don't need to be skewered), until charred on all sides. This will take 2 to 3 minutes per side for the garlic and habaneros, 4 minutes per side for the onions, and 4 to 6 minutes per side for the bell peppers. Transfer the vegetables to a plate and let cool. When cool, remove the vegetables from the skewers.

4. Scrape the burnt skins off the vegetables. (Don't worry about removing every last bit; a few specks of black add

character.) Finely chop the onions and garlic. For a milder relish, seed the habaneros and finely chop; for a truly hellish relish, chop the habaneros, seeds and all. Stem and seed the bell peppers and cut into thin strips or ½-inch dice.

5. Place the vegetables in a nonreactive saucepan with the remaining ingredients. Bring to a boil over high heat, reduce the heat to medium, and simmer the relish, uncovered, until thick and richly flavored, about 5 minutes. Most of the juices should be absorbed by the vegetables. Correct the seasoning, adding salt, vinegar, or sugar as needed. Transfer the relish to clean jars, cover, cool to room temperature, and refrigerate. The relish will keep for several weeks.

Variation

Tuscan Relish: Omit the habaneros. Substitute flat-leaf parsley for the cilantro and balsamic vinegar for the distilled. Add 1 tablespoon drained capers and 2 tablespoons chopped black olives.

KENYAN TOMATO RELISH

YIELD: Makes 2 cups, enough to serve 4 to 6

Her name is Angela and she grew up in Nairobi, Kenya. She followed a man (long since gone) to America and now drives a cab in Atlanta. As is my wont, I asked about the barbecue of her homeland. (I ask many cabdrivers about the barbecue of his or her homeland.) According to Angela, Kenyans grill very simply—just meat and salt and fire. The creativity comes with the condiments. This fresh tomato relish will make your mouth pucker with lemon and make your brow sweat from the Kenyan version of a Scotch bonnet chile. (I call for more readily available Scotch bonnets or habaneros.) For the full effect, use vine-ripened heirloom tomatoes.

TRY THIS!

Serve with simply grilled beef, lamb, or goat. Have plenty of beer on hand to put out the fires.

INGREDIENTS

2 ripe tomatoes

½ medium-size red onion, peeled and finely chopped

½ to 2 Scotch bonnet or habanero chiles, seeded and minced (for a hotter relish leave the seeds in)

3 tablespoons chopped fresh flat-leaf parsley

3 tablespoons fresh lemon juice, or more to taste

½ teaspoon coarse salt (sea or kosher), or more to taste

½ teaspoon freshly ground black pepper

Cut the tomatoes into ¼-inch dice, working on a grooved cutting board to catch the juices. Transfer the tomatoes and juices to a serving bowl and stir in the remaining ingredients. Correct the seasoning, adding salt or lemon juice; the relish should be tart and highly seasoned. Serve within a few hours of making.

PICKLES AND SLAWS

PICKLED PLUMS

YIELD: Makes 1 quart

TRY THIS!

Pickled plums go great with all manner of smoked and grilled pork and poultry. Pickle other fruit, like peaches, nectarines, pears, etc., the same way.

Travel Planet Barbecue and you'll find pickles being served with grilled and smoked meats everywhere: from the sambal (page 318) served with saté in Bali to the sauerkraut (facing page) dished up with bratwurst in Bavaria to *encurdito* (pickled onions) piled on *tacos al pastor* in the Yucatán. The logic is simple: The acetic acid in pickles provides a welcome counterpoint to the rich fat meat. Case in point: the pickled plums served with smoked triple thick pork chops at 18th & Vine in Dallas.

INGREDIENTS

2 pounds ripe plums (purple, red, or green—your choice; what matters is ripeness)

2 cups sugar

2 cups cold water

4 whole cloves

4 allspice berries

1 cinnamon stick (3 inches)

2 cups distilled white vinegar

YOU ALSO NEED

Large clean canning jars for pickling

1. Rinse, dry, and stem the plums. Cut in quarters, discarding the pits. Place the plums in clean canning jars.

2. Make a simple syrup: Place the sugar, water, cloves, allspice berries, and cinnamon stick in a large heavy saucepan and bring to a boil over high heat. Reduce the heat and simmer the mixture until the sugar is dissolved, 2 minutes. Remove from the heat, stir in the vinegar, and let cool to room temperature.

3. Pour the pickling mixture over the plums and screw on the lids. Let pickle for at least 24 hours. (A purist might strain out the spices, but I like to find allspice berries and cloves in the pickles.) The pickled plums will keep for at least 2 weeks in the refrigerator.

JAKE'S SAUERKRAUT

YIELD: Makes about 2 quarts

Sausage without sauerkraut is like, well, choose your metaphor for indispensable. At Jake's Handcrafted in Brooklyn, my stepson Jake Klein makes and smokes all the sausage on the premises. No surprise there, but what may surprise you is the sheer ingenuity of his menu: a double-smoked brisket sausage chock-full of burnt ends; a Reuben sausage flavored with home-smoked corned beef (really!), Swiss cheese, and Russian dressing; an oysters Rockefeller sausage made with fresh oysters and spinach. Naturally, when it comes to sauerkraut, Jake

TRY THIS!

Serve Jake's Sauerkraut with all manner of grilled and smoked sausages, not to mention smoked pork chops, ham, pastrami, and corned beef. A Reuben sandwich would be poor stuff without it. Or make the cooked sauerkraut on page 313.

YOU ALSO NEED

A couple of heavy plates; a large ceramic crock (about 1 gallon); and a glass jug or large heavy-duty resealable plastic bag filled with water

ferments his own, and if you're accustomed to commercial kraut, you'll be amazed by its depth of flavor. What you may not realize is just how easy fresh sauerkraut is to make from scratch at home.

INGREDIENTS

3 pounds savoy cabbage

¼ cup coarse salt
(sea or kosher)

1 tablespoon caraway seeds
(optional)

1 tablespoon juniper berries,
lightly crushed with the
side of a knife (optional)

Spring water, if needed

1. Cut each cabbage in quarters from top to bottom using a large chef's knife. Cut out the core. Thinly slice the cabbage by hand, on a mandoline, or in a food processor fitted with a slicing disk.

2. Place the sliced cabbage in a large bowl and sprinkle with the salt, caraway seeds (if using), and juniper berries (if using). Mix well, kneading (make that pummeling) the cabbage with your hands. The idea is to bruise the cabbage so it releases its liquid more quickly. Place a heavy plate or saucepan on top to press the cabbage. Let the mixture macerate at room temperature for 3 hours. The cabbage should feel moist and spongy.

3. Transfer the salted cabbage to a clean crock and pack it as tightly as possible. Place

a clean weight, like a glass jug or a resealable plastic bag filled with water, on top. This weight helps force the water out of the cabbage and keeps it submerged under the brine (salty cabbage liquid). If after one night the cabbage is not completely submerged, add enough spring water to the crock to cover the cabbage (tap water can contain chemicals like chlorine that interfere with the fermenting process). Cover the crock with a clean cotton cloth to keep out airborne debris.

4. Allow the cabbage to ferment in a cool dark cabinet or in the basement for 2 to 4 weeks. The exact length of the fermentation depends on the time of year and precise storage conditions. Check the kraut every few days. Sometimes mold appears on the surface of the brine. Skim

as much as you can off the surface—it may break up and you might not be able to remove all of it. Don't worry about it— it's just a surface phenomenon. The sauerkraut itself is under the anaerobic protection of the brine.

5. Taste the cabbage at 1 week intervals. It will start to taste like sauerkraut after about a week. The flavor will continue to deepen over time. Once you get the amount of "funk" you like, remove the weight and drain the sauerkraut before serving. At this point, it's ready to eat and full of healthy probiotics. Stored, covered, in the refrigerator, it will keep for at least 1 month.

COOKED SAUERKRAUT

YIELD: Makes about 2 quarts

Takes Brooklyn fresh sauerkraut halfway to Alsatian choucroute. Serve with smoked and grilled sausage, ham, and other cured meats.

INGREDIENTS

2 tablespoons vegetable oil

2 teaspoons caraway seeds

1 medium-size onion, peeled and thinly sliced crosswise

2 quarts (8 cups) drained sauerkraut (page 311)

1 bottle (12 ounces) good lager-style beer

Heat the oil in a large heavy saucepan. Add the caraway seeds and cook over medium heat for 1 minute. Add the onion and cook until soft but not brown, 3 minutes. Stir in the sauerkraut and beer and gently simmer, covered, until the kraut is tender and richly flavored, 20 to 30 minutes. Serve warm or cooled to room temperature. Any leftovers will keep, covered, in the refrigerator for at least 3 days.

KIMCHI

YIELD: Makes about 1 quart

TRY THIS!

Serve kimchi with *bul kogi* (Korean grilled rib eye) or *kalbi ku*i (Korean grilled short ribs). Pile it with grilled beef or pork on tortillas to make Korean-style tacos. Serve it with the Korean Pulled Pork on page 224. It goes equally well with Western-style slow-smoked proteins, such as pork shoulder, brisket, and pork or lamb belly.

Kimchi (sometimes spelled kimchee) looms large in Korea's foodie universe, playing the role that sauerkraut (page 311) does in Germany, pickles do in Eastern Europe, and *encurdito* (vinegar-cured vegetables) does in Latin America. That is to say, a sour-spicy condiment loaded with soulful fermented flavors that go great with Asian grilled meats.

Koreans make literally hundreds of different kinds of kimchi, ranging from the familiar napa cabbage version to exotic fermented seafood kimchis, each with its own unique constellation of flavors. Like all fermented vegetables, it is alive and changing—crunchy and tart when fresh, and acquiring deep funky flavors as it ages. Sure, you can buy kimchi at Asian markets and in the produce section of many supermarkets, but it's easy—and satisfying—to make at home. You'll need one special ingredient—*gochugaru* (Korean chile flakes), which you can purchase at a Korean market or online from Amazon. For a vegetarian version, substitute miso for the fish sauce. Here's how my assistant, Nancy Loseke—a Korean food fanatic—makes it.

INGREDIENTS

1 head napa cabbage (about 1¼ pounds)

2 carrots, peeled and cut on the diagonal into ½-inch slices

2 pickling cucumbers, scrubbed and cut on the diagonal into ½-inch slices

1 red bell pepper, cored and cut into ½-inch-wide strips

¼ cup coarse salt (sea or kosher) plus 1 tablespoon

Spring water, as needed

3 cloves garlic, peeled and minced

4 scallions (white and green parts), trimmed and cut diagonally into ½-inch slices

1 piece fresh ginger (1 inch), peeled and minced

3 to 5 tablespoons gochugaru (Korean chile flakes—in a pinch, you could use hot paprika)

2 teaspoons fish sauce, or 1 tablespoon Asian oyster-flavored sauce

1. Remove and discard any blemished leaves from the napa cabbage. Cut the cabbage lengthwise in quarters and remove the core. Cut crosswise into 1-inch-wide slices and place in a large bowl. Add the carrots, cucumbers, and bell pepper.

2. Pour the ¼ cup salt over the vegetables and massage with your hands until the cabbage softens slightly. You may want to wear gloves. Pour 3 cups spring water (tap water can contain chemicals like chlorine that interfere with the fermenting process) over the vegetables and let sit at room temperature for 3 hours, stirring occasionally. Place a resealable plastic bag filled with water on top to keep the vegetables submerged in the brine.

3. Drain the vegetables in a colander. Rinse and drain again. Return the vegetables to the bowl. Stir in the garlic, scallions, and ginger.

4. Make the chile paste: In a small bowl, combine the *gochugaru*, remaining 1 tablespoon salt, fish sauce, and ¼ cup spring water and whisk to mix. Pour over the vegetable mixture. With gloved hands, gently massage the mixture until the chile paste coats the vegetables. Pack tightly into the canning jar leaving 1 inch of headroom. Seal the jar.

5. Leave the jar on the countertop for 24 hours, occasionally turning it upside down, then right side up again to distribute the juices. The vegetables will "melt" as they ferment; you'll notice the liquids bubbling slightly.

6. Transfer the kimchi to the refrigerator and ferment for at least 1 week. Loosen, then retighten the lid each day to release the gases built up through lacto-fermentation. The kimchi will be ready after 1 week, but you can continue to ferment it for up to a month in the refrigerator—the longer, the tarter and richer the flavor. Refrigerated, it will keep for several months.

YOU ALSO NEED

A sterilized 1-quart canning jar, a fermentation jar, or a stoneware crock; food-safe gloves (optional)

ONE SLAW
THREE DRESSINGS

TRY THIS!

Serve vinegar slaw atop
pulled pork on a bun
to make a traditional
Carolina pork sandwich;
do the same with mustard
slaw and mustard sauce
to make a Georgia-style
pork sandwich. All three
slaws go great with
barbecued brisket, ribs,
chicken, and fish.

Coleslaw has accompanied American barbecue for as long as there's been an America—and likely before. A "Koolsla" (from the Dutch words *kool* for cabbage and *sla* for salad) appears in the first American cookbook, *American Cookery,* written by Amelia Simmons and published in Hartford, Connecticut, in 1796. But which slaw to serve depends on where you smoke and eat your meat. Vinegar slaw turns up, logically, in North Carolina, flavored with that state's distinctive vinegar barbecue sauce (page 186). Mustard slaw goes on pork sandwiches in South Carolina and Georgia, home of an equally unique mustard-based barbecue sauce (page 188). Creamy coleslaw is popular just about everywhere else.

BASIC SLAW MIXTURE

YIELD: Serves 4 to 6 (more if used on a sandwich)

INGREDIENTS

1 small or ½ large green
cabbage, cored and finely
chopped or shredded
(5 cups)

1 carrot, peeled and coarsely
grated

1 apple, peeled, cored, and
coarsely grated

⅓ cup golden or dark raisins
(optional)

Creamy Slaw Dressing or
Vinegar Slaw Dressing or
Mustard Slaw Dressing
(recipes follow)

Place the cabbage, carrot, apple, and raisins (if using) in a large mixing bowl and stir to mix.

Add the dressing of choice and stir to mix.

CREAMY COLESLAW DRESSING

YIELD: Makes about 1 cup

INGREDIENTS

⅔ cup mayonnaise, preferably homemade (page 251), or Hellmann's (aka Best Foods)

3 tablespoons sugar

2 tablespoons distilled vinegar, or to taste

1 teaspoon poppy seeds (optional)

½ teaspoon celery seeds

½ teaspoon freshly ground black pepper

Coarse salt (sea or kosher), to taste

Place the mayonnaise in a large bowl. Whisk in the sugar, vinegar, poppy and celery seeds, and pepper. Add salt to taste: The slaw should be highly seasoned.

VINEGAR COLESLAW DRESSING

YIELD: Makes about ¾ cup

INGREDIENTS

⅔ cup distilled white vinegar

1 to 3 tablespoons brown sugar (light or dark), or to taste

2 teaspoons red pepper flakes

1½ teaspoons coarse salt (sea or kosher)

1 teaspoon freshly ground black pepper

1 tablespoon hot sauce, such as Crystal, or to taste

Several tablespoons water (optional)

Combine the vinegar, sugar, red pepper flakes, salt, pepper, and hot sauce in a mixing bowl and whisk until the sugar and salt are dissolved. Correct the seasoning, adding sugar, salt, or hot sauce to taste; the dressing should be piquant but not quite sour. If too acidic, whisk in more sugar or a few tablespoons of water.

MUSTARD COLESLAW DRESSING

YIELD: Makes about 1 cup

INGREDIENTS

⅓ cup Dijon mustard

3 tablespoons sugar, or to taste

3 tablespoons vegetable oil

2 tablespoons distilled white vinegar, or to taste

1 to 2 tablespoons hot sauce, like Texas Pete, or to taste

1 teaspoon celery seeds

Coarse salt (sea or kosher) and freshly ground black pepper, to taste

Place the mustard in a bowl. Whisk in the sugar, vinegar, oil, hot sauce, celery seeds, salt, and pepper. Whisk until the sugar and salt are dissolved. Correct the seasoning, adding sugar, vinegar, salt, or hot sauce to taste; the dressing should be highly seasoned.

SAMBALS, CHUTNEYS, AND JAMS

SHALLOT SAMBAL

YIELD: Makes 1 cup, enough to serve 4

Sambal embraces a large family of relishes, sauces, and chile pastes that accompany saté and other grilled fare in Indonesia, Malaysia, and Singapore. A simple sambal might consist of nothing more than roasted shrimp paste and chiles. A more elaborate version might contain any of a dozen fruits or vegetables or even fried fish, squid, or shrimp.

Here's a simple shallot sambal you'll find in Jakarta.

INGREDIENTS

2 tablespoons canola or other
vegetable oil

1 teaspoon shrimp paste, or
1 anchovy fillet, chopped

1 cup thinly sliced shallots
(4 to 6)

4 to 8 hot chiles such as Thai
chiles or jalapeños, seeded
and minced (for a hotter
sambal leave in the seeds)

2 cloves garlic, peeled and
minced

3 tablespoons fresh lime juice

Coarse salt (sea or kosher) and
freshly ground black pepper
to taste

TRY THIS!

Serve this Shallot Sambal
at room temperature as
you would Grilled Tomato
Sambal on page 320. The
briny tang of the shrimp
paste makes it especially
good for grilled seafood
and shrimp.

1. Heat the oil in a nonreactive
wok or small skillet over
medium heat. Add the shrimp
paste and cook until fragrant,
30 seconds to 1 minute. Add
the shallots, chiles, and garlic
and cook until golden brown,
6 to 8 minutes, reducing the
heat if necessary to prevent the
shallots from burning.

2. Transfer the mixture to a
food processor and finely chop.
Add the lime juice and salt and
pepper. Transfer to a jar, cover,
and refrigerate. The sambal will
keep almost forever.

NOTE: Look for shrimp paste
at Asian markets and specialty
shops.

Variation

For a bolder, more in-your-face
sambal, cook half the chiles,
leaving the other half raw. Add
these raw chiles when you chop
the sambal.

GRILLED TOMATO SAMBAL

YIELD: Makes a scant 2 cups, enough to serve 6 to 8

TRY THIS!

Serve this sambal at room temperature with satés and other Asian-style grilled fare.

Grilling tomatoes and chiles adds a smoky dimension to this sambal, a condiment I discovered in Bali. Horn chiles, which are shaped like a ram's or a steer's horn, are available at most supermarkets and they're easier to grill than smaller chiles. Masochists can leave the seeds in.

INGREDIENTS

4 plum tomatoes

2 to 4 horn peppers

3 tablespoons vegetable oil

2 cloves garlic, peeled and minced

1 large shallot, peeled and minced

1 stalk lemongrass, trimmed and minced, or ½ teaspoon grated lemon zest

2 teaspoons minced fresh ginger

½ teaspoon shrimp paste, or fish sauce

2 tablespoons distilled white vinegar, or more to taste

½ teaspoon sugar

Coarse salt (sea or kosher) and freshly ground black pepper to taste

1. Set up a grill for direct grilling and preheat to high. Brush and oil the grill grate.

2. Place the tomatoes and chiles on the grate and grill until nicely browned on all sides, 6 to 8 minutes for the peppers, 10 to 12 minutes for the tomatoes. Transfer the vegetables to a plate to cool.

3. Scrape any really burned skin off the vegetables, leaving a little on for color and flavor. Stem and seed the peppers.

Coarsely purée the vegetables in a food processor.

4. Heat the oil in a wok or small skillet over medium heat. Add the garlic, shallot, lemongrass, ginger, and shrimp paste and cook until golden brown, 4 minutes. (If using fish sauce instead of shrimp paste, don't add it yet.) Stir in the tomato-chile mixture and cook until thick and flavorful, 4 minutes. If using fish sauce, add it now. Add the vinegar and sugar and bring to a boil.

Correct the seasoning, adding salt, pepper, or vinegar. Cool to room temperature. Transfer the sambal to bowls, if serving immediately. Or, transfer to a large jar, cover, and refrigerate. Bring to room temperature before serving. The sambal will keep for several weeks.

GINGER-PEAR CHUTNEY

YIELD: Makes about 3 cups, enough to serve 6 to 8

first tasted this gingery sweet-sour chutney at a game dinner in central Florida. I find that it goes equally well with smoked turkey, spit-roasted duck, grilled ham steaks, and barbecued or grilled pork.

TRY THIS!

Serve this chutney with grilled or barbecued poultry, especially game birds, like quail, pheasant, or partridge.

INGREDIENTS

3 pounds ripe pears

1 lemon, scrubbed, cut in half, and seeded

1½ cups packed dark brown sugar, or more to taste

1½ cups cider vinegar, or more to taste

6 ounces dark raisins (about 1 cup)

3 tablespoons thinly slivered candied ginger

⅓ cup toasted walnut pieces (see box, page 112)

2 cloves garlic, peeled and minced

1½ tablespoons pure chile powder

1 to 2 teaspoons red pepper flakes

1 teaspoon coarse salt (sea or kosher), or more to taste

½ teaspoon ground cinnamon

¼ teaspoon ground allspice

¼ teaspoon ground cloves

¼ teaspoon freshly grated nutmeg

1. Peel, halve, and core the pears, rubbing each piece with cut lemon to prevent browning. Cut the pears into ½-inch dice; you should have about 4 cups. Cut the lemon, rind and all, into ¼-inch dice. Discard the seeds.

2. Combine the brown sugar and vinegar in a large, heavy, nonreactive saucepan and bring to a boil over medium heat. Add the pears, lemon, and remaining ingredients and bring to a boil. Reduce the heat to medium-low and gently simmer, partially covered, stirring from time to time, for 20 minutes. Uncover the pan and continue simmering until the chutney is thick and flavorful, 10 minutes more.

3. Correct the seasoning, adding vinegar, sugar, or salt; the chutney should be highly seasoned. Transfer to jars, cover, cool to room temperature, and refrigerate. The chutney will keep for several weeks.

PEACH-PECAN CHUTNEY

YIELD: Makes 3 cups, enough to serve 6 to 8

TRY THIS!

Peach chutney goes great with such Southern fare as grilled chicken, turkey, and pork.

This Southern chutney plays the sweetness of ripe summer peaches against the bite of jalapeños and rice vinegar. For even more flavor, use smoked pecans.

INGREDIENTS

4 pounds ripe peaches

1 cinnamon stick (3 inches)

4 allspice berries

4 whole cloves

10 black peppercorns

½ small red onion, peeled and finely chopped (½ cup)

½ red bell pepper, stemmed, seeded, and cut into ½-inch dice

½ yellow bell pepper, stemmed, seeded, and cut into ½-inch dice

2 to 4 jalapeño peppers, seeded and diced (for a spicier chutney leave the seeds in)

2 slices candied ginger, finely chopped

½ cup dried cranberries

½ cup toasted pecan pieces (see box, page 112)

¼ cup rice vinegar or cider vinegar, or more to taste

¼ cup packed dark brown sugar, or more to taste

3 tablespoons chopped fresh cilantro or mint leaves

1. Bring a deep pot of water to a boil over high heat. Plunge the peaches into the water for 30 seconds. Transfer them to a colander, rinse under cold water, and slip off the skins. Cut the peaches into 1-inch pieces, discarding the pits.

2. Tie the cinnamon, allspice, cloves, and peppercorns in a piece of cheesecloth (or see Try This! on page 325).

3. Place the peaches, spices, and remaining ingredients in a heavy nonreactive saucepan and bring to a simmer over medium heat. Reduce the heat and simmer, partially covered, until the peaches are soft, 10 minutes. Correct the seasoning, adding sugar or vinegar; the chutney should be a little sweet and a little sour. Discard the spice bag and transfer the chutney to sterile jars. Cover, cool to room temperature, and refrigerate. The chutney will keep for several months.

FRESH MANGO CHUTNEY

YIELD: Makes 2 cups, enough to serve 6 to 8

To most people, mango chutney calls forth visions of a thick sweet jam-like mixture of mangos and spices. Here's a chutney to spoon over grilled chicken or fish like a sauce. Use ripe mangos: Leave them in a paper bag at room temperature until fragrant and soft. Note that if you have sensitive skin, wear rubber gloves when peeling the mangos. The oils in the mango skin can cause a poison ivy-like rash.

This fruity chutney comes from India, so tandoori and other Indian-style barbecue are the first uses that come to mind. The complex flavor (sweet, sour, fruity, hot, and aromatic) goes well with rich grilled and smoked meats, from salmon to poultry to pork.

INGREDIENTS

2 to 4 very ripe mangos (enough to make 1½ cups strained purée)

3 to 4 tablespoons cold water, as needed

2 tablespoons vegetable oil

2 shallots, peeled and minced

1 clove garlic, peeled and minced

1 tablespoon minced fresh ginger

1 jalapeño pepper, seeded and minced

¼ cup minced fresh cilantro leaves

2 tablespoons fresh lime juice, or more to taste

1 to 3 teaspoons Thai chile paste or chile sauce

1 tablespoon light brown sugar, or more to taste

Coarse salt (sea or kosher) and freshly ground black pepper, to taste

1. Peel the mangos and cut the flesh off the pits. Transfer the mango flesh to a food processor and process to a smooth purée. Strain through a strainer into a large measuring cup. You should have 1½ cups. (If the mango is too thick to purée and strain, stir in a few tablespoons water and then strain.)

2. Heat the oil in a saucepan over medium heat. Add the shallots, garlic, ginger, and jalapeño and cook until soft but not brown, 3 minutes. Add the mango purée and simmer for 3 minutes. Add the cilantro, lime juice, chile paste, and sugar and simmer for 2 minutes. Correct the seasoning, adding salt and pepper. For a sweeter chutney, add more sugar; for a tarter chutney, more lime juice. Transfer to jars, cover, cool to room temperature, and refrigerate. The chutney will keep for several weeks.

APPLE-FIG CHUTNEY

YIELD: Makes 4 cups, enough to serve 8 to 10

Here's an autumnal chutney with apples, cider, and apple-jack. The seeds in the dried figs give it crunch.

TRY THIS!

If you don't have cheesecloth for tying up the spices, wrap them in foil and perforate the package with a fork.

INGREDIENTS

2 cups apple cider, or more as needed

2 cups dried figs

1 cup dark raisins

6 whole cloves

6 allspice berries

6 blades mace, or ¼ teaspoon freshly grated nutmeg

1 cinnamon stick (3 inches)

2 apples, peeled, cored, and coarsely chopped

½ teaspoon grated lemon zest

1 cup packed dark brown sugar, or more to taste

1 cup cider vinegar, or more to taste

2 tablespoons finely chopped candied ginger

1 clove garlic, peeled and minced

1 tablespoon pure chile powder

¼ teaspoon ground cayenne pepper, or more to taste

½ cup applejack or apple brandy

Pinch of coarse salt (sea or kosher)

1. Warm the cider in a large, heavy, nonreactive saucepan over medium heat. Remove the pan from the heat, add the figs and raisins, and let soften for 15 minutes.

2. Tie the cloves, allspice, mace, and cinnamon in a square of cheesecloth (or see Try This!). Add to the cider mixture.

3. Add the remaining ingredients to the cider and bring to a boil over medium heat. Reduce the heat to medium-low, and gently simmer, partially covered, 20 minutes. Uncover the pan and continue simmering until the chutney is richly flavored, 5 minutes more. If it gets too thick, add a little more cider.

4. Correct the seasoning, adding sugar or vinegar. Transfer to jars, cover, cool to room temperature, and refrigerate. The chutney will keep for several weeks.

CILANTRO-MINT CHUTNEY

YIELD: Makes 1 cup, enough to serve 4

TRY THIS!

Serve with any type of tandoori or Central or South Asian-style barbecue. Lamb is the most common meat in these parts, but don't pass it up as a sauce for grilled chicken, beef, or fish.

This bright green chutney turns up wherever sizzling skewers emerge from a tandoor, an Indian barbecue pit. The mint cools and refreshes your mouth, while the cilantro and garlic provide the requisite aromatics. On top of that, the chutney takes all of five minutes to prepare, which makes it a winner in my book.

INGREDIENTS

1 bunch fresh mint, rinsed, stemmed, and dried (about 1 cup packed)

½ bunch fresh cilantro, rinsed, stemmed, and dried (about ½ cup packed)

2 cloves garlic, peeled and chopped

1 to 3 jalapeño chiles, seeded and chopped

1 tablespoon chopped onion

¼ cup fresh lemon juice, or more to taste

1 tablespoon vegetable oil

Scant 1 teaspoon coarse salt (sea or kosher), or more to taste

½ teaspoon sugar

Freshly ground black pepper, to taste

3 tablespoons cold water, or more as needed

Combine all the ingredients in a blender and purée to a paste, scraping down the sides of the blender a few times and adding water as needed to obtain a pourable sauce. Correct the seasoning, adding salt or lemon juice; the chutney should be flavorful and piquant. This chutney will keep for several days, covered, in a jar, in the refrigerator, but I find it tastes best served within a few hours of making.

Variations

Yogurt-Mint Chutney: Add 1 cup plain Greek-style yogurt and ½ tablespoon minced fresh ginger to the blender with the other ingredients.

Afghan Cilantro-Mint Chutney: Afghans make a similar chutney to serve with shish kebabs and grilled fish. Prepare as for Cilantro-Mint Chutney, adding ½ cup walnut pieces. You'll likely need a little more water to obtain a pourable sauce and more lemon juice for tartness. Some Afghan kebabi men use vinegar instead of lemon juice.

TOMATO CHUTNEY

YIELD: Makes 1½ cups, enough to serve 4 to 6

When you're tired of ketchup and you can't look at another bottle of barbecue sauce, try this vibrant tomato chutney from India. The tomatoes are charred on the grill, which gives them a smoky flavor. The onions are soaked in cold water to rid them of their pungency while preserving their moist crisp crunch. The perfect accompaniment not just to Indian tandoori but to any Central Asian-style grilled poultry, seafood, and lamb.

TRY THIS!

Although this chutney comes from India, it's versatile enough to go with Western-style grilled chicken, pork, and lamb. I like to serve it in place of cocktail sauce on a platter of grilled shrimp.

INGREDIENTS

1 medium-size red onion

Ice water

4 medium-size ripe tomatoes

2 cloves garlic, peeled and minced

2 teaspoons minced fresh ginger

1 teaspoon coarse salt (sea or kosher), or more to taste

½ teaspoon sugar

2 tablespoons fresh lemon juice, or to taste

3 tablespoons minced fresh cilantro leaves

Freshly ground black pepper, to taste

1. Finely dice the onion and place it in a bowl with ice water to cover. Let soak for 1 hour, changing the water 2 or 3 times. Drain the onions in a colander and gently squeeze dry with your fingers.

2. Meanwhile, set up a grill for direct grilling and preheat to high. For the best results make a wood fire. Brush and oil the grill grate.

3. Grill the tomatoes until charred on all sides, about 2 minutes per side (6 to 8 minutes in all). Transfer to a plate to cool. Scrape off the burnt skins (you don't need to remove every last bit; a few bits of black add character). Finely chop the tomatoes.

4. Place the garlic, ginger, salt, and sugar in a bowl and mash to a paste with the back of a spoon. Place this mixture in a nonreactive saucepan and stir in the tomatoes and lemon juice. Cook, uncovered, over medium heat until thick and fragrant, about 4 minutes. Add the cilantro and cook for 1 minute more. Remove the pan from the heat and stir in the onions. Correct the seasoning, adding salt or pepper. Cool completely, then transfer to tiny individual serving bowls. Or transfer to a large jar, cover, and refrigerate. The chutney will keep for several days.

APRICOT BLATJANG

YIELD: Makes about 3 cups, enough to serve 6 to 8

TRY THIS!

Serve *blatjang* as you would any fruit chutney—it goes particularly well with grilled or smoked chicken, pork, and lamb.

I'm always fascinated by the cultural and geographic migrations of barbecue. Consider the chutney-like condiment served at South African barbecues, *blatjang*. *Blacan* is the Malay word for shrimp paste. Malay laborers brought it to South Africa at the turn of the last century, when they came there to work in the gold and diamond mines. *Blacan* gave its name to *blatjang* and as time passed, the shrimp paste was supplanted by more European ingredients, like apricots, raisins, and onions.

INGREDIENTS

2 tablespoons vegetable oil

3 shallots or 1 small onion, peeled and thinly sliced

2 cloves garlic, peeled and thinly sliced

1 tablespoon minced fresh ginger

1 to 2 jalapeño peppers or other hot chiles, seeded and minced (for a hotter blatjang, leave the seeds in)

2 cups dried apricots, quartered

½ cup (4 ounces) dark raisins

5 tablespoons packed dark brown sugar, or more to taste

3 tablespoons chopped fresh cilantro leaves

1½ teaspoons ground coriander

6 tablespoons cider vinegar

2 strips of lemon zest

2 tablespoons fresh lemon juice

1 cup cold water, or more as needed

½ cup chopped dry-roasted peanuts

Coarse salt (sea or kosher), to taste

Heat the oil in a heavy nonreactive saucepan over medium heat. Add the shallots, garlic, ginger, and jalapeño and cook until lightly browned, 5 minutes. Add the remaining ingredients and bring to a boil. Reduce the heat and simmer, uncovered, until the apricots are soft and the mixture has thickened to the consistency of jam, about 15 minutes. If it starts to get too thick, add a little more water. Correct the seasoning, adding any of the ingredients to taste. Transfer to jars, cover, cool to room temperature, and refrigerate. The *blatjang* will keep for several weeks.

OKLAHOMA BRUSCHETTA

YIELD: Serves 4 to 6

Bruschetta, grilled bread, is one of Italy's great contributions to global grilling. (The name comes from Italian *bruscare*, "to char" or "burn.") This one comes topped with bacon jam and a dollop of Chinese Mustard Cream.

INGREDIENTS

BREAD (SEE NOTE)

1 baguette

3 tablespoons melted butter, or reserved bacon fat

1½ cups Bacon Jam (facing page), at room temperature

CHINESE MUSTARD CREAM

½ cup mayonnaise, preferably homemade or Hellmann's (aka Best Foods)

¼ cup prepared Chinese mustard or Dijon mustard

1 tablespoon sriracha, or your favorite hot sauce

2 scallions, trimmed and thinly sliced on the diagonal

1. Set up a grill for direct grilling and preheat to medium-high. Brush and oil the grill grate.

2. Cut the baguette crosswise on the diagonal into finger-thick slices. Lightly brush each slice on both sides with melted butter or bacon fat.

3. Make the Chinese Mustard Cream: Combine the mayonnaise, mustard, and sriracha in a bowl and whisk to mix.

4. Arrange the bread slices on the grate and grill the bread until browned on both sides, 1 to 2 minutes per side.

5. Transfer the grilled bread to a platter. Spread each slice with Bacon Jam. Top with a dollop of Chinese Mustard Cream and a few scallion slices.

NOTE: For an interesting variation, substitute cornbread for the baguette. Because cornbread is more crumbly than French bread, it helps to grill it in a grill basket.

BACON JAM

YIELD: Makes 3 cups

Tulsa, Oklahoma, may not top your must-visit travel list, but this lively oil town boasts a terrific Woody Guthrie museum, a fine art museum (the Philbrook), a monumental piece of folk art (the Golden Driller, a three-story tall statue of an oil man), a singular grill manufacturer (Hasty Bake), and enough great barbecue joints to keep you sated for a week. What I remember most from a recent visit was one of the coolest uses I've ever found for bacon: the bacon jam served at Smoke Woodfire Grill. Smoke chef-owner Erik Reynolds brings a tweezers sensibility to traditional Oklahoma barbecue. He cures and smokes his own bacon, and developed the jam as a way to take advantage of all the smoky trimmings. If you can't make your own, use a good artisanal bacon, like Nueske's.

TRY THIS!

Stuff Bacon Jam into a pork chop (cut a pocket in the side) or spoon it over grilled burgers or salmon steaks. It revolutionizes a grilled cheese sandwich. Hell, it's pretty awesome eaten straight off the spoon.

INGREDIENTS

1 pound bacon, thinly slivered crosswise

1 medium-size onion, peeled and diced

4 cloves garlic, peeled and minced

1 cup strong brewed coffee

¼ cup cider vinegar

¼ cup maple syrup

2 tablespoons molasses

2 tablespoons brown sugar (light or dark—your choice)

2 teaspoons freshly ground black pepper

Tabasco sauce, or your favorite hot sauce, to taste

1. Place the bacon in a large cold cast-iron skillet. Cook over medium heat until the bacon is browned and crisp, 5 minutes. Work in several batches, as needed.

2. Transfer the bacon to a colander set in a heatproof bowl and drain. Pour off all but 2 tablespoons bacon fat. (Reserve the remaining bacon fat for later use, like the Lean-and-Mean Texas Barbecue Sauce on page 167.)

3. Return the skillet to the stove and heat over medium-high heat. Add the onion and cook until lightly browned, 4 minutes, stirring with a wooden spoon. Stir in the garlic and cook until fragrant, 1 minute.

4. Return the bacon to the pan along with the coffee, vinegar, syrup, molasses, brown sugar, pepper, and hot sauce. Stir well and gradually bring the mixture to a boil, stirring often. Lower the heat and gently simmer the mixture, uncovered, until thick and syrupy, 15 to 20 minutes, stirring often.

5. For a chunky jam, use as is. For a smoother jam, purée the ingredients in a food processor, running the machine in short bursts.

6. Serve the bacon jam at once, either warm or at room temperature. Or transfer to a jar, cover, and cool to room temperature. The jam will keep refrigerated for at least 3 days, but for the best results, let it warm to room temperature before serving.

NOTE: For an extra kick, add a shot of bourbon.

CONVERSION TABLES

Please note that all conversions are approximate but close enough to be useful when converting from one system to another.

OVEN TEMPERATURES

FAHRENHEIT	GAS MARK	CELSIUS
250	½	120
275	1	140
300	2	150
325	3	160
350	4	180
375	5	190
400	6	200
425	7	220
450	8	230
475	9	240
500	10	260

NOTE: Reduce the temperature by 20°C (68°F) for fan-assisted ovens.

APPROXIMATE EQUIVALENTS

1 stick butter = 8 tbs = 4 oz = ½ cup = 115 g

1 cup all-purpose presifted flour = 4.7 oz

1 cup granulated sugar = 8 oz = 220 g

1 cup (firmly packed) brown sugar = 6 oz = 220 g to 230 g

1 cup confectioners' sugar = 4½ oz = 115 g

1 cup honey or syrup = 12 oz = 350 g

1 cup grated cheese = 4 oz = 125 g

1 cup dried beans = 6 oz = 175 g

1 large egg = about 2 oz or about 3 tbs

1 egg yolk = about 1 tbs

1 egg white = about 2 tbs

LIQUID CONVERSIONS

U.S.	IMPERIAL	METRIC
2 tbs	1 fl oz	30 ml
3 tbs	1½ fl oz	45 ml
¼ cup	2 fl oz	60 ml
⅓ cup	2½ fl oz	75 ml
⅓ cup + 1 tbs	3 fl oz	90 ml
⅓ cup + 2 tbs	3½ fl oz	100 ml
½ cup	4 fl oz	125 ml
⅔ cup	5 fl oz	150 ml
¾ cup	6 fl oz	175 ml
¾ cup + 2 tbs	7 fl oz	200 ml
1 cup	8 fl oz	250 ml
1 cup + 2 tbs	9 fl oz	275 ml
1¼ cups	10 fl oz	300 ml
1⅓ cups	11 fl oz	325 ml
1½ cups	12 fl oz	350 ml
1⅔ cups	13 fl oz	375 ml
1¾ cups	14 fl oz	400 ml
1¾ cups + 2 tbs	15 fl oz	450 ml
2 cups (1 pint)	16 fl oz	500 ml
2½ cups	20 fl oz (1 pint)	600 ml
3¾ cups	1½ pints	900 ml
4 cups	1¾ pints	1 liter

WEIGHT CONVERSIONS

US/UK	METRIC	US/UK	METRIC
½ oz	15 g	7 oz	200 g
1 oz	30 g	8 oz	250 g
1½ oz	45 g	9 oz	275 g
2 oz	60 g	10 oz	300 g
2½ oz	75 g	11 oz	325 g
3 oz	90 g	12 oz	350 g
3½ oz	100 g	13 oz	375 g
4 oz	125 g	14 oz	400 g
5 oz	150 g	15 oz	450 g
6 oz	175 g	1 lb	500 g

INDEX

Page references in *italics* refer to photographs.

A

Acids:
for marinades, 64
nonreactive containers for, 65
Adobo, 61
chipotle chile marinade, 58
Cuban garlic marinade, 60
Afghan cilantro-mint chutney, 326–27
African (flavors):
apricot *blatjang*, 328–29
Kenyan tomato relish, 309–10
monkey gland sauce, 218
piri-piri sauce, 287
see also Moroccan (flavors)
After-marinades, 275–80
"board sauce" for steak, 281–82
pesto, deconstructed, 275–76
Thai flavor, 277
Aïoli (garlic mayonnaise), 255
Aji amarillo chiles, 205
Peruvian yellow pepper sauce, 202–3
Aji dulce chiles, 204
Ajilimojili (Puerto Rican pepper sauce), 195–96
Allspice, 35
Ancho chiles, 205
Anchovy fillets/paste, 159
Anise seed, 35
A.1. Steak Sauce, 255
Appetizers:
Nashville hot wings, 121
Oklahoma bruschetta, 330
Singapore pork saté, *230*, 231
tandoori shrimp, *74*, 75
Apple:
barbecue sauce, B.B's Lawnside spicy, 166
fig chutney, 325
Apricot *blatjang*, 328–29
Argentine *chimichurri* (parsley-garlic sauce), 192–93
Asian (flavors):
brandy-brined turkey breast with tangerine lacquer glaze, *134*, 135
Central Asian seasoned salt, 16
chile paste and chile sauce, 303

curry oil, 142
5-4-3-2-1 rub, 26–27
injector sauce, 128–29
Korean honey-sesame marinade, 83
sesame-ginger-soy vinaigrette, 270
sesame grilled tofu, 78
sweet sesame-soy marinade, 77–79
tangerine lacquer glaze, 132
see also Chinese (flavors); Indian (flavors); Japanese (flavors); Southeast Asian (flavors); Thai (flavors)
Avocado:
peeling, pitting, and dicing, 305
salsa, 304

B

Baas, Rob, 148–49, 173
Bacon, 160
bourbon barbecue sauce, smoke wrangler's, 173
brining, 101
jam, 331–32
onion butter, 154–55
pastrami, 32, 107
Balinese (flavors):
grilled tomato sambal, 320–21
seasoned salt, 15
spice paste, 97–98
Balsamic:
drizzle, 274
vinegar, 158
Banana:
ketchup, 244
raita, 222
tamarind barbecue sauce, 181–82
Barbacoa (pit-roasted lamb or goat), *salsa borracha* (drunken salsa) for, 297
Barbecue:
bastes for, 109, 111–20; *see also* Bastes
finishing sauces for, 110, 146–49; *see also* Finishing sauces
flavored butters for, 110, 151–55; *see also* Butters, flavored
flavored oils for, 110, 136–45; *see also* Oils, flavored
glazes for, 110, 130–33; *see also* Glazes
injector sauces for, 110, 126–29; *see also* Injector sauces

mop and spray sauces for, 109–10, 122–25; *see also* mop sauces/spray sauces
rubs for, 19–33; *see also* Rubs, American
Barbecue burger, 174, *175*
Barbecue sauces, 4
building blocks of, 158–60
extending shelf life of, 172
safe handling of, 9
squirt bottles for, 183
Barbecue sauces, African, 216–18
charmoula (Moroccan herb and paprika sauce), 216
monkey gland sauce, 218
Barbecue sauces, American, 157–89
apple, B.B's Lawnside spicy, 166
bacon bourbon, smoke wrangler's, 173
Coca-Cola, 185
coffee, 184–85
doctor, 178
espresso, Aaron Franklin's, 164
guava, 179
jalapeño-mustard, 188–89
lean-and-mean Texas, 167
Memphis-style, 171–72
peach, 169–70
pig picker pucker, 186
sweet-and-smoky, 161
tamarind-banana, 181–82
Texa-Lina, 170–71
Texas, Kansas City style, 176–77
three C's, Jake's, 180–81
truffled porcini, Charlie Trotter's, 187–88
vinegar, bubba-lina, 189
Barbecue sauces, Asian, 219–37
Beijing, 219
Cambodian dipping sauce, 233
finadene (vinegar-soy barbecue sauce from Guam), 237
Korean (KB sauce), 223
mam nem (Vietnamese pineapple-shrimp dipping sauce), 235–36
miso, 228
peanut dipping sauce, rich, 229
quick peanut dipping sauce, 232
raita, 222
Vietnamese dipping sauce (*nuoc mam*), 234
yakitori, 226
Barbecue sauces, Caribbean and Latin, 192–208

Aji amarillo sauce (Peruvian yellow pepper sauce), 202–3

ajilimojili (Puerto Rican pepper sauce), 195–96

chimichurri (Argentine parsley-garlic sauce), 192–93

chirmol (Central American tomato sauce), 198–201

mojo (Cuban citrus-garlic sauce), 193–94

mole poblano (Mexican chocolate-chile sauce), 196–98

pebre (Chilean pepper sauce), 207

St. Barth, 208

salsa criolla (Colombian Creole sauce), 201–2

Barbecue sauces, European, 209–16
    red currant port, 213–14
    romesco, 212–13
    rouille (saffron–roasted pepper sauce), 210–11
    salsa verde (Italian green sauce), 209–10
    tkemali (Georgian rhubarb sauce), 215–16

Barbecue vinaigrette, 268

Basil, 88
    deconstructed pesto after-marinade, 275–76
    sweet, oil with garlic, 136–37

Bastes, 4, 109, 111–20
    chicken, Nashville hot, 120
    coconut curry, 118
    garlic butter, 111–12
    lemon-garlic, Greek, 119
    saffron butter, 117
    secret weapon basting sauce, 116–17
    sesame soy butter, 113

Basting, safety tips for, 9

Bay leaf, 88–89

BBQ Titans' brisket, 165

B.B's Lawnside spicy apple barbecue sauce, 166

Béarnaise sauce, 257–58

Beef:
    Berber spice paste for, 95
    grilled, salad, Thai (*yam nua*), 278, *279*
    jerky marinade for, 56
    kebabs, Persian saffron-yogurt marinade for, 71
    kebabs, *pincho* powder for, 41
    Kenyan tomato relish for, 309–10
    stock, 160

walnut-Roquefort butter for, 153
see also Brisket; Burger(s); Ribs, beef; Steak(s)

Beef, roast:
    horseradish mayonnaise for, 253
    horseradish mustard for, 250–51
    Lone Star steak rub for, 27
    volcanic horseradish sauce for, 260
    wasabi-horseradish butter for, 155

Beer:
    brine, 103
    butter beef injector sauce, 127
    marinade, Belgian, 66
    mustard butter, 153–54

Beijing barbecue sauce, 219

Beijing blast, 42

Belgian beer marinade, 66

Belissimo, Teressa, 124

Berber spice paste, 95

Beurre noisette, 111, 112

Bhut jolokia, 204

Black *recado* (*recado negro*), 93–94

Blatjang, apricot, 328–29

Blenders, 6

Bluefish, teriyaki marinade for, 81–82

Boar, wild game marinade with juniper and gin for, 69

"Board sauce" for steak, 281–82

Bourbon:
    bacon barbecue sauce, smoke wrangler's, 173
    cider squirt, 125

Bowls, mixing, 7

Brandy-brined turkey breast with tangerine lacquer glaze, *134*, 135

Brazilian (flavors):
    garlic marinade, 63
    hot sauce, 286

Bread, grilled:
    crostini, Mediterranean relish for, 306
    garlic, with walnut-Roquefort butter, 152
    pita, Yemenite pepper sauce (*zehug*) as dip for, 288
    see also Bruschetta

Bread, grilled, bastes and sauces for:
    fresh garlic oil, 136
    garlic butter baste, 111–12
    romesco sauce, 212–13
    saffron butter baste, 117
    smoked tomato sauce, 265–66

Brined meats, pastrami rub for, 32

Brines, 3, 101–6
    all-purpose, 102–3
    beer, 103
    flavorings for, 102
    function of, 101
    lemon-ginger cider, 104
    making, 101
    pastrami, 106

Brisket:
    BBQ Titans', 165
    beer-butter beef injector sauce for, 127
    Dalmatian rub/newspaper rub for, 21
    espresso barbecue sauce for, Aaron Franklin's, 164
    Fette Sau's coffee rub for, 28
    Kansas City sweet and smoky rub for, 24
    lean-and-mean Texas barbecue sauce for, 167
    Lone Star steak rub for, 27
    pastrami, 31, 32
    peach barbecue sauce for, 169–70
    sweet-and-smoky barbecue sauce for, 161
    Texas barb-b-que sauce, Kansas City style for, 176–77

Broth:
    butter injector sauce, 126
    see also Stock

Brown sugar, 158

Bruschetta:
    Hellas relish for, 307
    hellish relish for, 308–9
    Oklahoma, 330
    romesco sauce for, 212–13
    rouille (saffron–roasted pepper sauce) for, 210–11
    saffron butter baste for, 117

Bubba-lina vinegar sauce, 189

Budros, Jim, 185

Buffalo mop, 124

Burger(s):
    bacon jam for, 331–32
    bacon-onion butter for, 154–55
    barbecue, 174, *175*
    chipotle mayonnaise for, 253
    horseradish mustard for, 250–51
    sauce for grown-ups, 256
    walnut-Roquefort butter for, 153

Burke, Pat, 2

Butter, 160
    beer beef injector sauce, 127
    beurre noisette, 111, 112
    garlic, baste, 111–12

injector sauce, 126
saffron, baste, 117
sesame soy, baste, 113
Butters, flavored, 110, 151–55
  bacon-onion, 154–55
  making and storing, 151
  mustard-beer, 153–54
  tarragon-lemon, 151
  walnut-Roquefort, 153
  wasabi-horseradish, 155

C

Cabbage:
basic slaw mixture, 316
  Jake's sauerkraut, 311–13
  kimchi, 314–15
  xni pec, 282–83
Cajun (flavors):
  injector sauce, 129
  rémoulade, 261
  rub, 33
  tuna, 262, *263*
Cambodian dipping sauce, 233
Cane syrup, 158
Capers, 159
Caprese salad, smokehouse, 265
Cardamom, 36
Caribbean (flavors):
  ajilimojili (Puerto Rican pepper sauce), 195–96
  banana ketchup, 244
  Cuban garlic marinade (adobo), 60
  French West Indian Scotch bonnet–lime marinade, 61–62
  island seasonin', 84–85
  Jamaican jolt, 38
  mojo (Cuban citrus-garlic sauce), 193–94
  Paramin seasonin' from Trinidad, 85
  St. Barth barbecue sauce, 208
  sazón (Puerto Rican pig powder), 34
Carnitas:
  fresh *chirmol* for, 199
  Mexican chile oil for, 144
Carroll, Joe, 28
Carrot raita from Goa, 222
Cascabel chiles, 205
Cassia, 36
Cast-iron skillets, 6
  acids and, 65
Catalan (flavors):
  romesco sauce, 212–13
  vinaigrette, 269

Cayenne, 159, 205
Celery, 159
Central American (flavors):
  jalapeño sauce, 283–84
  tomato sauce (*chirmol*), 198–201
Central Asian seasoned salt, 16
Chambrette, Fernand, 69
Charlie Trotter's truffled porcini BBQ sauce, 187–88
Charmoula (Moroccan herb and paprika sauce), 216
Char siu:
  chicken thighs, 55
  marinade, 53–54
Cheesecloth, 6
Cherries, in Jake's three C's barbecue sauce, 180–81
Chicken:
  all-purpose brine for, 102–3
  Asian injector sauce for, 128–29
  Balinese spice paste for, 97–98
  basic mop sauce for, 122–23
  Beijing barbecue sauce for, 219
  Berber spice paste for, 95
  Brazilian garlic marinade for, 63
  Buffalo mop for, 124
  butter injector sauce for, 126
  Cajun injector sauce for, 129
  Chinese five-spice powder for, 42
  French West Indian Scotch bonnet–lime marinade for, 61–62
  fresh mango chutney for, 323–24
  fruit + booze glaze for, 133
  green tandoori spice paste for, 96–97
  guava barbecue sauce for, 179
  honey cure for, 100
  Indian tandoori marinade for, 76–77
  island seasonin' for, 84–85
  Jamaican jerk seasoning for, 85–86
  Kansas City sweet and smoky rub for, 24
  kebabs (*spiedies*), 272–73
  kebabs, *pincho* powder for, 41
  melon-mint relish for, 299
  Nashville hot baste for, 120
  not-just-for-ham glaze for, 130
  peach-pecan chutney, 322–23
  recado rojo (Yucatán red spice paste) for, 90–92
  red currant port sauce for, 213–14
  sandwiches, mustard mayonnaise for, 252

stock, 160
  tangerine lacquer glaze for, 132
  thighs, char siu, 55
  wings, Buffalo mop for, 124
  wings, Nashville hot, 121
  yakitori, 227
Chile(s), 159, 204–6
  aji amarillo sauce (Peruvian yellow pepper sauce), 202–3
  chocolate sauce, Mexican (*mole poblano*), 196–98
  dried, canned, and preserved, 205–6
  fresh, 204–5
  habaneros, in hellish relish, 308–9
  habaneros, in *xni pec*, 282–83
  handling safely, 62
  oil, Mexican, 144
  paste and sauce, Asian, 303
  pebre (Chilean pepper sauce), 207
  rocotillo, in *ajilimojili* (Puerto Rican pepper sauce), 195–96
  smoky two-chile salsa, 295–96
  see also Chipotle chile(s); Jalapeño(s); Scotch bonnet chile(s)
Chilean pepper sauce (*pebre*), 207
Chili powder, 159
Chimichurri (Argentine parsley-garlic sauce), 192–93
Chinatown duck, 220, *221*
Chinatown marinade, 79–80
Chinese (flavors):
  Beijing blast, 42
  char siu chicken thighs, 55
  char siu marinade, 53–54
  Chinatown duck, 220, *221*
  Chinatown marinade, 79–80
  fire oil, 142–43
  five-spice powder, 42
  hot bean paste, 303
  mustard cream, 330
  sweet and licoricey duck rub, 46
Chinese dried chiles, 205
Chipotle chile(s), 205
  Jake's three C's barbecue sauce, 180–81
  marinade, 58
  mayonnaise, 253
Chirmol (Central American tomato sauce), 198–201
Chives, 89
Chocolate:
  chile sauce, Mexican (*mole poblano*), 196–98

Jake's three C's barbecue sauce, 180–81
Chutneys, 5, 291–92, 321–28
  apple-fig, 325
  apricot *blatjang*, 328–29
  cilantro-mint, 326–27
  ginger-pear, 321–22
  mango, fresh, 323–24
  monkey gland sauce, 218
  peach-pecan, 322–23
  tomato, 327–28
  yogurt-mint, 326
Cider:
  brine, lemon-ginger, 104
  -brined pork chops, 105
  squirt, 125
Cider vinegar, 158
Cilantro, 88, 89
  charmoula (Moroccan herb and paprika sauce), 216
  mint chutney, 326–27
Cinnamon (sticks), 36
  orange marinade, 67
Citrus-garlic sauce, Cuban (*mojo*), 193–94
City Barbeque and Catering restaurants, 185
Cloves, 36
Coca-Cola barbecue sauce, 185
Cocktail sauce, tomato chutney as, 327–28
Coconut curry baste, 118
Coffee:
  barbecue sauce, 184–85
  in barbecue sauces, 160
  double, skirt steaks or venison, 29
  espresso barbecue sauce, Aaron Franklin's, 164
  rub, Fette Sau's, 28
Coleslaw, 316–18
  basic mixture for, 316
  creamy dressing for, 317
  mustard dressing for, 318
  vinegar dressing for, 317
Colombian Creole sauce (*salsa criolla*), 201–2
Condiments, 5
  see also specific condiments
Cooking in Paradise (St. Barthélemy), 208
Coriander, 36
Corn:
  grilled, with sesame soy butter, 114, *115*
  relish, spicy, 302–3
Cornish game hens:
  grilled (*tabaka*), 68

Persian saffron-yogurt marinade for, 71
Corn syrup, 158
Corrosion protection, 172
Cream sauce, peppery, for grilled steak, 259
Creamy coleslaw dressing, 317
Creole sauce, Colombian (*salsa criolla*), 201–2
Cross contamination, avoiding, 9
Crostini:
  Mediterranean relish for, 306
  see also Bruschetta
Cuban (flavors):
  garlic marinade (adobo), 60
  mojo (citrus-garlic sauce), 193–94
Cucumber(s):
  Hellas relish, 307
  melon-mint relish, 299
  peeling and seeding, 299
  raita, 222
  relish, Thai, 298
Cumin, 36
Cures, 3–4
  fish, failproof, 30
  honey, 100
  salt, 101
  using rub as, 25
Curry:
  coconut baste, 118
  oil, 142
Cutting boards, 6–7
  safe handling of, 9

D

Dady, Jason, 169
Dairy products, cultured:
  in marinades, 64
  see also Yogurt
Daisy May's (New York), 281
Dallman, Matt, 265
Dalmatian ribs (salt and pepper beef ribs), 22, *23*
Dalmatian rub/newspaper rub, 21
Davis, Richard, 116
De árbol chiles, 205
Deconstructed pesto after-marinade, 275–76
Dessert(s):
  rub, 47
  spice-grilled pineapple with smoky whipped cream, *48*, 49
Dill (seed), 88, 89
Dipping sauces, 4
  Cambodian, 233
  peanut, quick, 232

peanut, rich, 229
pepper, Puerto Rican (*ajilimojili*), 195–96
pineapple-shrimp, Vietnamese (*mam nem*), 235–36
rouille (saffron–roasted pepper sauce), 210–11
Vietnamese (*nuoc mam*), 234
vinegar, Monroe County, 148–49
Doctor sauce, 178
Dressings:
  creamy coleslaw, 317
  Italian, from scratch, 271
  mustard coleslaw, 318
  vinegar coleslaw, 317
  see also Vinaigrettes
Drizzle, balsamic, 274
Drunken salsa (*salsa borracha*), 297
Duck:
  Asian 5-4-3-2-1 rub for, 26–27
  Balinese spice paste for, 97–98
  Chinatown, 220, *221*
  Chinatown marinade for, 79–80
  Chinese five-spice powder for, 42
  ginger-pear chutney for, 321–22
  guava barbecue sauce for, 179
  red currant port sauce for, 213–14
  rub, sweet and licoricey, 46
  tangerine lacquer glaze for, 132
Durney, Billy, 106

E

East Coast Grill (Cambridge, Mass.), 276
Eggplant, miso barbecue sauce for, 228
18th & Vine Barbeque (Dallas), 265, 310
Elk:
  double coffee, 29
  red currant port sauce for, 213–14
English, Todd, 241
Equipment, 6–8
Escamillo, Evaristo, 92
Espresso barbecue sauce, Aaron Franklin's, 164

F

Fajitas:
  Mexican chile oil for, 144
  salsa fresca for, 293
  smoky two-chile salsa for, 295–96

Fennel seed, 36
  Cajun rub with, 33
Fette Sau's coffee rub, 28
Fig-apple chutney, 325
Filet mignons:
  béarnaise sauce for, 257–58
  peppery cream sauce for, 259
Finadene (vinegar-soy barbecue
  sauce from Guam), 237
Finishing sauces, 4, 110, 146–49
  merlot-soy, 148
  Monroe County vinegar dip,
  148–49
  smoked stock for, 146–47
Fire oil, Chinese, 142–43
Fish and seafood:
  aïoli (garlic mayonnaise) for, 255
  barbecue rub for, 20
  Beijing blast for, 42
  Berber spice paste for, 95
  Cajun rémoulade for, 261
  Cajun rub for, 33
  coconut curry baste for, 118
  failproof fish cure for, 30
  finadene (vinegar-soy barbecue
  sauce from Guam) for, 237
  French West Indian Scotch
  bonnet–lime marinade for,
  61–62
  fresh mango chutney for, 323–24
  Greek lemon-garlic baste for, 119
  green tandoori spice paste for,
  96–97
  Hellas relish for, 307
  herbes de Provence for, 39
  honey cure for, 100
  Indian tandoori marinade for,
  76–77
  island seasonin' for, 84–85
  lemon pepper oil for, 141
  Mediterranean herb rub for, 40
  Mediterranean relish for, 306
  mustard mayonnaise for, 252
  recado rojo (Yucatán red spice
  paste) for, 90–92
  rouille (saffron–roasted pepper
  sauce) for, 210–11
  St. Barth barbecue sauce for,
  208
  salsa fresca for, 293
  salsa verde (Italian green sauce)
  for, 209–10
  Scotch bonnet sauce for, 289
  sesame-soy butter baste for, 113
  shallot sambal for, 318–19
  striped bass, grilled, with melon-
  mint relish, 300, *301*

  tarragon-lemon butter for, 151
  teriyaki marinade for, 81–82
  wasabi mayonnaise for, 254
  see also Lobster; Salmon;
  Shrimp; Tuna
Fish sauce, 159, 235
5-4-3-2-1 rubs, 26–27
Five-spice powder, Chinese, 42
Flame-charred *salsa verde*,
  294–95
Food processors, 7
Franklin, Aaron, 164
French (flavors):
  aïoli (garlic mayonnaise), 255
  béarnaise sauce, 257–58
  beurre noisette, 111, 112
  herbes de Provence, 39
  peppery cream sauce for grilled
  steak, 259
  rouille (saffron–roasted pepper
  sauce), 210–11
  tarragon-lemon butter, 151
  wild game marinade with
  juniper and gin, 69
French West Indian (flavors):
  St. Barth barbecue sauce, 208
  Scotch bonnet–lime marinade,
  61–62
Fruit:
  + booze glaze, 133
  dessert rub for, 47
  juices, in marinades, 64
  see also specific fruits

G

Galangal (aka galanga), 36
Game:
  double coffee, 29
  fruit + booze glaze for, 133
  guava barbecue sauce for, 179
  red currant port sauce for,
  213–14
  wild, marinade with juniper and
  gin, 69
  see also Venison
Game birds:
  cinnamon-orange marinade
  for, 67
  ginger-pear chutney for, 321–22
  Persian saffron-yogurt marinade
  for, 71
  red currant port sauce for,
  213–14
  saffron butter baste for, 117
  tabaka (grilled game hens), 68
  see also Quail

Garlic, 159
  bread, grilled, with walnut-
  Roquefort butter, 152
  butter baste, 111–12
  citrus sauce, Cuban (*mojo*),
  193–94
  fresh, oil, 136
  fried, oil, 137
  lemon baste, Greek, 119
  marinade, Brazilian, 63
  marinade, Cuban (*adobo*), 60
  mayonnaise (*aïoli*), 255
  parsley sauce, Argentine
  (*chimichurri*), 192–93
  peeling and smashing, 138
  pineapple glaze, 131
  roasted, oil, 138
  sweet basil oil with, 136–37
  yogurt marinade, Turkish, 70
Georgian (flavors):
  cinnamon-orange marinade, 67
  tabaka (grilled game hens), 68
  tkemali (rhubarb sauce), 215–16
Ghost peppers, 204
Gin, wild game marinade with
  juniper and, 69
Ginger, 159
  lemon cider brine, 104
  pear chutney, 321–22
  -sesame-soy vinaigrette, 270
Glazes, 4, 110, 130–33
  fruit + booze, 133
  not-just-for-ham, 130
  pineapple garlic, 131
  tangerine lacquer, 132
Glazing, safety tips for, 9
Gloves, rubber or plastic, 9
Goa, carrot raita from, 222
Goat:
  French West Indian Scotch
  bonnet–lime marinade for,
  61–62
  Kenyan tomato relish for,
  309–10
  salsa borracha (drunken salsa)
  for, 297
Gochugaru, 36
Gochujang in KB sauce (Korean
  barbecue sauce), 223
Gottlich, Scott, 265
Grapefruit-mint *mojo*, 194
Greek (flavors):
  Hellas relish, 307
  lemon-garlic baste, 119
Green peppercorn mustard, 249
Green sauce, Italian (*salsa verde*),
  209–10

Green tandoori spice paste, 96–97
Grilled cheese sandwiches with
    bacon jam, 331–32
Guajillo chiles, 205–6
Guam, vinegar-soy barbecue sauce
    from (*finadene*), 237
Guava barbecue sauce, 179

H

Habaneros, 204
  handling safely, 62
  hellish relish, 308–9
  xni pec, 282–83
Ham:
  brining, 101
  cooked sauerkraut for, 313
  ginger-pear chutney for, 321–22
  Jake's sauerkraut for, 311–13
  not-just-for-ham glaze for, 130
Hart, Bob, 104, 105
Heat, ingredients for, 159
H. J. Heinz Company, 245
Heirloom Market BBQ (Atlanta),
    223
Hellas relish, 307
Hellish relish, 308–9
Hell's fury, 284–85
Herb(s):
  in barbecue sauce, 159
  dried, 88
  fresh, cooking with, 88–89
  freshness of, 25
  herbes de Provence, 39
  and paprika sauce, Moroccan
    (*charmoula*), 216
  rinsing and storing, 88
  rub, Mediterranean, 40
  stalks, using as skewers, 88
  vinaigrette, basic, 266–67
  see also specific herbs
Herbes de Provence, 39
Hoisin sauce, 159
  Beijing barbecue sauce, 219
Hometown Bar-B-Que, Red Hook,
    Brooklyn, 107
Honey, 158
  cure, 100
  sesame marinade, Korean, 83
Horn peppers, 204
Horseradish, 159
  mayonnaise, 253
  mustard, 250–51
  sauce, volcanic, 260
  wasabi butter, 155
Hot sauces, 159, 282–89
  Brazilian, 286

hell's fury, 284–85
jalapeño, 283–84
piri-piri, 287
Scotch bonnet sauce, 289
xni pec, 282–83
zehug (Yemenite pepper sauce),
    288
Husbands, Andy, 127

I

Indian (flavors):
  cilantro-mint chutney, 326–27
  fresh mango chutney, 323–24
  green tandoori spice paste,
    96–97
  raita, 222
  tandoori marinade, 76–77
  tandoori shrimp, *74*, 75
  tomato chutney, 327–28
  yogurt-mint chutney, 326
Indonesian (flavors):
  sambal ulek (or *oelek*), 303
  sesame soy butter baste, 113
  shallot sambal, 318–19
  see also Balinese (flavors)
Injectors, 7
  how to use, 128
Injector sauces, 110, 126–29
  Asian, 128–29
  beer-butter beef, 127
  butter, 126
  Cajun, 129
  pastrami, 106
Island seasonin', 84–85
Italian (flavors):
  salsa verde (green sauce),
    209–10
  spiedies (chicken kebabs),
    272–73
  Tuscan relish, 309
  see also Bruschetta
Italian dressing from scratch, 271

J

Jack's Firehouse (Philadelphia),
    188
Jake's Handcrafted (Brooklyn),
    120, 180, 311
Jake's sauerkraut, 311–13
Jake's three C's barbecue sauce,
    180–81
Jalapeño(s), 204
  mustard barbecue sauce, 188–89
  sauce, 283–84
  tartar sauce, 264

zehug (Yemenite pepper sauce),
    288
Jamaican (flavors):
  jerk leg of lamb, 87
  jerk seasoning, 85–86
  jolt, 38
Jams, 158
  bacon, 331–32
Japanese (flavors):
  grilled corn with sesame soy
    butter, 114, *115*
  miso barbecue sauce, 228
  teriyaki marinade, 81–82
  wasabi-horseradish butter, 155
  yakitori chicken, 227
  yakitori sauce, 226
Jars, 7
Jellies, 158
Jerk:
  leg of lamb, 87
  seasoning, Jamaican, 85–86
Jerky:
  marinade, 56
  venison, smoked, 57
Joe's Kansas City Barbecue, 189
Juniper, wild game marinade with
    gin and, 69

K

Kaffir lime leaf, 89
Kansas City Barbecue Society
    (KCBS), 24, 161
Kansas City style:
  sweet and smoky rub, 24
  Texas barb-b-que sauce, 176–77
KB sauce (Korean barbecue
    sauce), 223
Kebabs:
  chicken (*spiedies*), 272–73
  lamb, Moroccan, 217
  Persian saffron-yogurt marinade
    for, 71
  pincho powder for, 41
Kenyan tomato relish, 309–10
Ketchups, 4, 239–45
  banana, 244
  history of, 245
  made-from-scratch, 241–42
  mango-mint, 242–43
Kimchi, 314–15
Kingfish, Belgian beer marinade
    for, 66
Klein, Jake, 120, 311–13
Knives, 7
Korean (flavors):
  barbecue sauce, 223

honey-sesame marinade, 83
kimchi, 314–15
pulled pork, 224–25
Kukonis, Paul, 103

L

Lago de los Cisnos, El
    (Mexico City), 304
Lamb:
  béarnaise sauce for, 257–58
  Brazilian garlic marinade for, 63
  carrot raita from Goa for, 222
  cilantro-mint chutney for,
    326–27
  doctor sauce for, 178
  green tandoori spice paste for,
    96–97
  Hellas relish for, 307
  herbes de Provence for, 39
  Indian tandoori marinade for,
    76–77
  island seasonin' for, 84–85
  Kenyan tomato relish for,
    309–10
  Mediterranean relish for, 306
  salsa borracha (drunken salsa)
    for, 297
  Turkish garlic-yogurt marinade
    for, 70
  walnut-Roquefort butter for, 153
Lamb chops:
  Berber spice paste for, 95
  monkey gland sauce for, 218
  Persian saffron, 72, *73*
  tarragon-lemon butter for, 151
Lamb kebabs:
  Moroccan, 217
  Persian saffron-yogurt marinade
    for, 71
  pincho powder for, 41
Lang, Adam Perry, 281
Lard, 160
Latin (flavors):
  aji amarillo sauce (Peruvian
    yellow pepper sauce), 202–3
  Brazilian garlic marinade, 63
  Brazilian hot sauce, 286
  chimichurri (Argentine parsley-
    garlic sauce), 192–93
  chirmol (Central American
    tomato sauce), 198–201
  jalapeño sauce, 283–84
  mole poblano (Mexican
    chocolate-chile sauce), 196–98
  pebre (Chilean pepper sauce),
    207

salsa criolla (Colombian Creole
    sauce), 201–2
Lean-and-mean Texas barbecue
  sauce, 167
Ledée, 208
Lee, Jiyeon "Jiji," 223
Lemon(s):
  garlic baste, Greek, 119
  ginger cider brine, 104
  juice, 64, 158
  juicing, 53
  pepper, 17
  pepper oil, 141
  tarragon butter, 151
  zest, 53
Lemongrass, 89, 99
  stalks, as basting brushes or
    skewers, 88
Lime:
  juice, 64, 159
  Scotch bonnet marinade,
    French West Indian, 61–62
Lindsay, Robert, 101
Liquid smoke, 116, 160
Lobster:
  finadene (vinegar-soy barbecue
    sauce from Guam) for, 237
  Scotch bonnet sauce for, 289
  spiny, St. Barth barbecue sauce
    for, 208
Lone Star steak rub, 27
Loseke, Nancy, 314

M

Mace, 36
Mackerel, teriyaki marinade for,
  81–82
Main courses:
  barbecue burger, 174, *175*
  BBQ Titans' brisket, 165
  brandy-brined turkey breast
    with tangerine lacquer glaze,
    134, 135
  Cajun tuna, 262, *263*
  char siu chicken thighs, 55
  Chinatown duck, 220, *221*
  cider-brined pork chops, 105
  Dalmatian ribs (salt and pepper
    beef ribs), 22, *23*
  double coffee skirt steaks, 29
  grilled striped bass with melon-
    mint relish, 300, *301*
  jerk leg of lamb, 87
  Korean pulled pork, 224–25
  Moroccan lamb kebabs, 217
  Nashville hot wings, 121

pastrami bacon, 107
Persian saffron lamb chops,
  72, *73*
righteous ribs, *162*, 163
sesame grilled tofu, 78
Singapore pork saté, *230*, 231
smoky marinated pork
  tenderloin with spicy corn
  relish, 59
spiedies (chicken kebabs),
  272–73
tabaka (grilled game hens), 68
tandoori shrimp, *74*, 75
yakitori chicken, 227
Malagueta chiles, 206
Malaysian (flavors):
  coconut curry baste, 118
  rich peanut dipping sauce, 229
Mam nem (Vietnamese pineapple-
  shrimp dipping sauce), 235–36
Mango:
  chutneys, fresh, 323–24
  hell's fury, 284–85
  mint ketchup, 242–43
Mangum, Hugh, 170
Maple sugar/maple syrup, 158
Marinades, 3, 51–83
  adobos, 61
  beer, Belgian, 66
  char siu, 53–54
  Chinatown, 79–80
  chipotle chile, 58
  cinnamon-orange, 67
  components of, 64
  containers for, 6, 65
  cooking, 64, 65
  garlic, Brazilian, 63
  garlic, Cuban (adobo), 60
  garlic-yogurt, Turkish, 70
  herb vinaigrette, basic, 266–67
  honey-sesame, Korean, 83
  Italian dressing from scratch, 271
  jerky, 56
  marinating times and, 54
  the only marinade you'll ever
    need, 52
  safety tips for, 9, 65
  saffron-yogurt, Persian, 71
  saté, Thai, 80–81
  Scotch bonnet–lime, French
    West Indian, 61–62
  sesame-soy, sweet, 77–79
  tandoori, Indian, 76–77
  teriyaki, 81–82
  wild game, with juniper and
    gin, 69
  see also After-marinades

Marjoram, 88, 89
Mayonnaise, 239–40, 251–58
    burger sauce for grown-ups, 256
    Cajun rémoulade, 261
    Chinese mustard cream, 330
    chipotle, 253
    garlic (aïoli), 255
    homemade, 251–52
    horseradish, 253
    jalapeño tartar sauce, 264
    mustard, 252
    sriracha, 254
    variations, 251
    wasabi, 254
McDavid, Jack, 188
Measuring cups and spoons, 7
Meat drippings, 160
Mediterranean (flavors):
    herb rub (rosemary, oregano,
        sage, and mint), 40
    relish, 306
Melon-mint relish, 299
Memphis-style barbecue sauce,
    171–72
Merlot-soy finishing sauce, 148
Mexican (flavors):
    avocado salsa, 304
    chile oil, 144
    chipotle chile marinade, 58
    flame-charred *salsa verde*, 294–95
    mole poblano (chocolate-chile
        sauce), 196–98
    recado de bistec (steak *recado*),
        92–93
    recado negro (black *recado*),
        93–94
    recado rojo (Yucatán red spice
        paste), 90–92
    salsa, 5
    salsa borracha (drunken salsa),
        297
    salsa fresca (aka salsa Mexicana
        or *pico de gallo*), 293
    smoky marinated pork
        tenderloin with spicy corn
        relish, 59
    smoky two-chile salsa, 295–96
    xni pec, 282–83
Mezcal, in *salsa borracha*
    (drunken salsa), 297
Michiba, Rokusaburo, 116
Mint, 88, 89
    cilantro chutney, 326–27
    grapefruit *mojo*, 194
    mango ketchup, 242–43
    melon relish, 299
    yogurt chutney, 326

Miso, 159
    barbecue sauce, 228
Mixing bowls, 7
Mojo (Cuban citrus-garlic sauce),
    193–94
    grapefruit-mint, 194
Molasses, 158
Mole poblano (Mexican chocolate-
    chile sauce), 196–98
Monkey gland sauce, 218
Monroe County vinegar dip,
    148–49
Mop sauces/spray sauces, 109–10,
    122–25
    basic mop sauce, 122–23
    Buffalo mop, 124
    cider squirt, 125
Moroccan (flavors):
    Berber spice paste, 95
    charmoula (herb and paprika
        sauce), 216
    lamb kebabs, 217
Mortar and pestles, 7–8
Mozzarella, in smokehouse
    Caprese salad, 265
Mulato chiles, 206
Mustard(s), 4, 159, 239–40,
    246–51
    beer butter, 153–54
    Chinese, cream, 330
    coleslaw dressing, 318
    green peppercorn, 249
    history of, 247
    horseradish, 250–51
    jalapeño barbecue sauce, 188–89
    mayonnaise, 252
    purple, 248
    sun-dried tomato, 251
    sweet and spicy, 246–47
Mustard seeds, 36, 247

N

Naranja agria. See Orange, sour
Nashville hot chicken baste, 120
Nashville hot wings, 121
Newspaper rub/Dalmatian rub, 21
Nonreactive containers, 65
North Carolina–style:
    bubba-lina vinegar sauce, 189
    pig picker pucker sauce, 186
Not-just-for-ham glaze, 130
Nuoc mam (Vietnamese dipping
    sauce), 234
Nutmeg, 36
Nut oils, 64
Nuts, toasting, 112

O

Oils:
    in barbecue sauces, 160
    in marinades, 64
Oils, flavored, 4, 136–45
    chile, Mexican, 144
    Chinese fire, 142–43
    curry, 142
    garlic, fresh, 136
    garlic, fried, 137
    garlic, roasted, 138
    lemon pepper, 141
    sweet basil, with garlic, 136–37
    truffle, 145
Oklahoma bruschetta, 330
Olive oil, 64
Olives, 159
Onion(s), 159
    bacon butter, 154–55
    jalapeño sauce, 283–84
Orange:
    cinnamon marinade, 67
    juice, 159
    teriyaki marinade, 82
Orange, sour (*naranja agria*),
    159, 194
    adobo (Cuban garlic marinade),
        60
    mojo (Cuban citrus-garlic
        sauce), 193–94
    recado rojo (Yucatán red spice
        paste), 90–92
Oregano, 88, 89

P

Paprika, 36
    and herb sauce, Moroccan
        (*charmoula*), 216
    smoked (pimentón), 37
Paramin seasonin' from Trinidad,
    85
Parmigiano-Reggiano, in
    deconstructed pesto after-
    marinade, 275–76
Parsley, 88, 89
    charmoula (Moroccan herb and
        paprika sauce), 216
    garlic sauce, Argentine
        (*chimichurri*), 192–93
    salsa verde (Italian green
        sauce), 209–10
Partridge:
    ginger-pear chutney for, 321–22
    red currant port sauce for,
        213–14

Pasilla chiles, 206
  salsa borracha (drunken salsa),
    297
Pastrami:
  bacon, 107
  brine and injector sauce, 106
  brining, 101
  rub, 31
  rub for brined meats, 32
Peach:
  barbecue sauce, 169–70
  pecan chutney, 322–23
Peanut:
  butter, in barbecue sauce, 160
  dipping sauce, quick, 232
  dipping sauce, rich, 229
Pear-ginger chutney, 321–22
Pebre (Chilean pepper sauce), 207
Pecan-peach chutney, 322–23
Peelers, vegetable, 8
Pepper(corn)(s), 159
  green, mustard, 249
  how to crack, 21
  lemon, 17
  lemon oil, 141
  peppery cream sauce for grilled
    steak, 259
  Sichuan, 37
  six pepper blend, 18
Peppers (bell), 159
  hellish relish, 308–9
  red, in *rouille* (saffron–roasted
    pepper sauce), 210–11
  Tuscan relish, 309
Peppers, chile. *See* Chile(s)
Pequin chiles, 206
Persian (flavors):
  saffron butter baste, 117
  saffron lamb chops, 72, *73*
  saffron-yogurt marinade, 71
Peruvian aji amarillo (yellow
    pepper sauce), 202–3
Pesto, 64
  after-marinade, deconstructed,
    275–76
Pheasant:
  ginger-pear chutney for, 321–22
  red currant port sauce for,
    213–14
Pickled plums, 310–11
Pickle juice, 159
Pickles, 5
Pico de gallo (salsa Mexicana or
    salsa fresca), 293
Pig picker pucker sauce, 186
Piloncillo, 158
Pimentón, 37

Pincho powder, 41
Pineapple:
  garlic glaze, 131
  raita, 222
  shrimp dipping sauce,
    Vietnamese (*mam nem*),
    235–36
  spice-grilled, with smoky
    whipped cream, *48*, 49
Pink curing salt (Prague powder
    #1), 37, 101
Piri-piri sauce, 287
Platters and plates, safe handling
    of, 9
Plums, pickled, 310–11
Poblano chiles, 159, 204
Polenta, grilled:
  Charlie Trotter's truffled porcini
    BBQ sauce for, 187–88
  truffle oil for, 145
Porcini BBQ sauce, truffled,
    Charlie Trotter's, 187–88
Pork:
  all-purpose brine for, 102–3
  Asian injector sauce for, 128–29
  belly, making pastrami bacon
    with, 32, 107
  Brazilian garlic marinade for, 63
  brined grilled, *xni pec* for,
    282–83
  Chinese five-spice powder for, 42
  ginger-pear chutney for, 321–22
  herbes de Provence for, 39
  Jamaican jerk seasoning for,
    85–86
  kebabs, *pincho* powder for, 41
  peach-pecan chutney, 322–23
  sandwiches, slaws for, 316–18
  saté, Singapore, *230*, 231
  tenderloin, Asian 5-4-3-2-1 rub
    for, 26–27
  tenderloin, smoky marinated,
    with spicy corn relish, 59
  see also Bacon; Ham; Pulled
    pork; Ribs, pork; Sausages;
    Suckling pig
Pork chops and pork loin:
  B.B's Lawnside spicy apple
    barbecue sauce for, 166
  Catalan vinaigrette for, 269
  cider-brined, 105
  fruit + booze glaze for, 133
  Jamaican jolt for, 38
  not-just-for-ham glaze for, 130
  recado rojo (Yucatán red spice
    paste) for, 90–92
  stuffed with bacon jam, 331–32

Pork shoulder:
  Balinese spice paste for, 97–98
  basic mop sauce for, 122–23
  Brazilian garlic marinade for, 63
  char siu marinade for, 53–54
  Fette Sau's coffee rub for, 28
  Kansas City sweet and smoky
    rub for, 24
  KB sauce (Korean barbecue
    sauce) for, 223
  Memphis-style barbecue sauce
    for, 171–72
  pig picker pucker sauce for,
    186
  steaks, Monroe County vinegar
    dip for, 148–49
  steaks, vinegar-dipped, 150
  wild game marinade with
    juniper and gin for, 69
Port:
  purple mustard, 248
  red currant sauce, 213–14
Prague powder #1, 37, 100
Prawns, *finadene* (vinegar-soy
    barbecue sauce from Guam)
    for, 237
Project Smoke, 173
Puerto Rican (flavors), 44
  ajilimojili (pepper sauce),
    195–96
  pig powder (*sazón*), 34
Pulled pork:
  bubba-lina vinegar sauce for,
    189
  Korean, 224–25
  pig picker pucker sauce for, 186
  slaws for, 316–18
  smoke wrangler's bacon bourbon
    barbecue sauce for, 173
Purple mustard, 248

Q

Quail:
  Chinatown marinade for,
    79–80
  ginger-pear chutney for,
    321–22
  mole poblano (Mexican
    chocolate-chile sauce) for,
    196–98
  not-just-for-ham glaze for, 130
  Persian saffron-yogurt marinade
    for, 71
  red currant port sauce for,
    213–14
  saffron butter baste for, 117

R

Raita, 222
Recados (Yucatán spice pastes),
   90–94
   de bistec (steak *recado*), 92–93
   negro (black *recado*), 93–94
   rojo (red *recado*), 90–92
Red currant port sauce, 213–14
Redfish, Cajun rémoulade for, 261
Red naga, 204
Red pepper flakes, 159
Relishes, 5, 291–92, 298–310
   avocado salsa, 304
   corn, spicy, 302–3
   cucumber, Thai, 298
   extending shelf life of, 172
   Hellas, 307
   hellish, 308–9
   Mediterranean, 306
   melon-mint, 299
   tomato, Kenyan, 309–10
   Tuscan, 309
Rémoulade, Cajun, 261
Reynolds, Erik, 331
Rhubarb sauce, Georgian
   (*tkemali*), 215–16
Ribs, beef:
   Dalmatian (salt and pepper beef
      ribs), 22, *23*
   Dalmatian rub/newspaper rub
      for, 21
   Korean honey-sesame marinade
      for, 83
   Texa-Lina barbecue sauce for,
      170–71
Ribs, pork:
   basic mop sauce for, 122–23
   Beijing barbecue sauce for, 219
   Fette Sau's coffee rub for, 28
   fruit + booze glaze for, 133
   Jamaican jolt for, 38
   Kansas City sweet and smoky
      rub for, 24
   Memphis-style barbecue sauce
      for, 171–72
   righteous, *162*, 163
   sweet-and-smoky barbecue
      sauce for, 161
Ribs, veal, coffee barbecue sauce
   for, 184–85
Rice syrup, 158
Rocotillo chiles, 204
   ajilimojili (Puerto Rican pepper
      sauce), 195–96
Romesco sauce, 212–13
Roquefort-walnut butter, 153

Rosemary, 88, 89
Rouille (saffron–roasted pepper
   sauce), 210–11
Rubs, 3, 11, 19–47
   history of, 44
   maximizing performance of, 25
   safe handling of, 9
   using, 25, 44–45
   see also Wet rubs and spice
      pastes
Rubs, American, 19–33
   barbecue, basic, 19
   barbecue, customizing, 20
   Cajun, 33
   coffee, Fette Sau's, 28
   Dalmatian/newspaper, 21
   fish cure, failproof, 30
   5-4-3-2-1, 26
   Kansas City sweet and smoky, 24
   pastrami, 31
   pastrami, for brined meats, 32
   regional differences in, 44
   steak, Lone Star, 27
Rubs, world, 34–42, 44
   Asian 5-4-3-2-1, 26–27
   Beijing blast, 42
   dessert, 47
   duck, sweet and licoricey, 46
   herbes de Provence, 39
   Jamaican jolt, 38
   Mediterranean herb (rosemary,
      oregano, sage, and mint), 40
   pincho powder, 41
   sazón (Puerto Rican pig
      powder), 34
   Singapore saté, 46–47

S

Safety concerns, 8–9
Saffron, 37
   butter baste, 117
   buying, 117
   lamb chops, Persian, 72, *73*
   –roasted pepper sauce (*rouille*),
      210–11
   yogurt marinade, Persian, 71
St. Barth barbecue sauce, 208
Salads:
   grilled beef, Thai (*yam nua*),
      278, *279*
   smokehouse Caprese, 265
Salmon:
   bacon jam for, 331–32
   balsamic drizzle for, 274
   béarnaise sauce for, 257–58
   Belgian beer marinade for, 66

   Berber spice paste for, 95
   brining, 101
   Catalan vinaigrette for, 269
   coffee barbecue sauce for, 184–85
   honey cure for, 100
   miso barbecue sauce for, 228
   pastrami, 31, 32
   smoked, failproof fish cure for, 30
   tkemali (Georgian rhubarb
      sauce) for, 215–16
   walnut-Roquefort butter for, 153
   wasabi-horseradish butter for,
      155
Salsa criolla (Colombian Creole
   sauce), 201–2
Salsas, 5, 291–97
   avocado, 304
   flame-charred *salsa verde*, 294–95
   jalapeño sauce, 283–84
   pebre (Chilean pepper sauce), 207
   salsa borracha (drunken salsa),
      297
   salsa fresca (salsa Mexicana or
      pico de gallo), 293
   smoky two-chile, 295–96
   xni pec, 282–83
Salsa verde (Italian green sauce),
   209–10
Salt, 14, 159
   brining and, 101
   pink (Prague powder #1), 37, 101
Salt curing, 101
Salts, seasoned, 12–17
   all-purpose, 12
   Balinese, 15
   Central Asian, 16
   sesame, 16–17
   smoked, 13–14
Sambals, 291–92, 318–20
   grilled tomato, 320–21
   shallot, 318–19
Samuelsson, Marcus, 184
Saté(s):
   coconut curry baste for, 118
   grilled tomato sambal for, 320–21
   marinade, Thai, 80–81
   peanut dipping sauce for, quick,
      232
   peanut dipping sauce for, rich,
      229
   pork, Singapore, *230*, 231
   rub, Singapore, 46–47
   Scotch bonnet sauce for, 289
Saucepans, 8
Sauerkraut:
   cooked, 313
   Jake's, 311–13

Sausages, accompaniments for:
  cooked sauerkraut, 313
  green peppercorn mustard, 249
  horseradish mustard, 250–51
  Jake's sauerkraut, 311–13
  purple mustard, 248
  sweet and spicy mustard,
    246–47
Sazón (Puerto Rican pig powder),
  34
Scales, 8
Scallops:
  Chinatown marinade for, 79–80
  lemon pepper oil for, 141
Schlesinger, Chris, 276, 280
Scorpion peppers, 204
Scotch bonnet chile(s), 205
  handling safely, 62
  hell's fury, 284–85
  sauce, 289
  lime marinade, French West
    Indian, 61–62
  pebre (Chilean pepper sauce),
    207
  St. Barth barbecue sauce, 208
Scotch whisky, in secret weapon
    basting sauce, 116–17
Seafood. *See* Fish and seafood
Seasonings, 3, 11–18
  for barbecue sauces, 159
  Chinese five-spice powder, 42
  using rub as, 25, 44–45
  see also Pepper(corn)(s); Rubs;
    Salts, seasoned
Secret weapon basting sauce,
  116–17
Serrano chiles, 205
Sesame (seeds):
  -ginger-soy vinaigrette, 270
  grilled tofu, 78
  honey marinade, Korean, 83
  salt, 16–17
  soy butter baste, 113
  soy marinade, sweet, 77–79
  toasting, 112
Sesame oil, 64
Shallot sambal, 318–19
Shannon, Lindsey, 166
Shrimp:
  all-purpose brine for, 102–3
  Cajun rémoulade for, 261
  Catalan vinaigrette for, 269
  Chinatown marinade for, 79–80
  chipotle mayonnaise for, 253
  grilled, with deconstructed pesto
    after-marinade, 280
  lemon pepper oil for, 141

marinating, 45, 54
Mediterranean herb rub for, 40
pastrami, 31, 32
pineapple dipping sauce,
  Vietnamese (*mam nem*),
  235–36
Scotch bonnet sauce for, 289
shallot sambal, 318–19
tandoori, *74*, 75
teriyaki marinade for, 81–82
tomato chutney as cocktail
  sauce for, 327–28
Sichuan peppercorns, 37
Simmons, Amelia, 316
Singapore (flavors):
  pork saté, *230*, 231
  saté rub, 46–47
Six pepper blend, 18
Skewers:
  herb stalks as, 88
  see also Kebabs; Saté(s)
Skillets. *See* Cast-iron skillets
Skirt steaks, double coffee, 29
Slather sauces, 4, 239–89
  A.1. Steak Sauce, 255
  balsamic drizzle, 274
  béarnaise, 257–58
  burger sauce for grown-ups, 256
  Cajun rémoulade, 261
  horseradish, volcanic, 260
  Italian dressing from scratch,
    271
  jalapeño tartar, 264
  peppery cream, for grilled steak,
    259
  tomato, smoked, 265–66
  volcanic horseradish, 260
  see also After-marinades;
    Ketchups; Mayonnaise;
    Mustard(s); Vinaigrettes
Slaws, 316–18
  basic mixture for, 316
  creamy coleslaw dressing for, 317
  mustard coleslaw dressing for,
    318
  vinegar coleslaw dressing for, 317
Smoke:
  liquid, 116, 160
Smoked salt, 13–14
Smoked stock, 146–47
Smoked tomato sauce, 265–66
Smoke Woodfire Grill (Tulsa), 331
Smoke wrangler's bacon bourbon
    barbecue sauce, 173
Smoky two-chile salsa, 295–96
Snapper:
  banana ketchup for, 244

Cajun rémoulade for, 261
xni pec for, 282–83
Soda, in barbecue sauce, 160
Sodium nitrate, 101
Sodium nitrite, 37, 101
Sonny Bryan's (Dallas), 167
Souring agents, for barbecue
  sauces, 158–59
Sour orange. *See* Orange, sour
South African (flavors):
  apricot *blatjang*, 328–29
  monkey gland sauce, 218
  piri-piri sauce, 287
South American (flavors). *See*
  Latin (flavors)
Southeast Asian (flavors):
  Balinese seasoned salt, 15
  Balinese spice paste, 97–98
  Cambodian dipping sauce, 233
  coconut curry baste, 118
  fish sauce, 159, 235
  grilled tomato sambal, 320–21
  lemongrass, 88, 99
  mam nem (Vietnamese
    pineapple-shrimp dipping
    sauce), 235–36
  peanut dipping sauce, quick, 232
  peanut dipping sauce, rich, 229
  shallot sambal, 318–19
  Singapore pork saté, *230*, 231
  Singapore saté rub, 46–47
  spicy corn relish, 302–3
  Vietnamese dipping sauce
    (*nuoc mam*), 234
Soy (sauce), 159
  merlot finishing sauce, 148
  sesame butter baste, 113
  -sesame-ginger vinaigrette, 270
  sesame marinade, sweet, 77–79
  vinegar barbecue sauce from
    Guam (*finadene*), 237
Spanish (flavors):
  barbecue rub, 20
  pincho powder, 41
  romesco sauce, 212–13
  vinaigrette, 269
Spice(s), 35–37
  in barbecue sauce, 160
  buying, 35
  freshness of, 25, 35
  -grilled pineapple with smoky
    whipped cream, *48*, 49
  grinding just before using, 35
  pastes. *See* Wet rubs
  roasting, 35
Spice mills, 8
Spiedies (chicken kebabs), 272–73

Spirits:
  in barbecue sauce, 160
Spoons, wooden, 8
Spray bottles, 183
Spray sauces. *See* Mop sauces/
  spray sauces
Squirt bottles, 183
Squirts. *See* Mop sauces/spray
  sauces
Sriracha, 303
  mayonnaise, 254
Star anise, 37
Steak(s):
  Berber spice paste for, 95
  horseradish mustard for,
    250–51
  Korean honey-sesame marinade
    for, 83
  monkey gland sauce for, 218
  recado (*recado de bistec*), 92–93
  rub, Lone Star, 27
  skirt, double coffee, 29
  tarragon-lemon butter for, 151
  volcanic horseradish sauce for,
    260
Steak sauces, 160, 257–60
  A.1., 255
  béarnaise, 257–58
  "board sauce," 281–82
  horseradish, volcanic, 260
  peppery cream, 259
Stehey, Jeff, 189
Stock:
  in barbecue sauce, 160
  smoked, 146–47
Striped bass, grilled, with melon-
  mint relish, 300, *301*
Sucanat, 158
Suckling pig:
  Balinese spice paste for, 97–98
  recado negro (black *recado*) for,
    93–94
  sazón (Puerto Rican pig
    powder), 34
Sugars, 158
Sumac, 37
Sweet-and-smoky barbecue sauce,
  161
Sweetbreads:
  chimichurri (Argentine parsley-
    garlic sauce) for, 192–93
  garlic butter baste for, 111–12
Sweeteners, 158
Sweet potatoes, not-just-for-ham
  glaze for, 130
Sweet sesame-soy marinade,
  77–79

Tabaka (grilled game hens), 68
Tabasco sauce, 123
Tacos:
  burger sauce for grown-ups for,
    256
  chipotle mayonnaise for, 253
  salsa fresca for, 293
  smoky two-chile salsa for, 295–96
Tamarind, 159
  banana barbecue sauce, 181–82
  purée, 182–83
Tandoori, 2
  cilantro-mint chutney for,
    326–27
  fresh mango chutney for, 323–24
  marinade, Indian, 76–77
  shrimp, *74*, 75
  spice paste, green, 96–97
Tangerine:
  lacquer glaze, 132
  teriyaki marinade, 82
Tarragon, 88, 89
  béarnaise sauce, 257–58
  lemon butter, 151
Tartar sauce, jalapeño, 264
Taylor, Cody, 223
Tequila, in *salsa borracha*
  (drunken salsa), 297
Teriyaki marinade, 81–82
  orange or tangerine, 82
Texa-Lina barbecue sauce, 170–71
Texas style:
  barb-b-que sauce, Kansas City
    style, 176–77
  lean-and-mean barbecue sauce,
    167
  Lone Star steak rub, 27
Tex-Mex barbecue rub, 20
Thai (flavors):
  after-marinade, 277
  cucumber relish, 298
  grilled beef salad (*yam nua*),
    278, *279*
  saté marinade, 80–81
  sriracha (chile garlic sauce), 303
  sriracha mayonnaise, 254
Thai chile pastes, 303
Thai chiles, 205
Thyme, 88, 89
Tkemali (Georgian rhubarb
  sauce), 215–16
Toasting sesame seeds and nuts,
  112
Tofu:
  Beijing blast for, 42

Cambodian dipping sauce for, 233
char siu marinade for, 53–54
Chinatown marinade for, 79–80
Chinese fire oil for, 142–43
curry oil for, 142
Korean honey-sesame marinade
  for, 83
miso barbecue sauce for, 228
sesame grilled, 78
sesame salt for, 16–17
sesame-soy butter baste for, 113
sweet sesame-soy marinade for,
  77–79
Thai flavor after-marinade for,
  277
Vietnamese dipping sauce (*nuoc
  mam*) for, 234
Tomaquera, La (Barcelona), 269
Tomatillos:
  avocado salsa, 304
  flame-charred *salsa verde*,
    294–95
Tomato(es):
  buying and storing, 285
  chutney, 327–28
  grilled, sambal, 320–21
  Hellas relish, 307
  made-from-scratch ketchup,
    241–42
  Mediterranean relish, 306
  monkey gland sauce, 218
  pebre (Chilean pepper sauce), 207
  peeling and seeding, 285
  relish, Kenyan, 309–10
  romesco sauce, 212–13
  salsa criolla (Colombian Creole
    sauce), 201–2
  salsa fresca (aka salsa Mexicana
    or *pico de gallo*), 293
  sauce, Central American
    (*chirmol*), 198–201
  smoked, sauce, 265–66
  smokehouse Caprese salad, 265
  sun-dried, 159
  sun-dried, mustard, 251
  xni pec, 282–83
  zehug (Yemenite pepper sauce),
    288
Trinidad, Paramin seasonin' from,
  85
Trotter, Charlie, 187
Trout, wasabi-horseradish butter
  for, 155
Truffle(d):
  oil, 145
  porcini BBQ sauce, Charlie
    Trotter's, 187–88

Tuna:
  Berber spice paste for, 95
  burgers, banana ketchup for, 244
  Cajun, 262, *263*
  green peppercorn mustard for, 249
  peppery cream sauce for, 259
  wasabi mayonnaise for, 254
Turbinado sugar, 158
Turkey:
  all-purpose brine for, 102–3
  breast, brandy-brined, with tangerine lacquer glaze, *134*, 135
  butter injector sauce for, 126
  Cajun injector sauce for, 129
  fruit + booze glaze for, 133
  ginger-pear chutney for, 321–22
  guava barbecue sauce for, 179
  honey cure for, 100
  jerky marinade for, 56
  melon-mint relish for, 299
  mole poblano (Mexican chocolate-chile sauce) for, 196–98
  not-just-for-ham glaze for, 130
  pastrami, 31, 32
  peach-pecan chutney for, 322–23
  recado negro (black *recado*) for, 93–94
Turkish garlic-yogurt marinade, 70
Turmeric, 37
Tuscan relish, 309
Two Bros BBQ Market and H&D Ice House (San Antonio), 169

V

Vanilla extract, 160
Veal:
  ribs, coffee barbecue sauce for, 184–85
  walnut-Roquefort butter for, 153
Veal chops:
  balsamic drizzle for, 274
  Dalmatian rub/newspaper rub for, 21
  Mediterranean relish for, 306
  smoked tomato sauce for, 265–66
  tarragon-lemon butter for, 151
  truffle oil for, 145
Vegetable peelers, 8
Vegetables, grilled:
  ajilimojili (Puerto Rican pepper sauce) for, 195–96
  Balinese seasoned salt for, 15
  balsamic drizzle for, 274

  banana ketchup for, 244
  Catalan vinaigrette for, 269
  corn with sesame soy butter, 114, *115*
  curry oil for, 142
  lemon pepper oil for, 141
  Lone Star steak rub for, 27
  rouille (saffron–roasted pepper sauce) for, 210–11
  sesame-ginger-soy vinaigrette for, 270
  tarragon-lemon butter for, 151
  Thai flavor after-marinade for, 277
  tkemali (Georgian rhubarb sauce) for, 215–16
  truffle oil for, 145
  walnut-Roquefort butter for, 153
Venison:
  Charlie Trotter's truffled porcini BBQ sauce for, 187–88
  double coffee, 29
  jerky, smoked, 57
  jerky marinade for, 56
  red currant port sauce for, 213–14
  wild game marinade with juniper and gin for, 69
Vietnamese (flavors):
  chile paste, 303
  dipping sauce (*nuoc mam*), 234
  mam nem (pineapple-shrimp dipping sauce), 235–36
Vinaigrettes, 266–70
  barbecue, 268
  Catalan, 269
  herb, basic, 266–67
  sesame-ginger-soy, 270
Vinegar(s), 64, 158
  coleslaw dressing, 317
  dip, Monroe County, 148–49
  -dipped pork steaks, 150
  sauce, bubba-lina, 189
  soy barbecue sauce from Guam (*finadene*), 237
Volcanic horseradish sauce, 260

W

Walnut-Roquefort butter, 153
Wasabi, 37
  horseradish butter, 155
  mayonnaise, 254
West Indian (flavors):
  barbecue rub, 20
  French West Indian Scotch bonnet–lime marinade, 61–62

  Jamaican jolt, 38
  St. Barth barbecue sauce, 208
Wet rubs and spice pastes, 3, 51, 64, 84–98
  Balinese spice paste, 97–98
  Berber spice paste, 95
  green tandoori spice paste, 96–97
  island seasonin', 84–85
  jerk seasoning, Jamaican, 85–86
  Paramin seasonin' from Trinidad, 85
  recado de bistec (steak *recado*), 92–93
  recado negro (black *recado*), 93–94
  recado rojo (Yucatán red spice paste), 90–92
Whipped cream, spiced smoked, 49
Whisks, 8
Wild game marinade with juniper and gin, 69
Willingham, John, 9, 171
Wine:
  in barbecue sauce, 160
  béarnaise sauce, 257–58
  merlot-soy finishing sauce, 148
  purple mustard, 248
Wine vinegar, 158
Wooden spoons, 8
Worcestershire powder, 37
Worcestershire sauce, 160, 168
Worgul, Doug, 176

X, Y, Z

Xni pec, 282–83

Yakitori:
  chicken, 227
  sauce, 226
Yam nua (Thai grilled beef salad), 278, *279*
Yellow pepper sauce, Peruvian (aji amarillo sauce), 202–3
Yemenite pepper sauce (*zehug*), 288
Yogurt:
  garlic marinade, Turkish, 70
  in marinades, 64
  mint chutney, 326
  raita, 222
  saffron marinade, Persian, 71
Yucatecan (flavors):
  spice pastes. See Recados
  xni pec, 282–83

Zehug (Yemenite pepper sauce), 288